NATIONAL
cycle
NETWORK

NATIONAL *cycle* NETWORK

Nick Cotton and John Grimshaw

sustrans

ROUTES FOR PEOPLE

35 KING STREET, BRISTOL BS1 4DZ

First published by Sustrans in 2000

Copyright © Sustrans 2000

All rights reserved. No part of this
publication may be reproduced, stored in a
retrieval system or transmitted by any
means, electronic, mechanical, photocopying
or otherwise, without the prior permission of
the publisher.

All maps are derived from Ordnance Survey
or Ordnance Survey Northern Ireland
material © Crown Copyright with all rights
reserved.

ISBN 1-901389-23-5

Printed in Italy by G. Canale & C. Turin

Sustrans is continually improving and
refining its routes, so some of the
routes may vary from the information
currently in this book.

CONTENTS

The National Cycle Network routes open June 2000

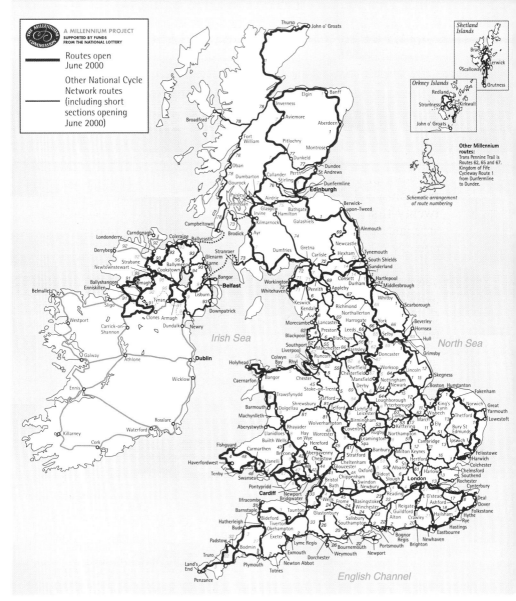

FOREWORD

I used to own a sepia photograph entitled 'The Trip'. Crowds of young men and women in Sunday-best clothes basked outside a pub, and in front of them, temporarily abandoned, lay hundreds of bicycles. The sun was shining, the trippers were jaunty, the photo spoke of a new modern world of independence, fun and healthy living.

A hundred years later that vision has been sullied by traffic jams and pollution. But the National Cycle Network offers us the chance to reclaim the sense of freedom our Edwardian ancestors felt, only this time in a twenty-first century context. It is weaving a network of safe and attractive cycling routes throughout the whole country.

This guide gives an introduction to the project. Many people – councils, landowners, funders, the Millennium Commission, enthusiasts, not to mention the dedicated team at Sustrans – have made this possible.

You will find extraordinary routes built to overcome barriers, as well as small details which weave their way through the heart of our towns and cities and out into the surrounding countryside. Although the project is only partly completed, by enjoying the National Cycle Network you will help create a world where once again cycling is recognised as a truly modern way of travelling through the next 100 years.

Tony Robinson

INTRODUCTION

Welcome to the Official Guide to the UK's National Cycle Network. 5,000 miles of route are now open, with thousands more miles under development.

This guide will help you find and use the Network – whether you want to learn to cycle from scratch, start cycling again, or venture out to places never before reached by bike. Over one third of the Network is on traffic-free routes, often on renovated railway tracks, riversides and forest paths – ideal for those newcomers wanting safety from traffic and idyllic for experienced cyclists too.

The Network is designed for you to use straight from home. The routes pass through the middle of most major towns and cities in the UK. A continuous programme of extensions is creating links to reach more and more railway stations, schools, offices and shops, as well as other Millennium and heritage sites. By 2005, the Network is forecast to pass within two miles of over 30 million people!

Every kind of journey is possible, whether cycling to work or to school, making local shopping trips, going on family leisure rides or undertaking long-distance "green tourism" trips.

The Network is a unique national asset, completely free and open to all. It gives countless historic landmarks like old railways, canals, bridges and viaducts a new lease of life. Everyone can help their environment by driving less and cycling and walking more – and fewer cars on the roads means cleaner air for everyone! Cycling is a great way to get fit and is enjoyed by all ages.

We very much hope you enjoy the National Cycle Network. Please respect other users and follow the advice in this book. Thank you.

HISTORY OF SUSTRANS AND THE NATIONAL CYCLE NETWORK

The National Cycle Network is a magnificent visionary scheme passing through all the major urban centres of the United Kingdom and linking these cities via 10,000 miles of traffic-free routes, quiet lanes and traffic-calmed city streets to form a comprehensive cycling network right across the country. It is a traffic partnership project par excellence – hundreds of bodies are involved, including local authorities, utility companies, landowners, heritage and wildlife bodies, rail operators and central government.

The origins of Sustrans, an abbreviated form of Sustainable Transport, can be traced back to the significant date of July 7th 1977 (7/7/77) when a group of Bristol environmentalists, driven by a desire to do something about the dangers to the environment recently highlighted by the oil crisis, set up a cycling group known as Cyclebag. Within two years the group started a programme of building cycle routes which has continued unabated, although now on a vastly expanded scale, over the last 20 years.

The dismantled railway line running between Bristol and Bath was the first railway path they converted for use by cyclists and walkers. The five-mile stretch near Saltford was where Sustrans' great enterprise started, a vision initially made possible by back-breaking work undertaken by enthusiastic volunteers. Since that modest beginning, what started as a single five-mile linear route will become a 10,000-mile network covering the whole country, built at a cost of more than £400 million.

View along Bristol & Bath Railway Path looking towards Bristol Temple Meads – opened 1984.

A Community Programme team constructing the York & Selby Path, 1985.

30 years of cycle planning and Sustrans is pursuing strategies to bring cycling back into the public domain.

Following its success on the Bristol & Bath Railway Path, Sustrans made full use of the various employment schemes available in the early 1980s such as Youth Opportunities Programmes and the Community Programme with hundreds of young people helping to build more paths in other cities such as Plymouth and Glasgow. At one stage, Sustrans was in the unusual position of having just one paid employee (John Grimshaw) and 800 people working on these very useful employment programmes! Many of those who supervised the early gangs have since gone on to become Regional Managers, responsible for building the Network. No one can accuse them of lacking hands-on experience!

Negotiations with British Waterways began in 1980. Although there are 2,000 miles of canal towpaths in the country, only a portion are passable by bike and in those days the useable mileage was even smaller. The Kennet & Avon Canal near Bath was covered in a foot of impassable sludge during the winter months. This was to be Sustrans' first towpath project and such was the state of the canal banks when work began

Sustrans is motivated by a desire to find solutions to the problems caused by the huge and relentless growth of traffic. Deaths, injuries, noise, pollution, the destruction of the environment and the creation of a lost generation of unfit children who will never have known the freedom offered by the bicycle, are all problems inherent in the traffic growth over the past 25 years. Every prediction indicates that things will get worse before they get better.

At the heart of the issue is the status and safety of cyclists and pedestrians in relation to the car. Proportionately, far more people cycle in Sweden, a country which is much colder, in Germany, which has a higher car ownership, and in Switzerland, which is considerably more hilly. Mile for mile, a cyclist in Britain is eight times more likely to be hurt in an accident than in Holland or Denmark.

In 1976 Denmark had the worst child accident rate in Europe – this led to an Act of Parliament which required local authorities to build safe cycle routes to school. Denmark is now one of the safest countries for cyclists in Europe. By contrast, Britain currently has the worst child accident rate in Europe and had to wait until 1998 before a Transport Bill was introduced that even mentioned Safe Routes to School. Britain has lost

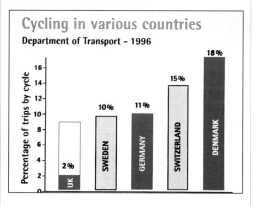

Cycling in various countries
Department of Transport - 1996

Diagram from Government's National Cycling Strategy showing cycling in various countries as a percentage of all trips. Government targets are to quadruple the low level of cycling in the UK by 2012, from 2% to +8%.

9

Detail from Ninth Legion by David Kemp showing use of old gas bottles and railway chairs.

The Ninth Legion, 17 miles from Glasgow Central on the Johnstone to Greenock Path.

that all new volunteers were told that their first job was to drive the dumper truck straight into the canal then retrieve it. The reason? The dumper truck had so often slipped into the water from the muddy 'path' that knowing how to get it out again was a most important skill to acquire! Over five years (1984-88) the path was rebuilt in stone from Bath all the way to Devizes. It is now tremendously popular as both a walking and cycling route.

Sustrans' reputation as path builders was growing year on year. More and more cities such as Derby, York, Liverpool and Sunderland had paths built through them. It became Sustrans' intention to have one quality route in each major city to show the government that the creation of attractive, safe cycle routes generated thousands of cycle journeys that might not otherwise have taken place, and enabled huge numbers of the public to learn to cycle again.

Great use was made of recycled materials in the construction of these cycle paths: bridges were made of concrete railway sleepers, sculptures were created from old JCBs and seats from wooden sleepers. Deliberate attempts were made to include attractive features such as causeways through cuttings, allowing ponds to be formed adjacent to the path, the creation of

*Path set on causeway through deep cutting on the
Lochwinnoch Loop Line south west from Glasgow.*

curves to break up the monotony of dead straight
lines and bending the route to weave a way
through mature trees. This concept of making
each ride full of interesting features became
known as the 'travelling landscape'.

After 15 years' experience of building paths,
Sustrans began to capture the public imagination
and launched a Supporter Programme. Supporter
numbers rose from 200 in 1993 to 40,000 in
1999. By 1995 Sustrans was in a position to make
a realistic bid to the Lottery for Millennium funds
for the National Cycle Network, a vast and
visionary scheme to create a 6,500-mile
countrywide network of safe cycle routes by the
year 2005 with 2,500 miles of the routes built by
the year 2000. (The figure of 6,500 miles has
since increased to 10,000 due to the enthusiasm
for the project shown by local authorities all over
the country).

The bid was successful and Sustrans was
awarded £43.5 million. Although this is a huge
amount, it only represents 20% of the total cost of
the first phase of the project and the remainder of
the funding comes from a variety of sources
including local authorities, development agencies,
the European Union, the Highways Agency, the
cycle trade and industry, and from generous
contributions from Sustrans supporters.

*End of the 2nd Trailblazing Ride, from Belfast to
Land's End, to promote the National Cycle Network.*

11

Advanced stop line in York.

Britain's roads are the busiest in Europe and predictions are that the situation will get worse, particularly in the countryside. Sustrans' aims in creating the Network are threefold: it should be attractive for novices, memorable for visitors and useful for everyday cyclists. The routes also promote a programme of sculpture and bring great economic benefit to many areas of the country.

The National Cycle Network is designed to encourage the public to start cycling again. Sustrans believes that to persuade non-cyclists to take up cycling it is essential to provide them with safe, traffic-free routes so they can regain confidence. These special paths can then connect (ideally) traffic-calmed urban roads with a network of routes through the countryside using quiet roads carrying less than 1,000 vehicles a day (this may sound busy but works out at less than one car a minute).

In the cities the main thrust of Sustrans' work is to increase the profile and status of the cyclist by re-allocating road space to favour the cyclist over the car, for example in the provision of Advanced Stop Lines at traffic lights, re-inforcing the idea that cyclists matter. Campaigning for lower speed limits in cities could lead to a drastic reduction in deaths and injuries to cyclists and pedestrians.

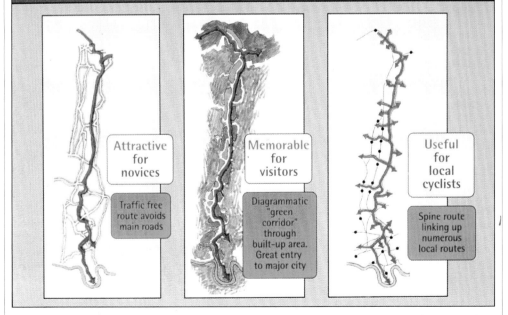

Diagram showing the three characteristics of the National Cycle Network (based on the Lee Valley Route, London).

Presentation of Millennium Milepost to the town of Odense (Denmark) to commemorate its Safe Routes to School exchange with Colchester.

The Safe Routes to Schools Project aims to change one of Britain's most shameful statistics: only 2% of journeys to school are made by bike, despite a huge majority of children wanting to get out of their parents' cars and onto their bikes. In Denmark the figure is 60%. Britain is one of the very few countries in Europe where more people cycle to work than to school. The benefits of reversing this trend are made patently clear at a school in Ipswich where 60% of the children arrive by bike. The school has won many sports competitions with other schools simply because the pupils are so much fitter.

Sculpture has come to be synonymous with the building of new sections of the Network. Starting in Consett, funded by Northern Arts, Andy Goldsworthy created the Lampton Worm, a long serpent sculpture running alongside the path. All over the country sculptures began appearing, carved from wood, sculpted from stone, welded from steel or built of brick. The Royal Bank of Scotland generously donated 1,000 mileposts with different versions designed by English, Scottish, Welsh and Irish sculptors.

Local economies have benefited enormously from the creation of Sustrans' long-distance routes. The first of these was the C2C (or Sea to Sea from the Cumbrian Coast to the North Sea) which led the way in featuring a mixture of traffic-free paths and on-road sections. Within a year of its opening 10,000 people had cycled the trail and spent over £1 million in the bed & breakfasts, Youth Hostels, pubs, cafes and shops along the way. In 1995 the C2C was the Global Winner of the 'British Airways Tourism for Tomorrow' awards. Since then many other long-distance routes have been opened and mapped, attracting many people to the idea of a cycling holiday for the first time in their lives and encouraging entrepreneurs to benefit from new business opportunities.

Sustrans has not restricted its vision to Britain alone. It is active in promoting EuroVelo which aims to link countries throughout Europe. The first of these European routes to open will be the North Sea Circuit taking in Norway, Sweden, Denmark, Holland and the East Coast of England and Scotland. A second major route, the Atlantic Arc Project will run from Cadiz in the south western tip of Spain through Portugal and the Atlantic Coast of France, crossing the Channel to Plymouth and running north to Ullapool in Scotland.

Route 5 – Reading to Holyhead and
Route 3 – Bristol to Land's End

How to use this guide

This guide helps you to explore the National Cycle Network. Perhaps you would like to try out a section of the Network close to home? Maybe you are interested in planning a longer ride of several days and would like to see which of the long-distance routes best meets your requirements. Might the Network offer a safe and attractive way for you to cycle to work? Perhaps it will act as a catalyst for you to visit a nearby friend: cycle there and catch the train back or vice versa (check which way the wind is blowing!). Use your bike on the Network to explore nearby villages, towns and cities, canals, forests and country parks, ancient monuments and historic homes. From the vantage point of a bike saddle, visit Britain's rich industrial past and see how the National Cycle Network has helped regenerate derelict wasteland into corridors of greenery, dotted with specially commissioned sculptures.

The Network near you

In this guide the country has been divided into nine regional chapters, each of which starts with a map showing the Network in the area. Each route of the Network has been given a number (you may have already seen numbers on local signposts). The map will show you how close you are to the nearest part of the Network and where it goes north, south, east and west. As an introduction to the Network you may simply wish to go for a there-and-back ride on the nearest section of traffic-free trail. As you gain confidence you will no doubt want to try out other parts of the Network which make use of quiet minor lanes.

The Day Rides in the book

The 29 Day Rides in the book offer a tremendous variety of rides showing the various different aspects of the Network. Some go right through cities, including one which runs alongside the Thames in West London, others explore some of the more rugged and remote scenery of Scotland and Wales.

Planning longer trips

You may wish to start from home and make a trip to visit a friend or relative who lives on or close to the Network or perhaps you would like to explore a different part of the country altogether. You have plenty of choice! The Network runs from Land's End to John o'Groats, from the spectacular coastline of West Wales to the Channel Ports of Dover and Ramsgate. Many of the long distance routes are covered by maps which enable you to complete a satisfying section of the Network. The most well-known of these is the C2C (Sea to Sea Route) from Whitehaven to Tynemouth but there are many others, the easiest being the Hull to Harwich route down the East Coast of the country. The hardest is probably Lôn Las Cymru (the Welsh National Route), crossing three ranges of mountains on its way from Holyhead to Cardiff. See page 218 for the Long Distance Maps already published or soon to be produced.

Sustrans Information Service

Based in Bristol, the Information Service offers a range of free information sheets covering many aspects of the National Cycle Network, including a Traffic-Free Paths Sheet, details about the Safe Routes to Schools Project, the Stamping Scheme, Millennium Mileposts plus a full selection of cycling literature which can be purchased. Goods for sale include the award-winning National Route Maps covering the long-distance routes within the National Cycle Network, packs of leaflets produced by local authorities and cycle guidebooks describing rides in many regions of the country.

The Information Service now has an on-line mail order service so you can place a credit card order for any product available in the catalogue 24 hours a day from anywhere in the world via the Internet site. The Web address is: www.sustrans.org.uk

Sustrans Information Service,
PO Box 21, Bristol BS99 2HA
Telephone: 0117 929 0888

The opening times of the office are 8.30am-5.30pm weekdays all year and 9am-1pm Saturdays from April to October.

The West Country

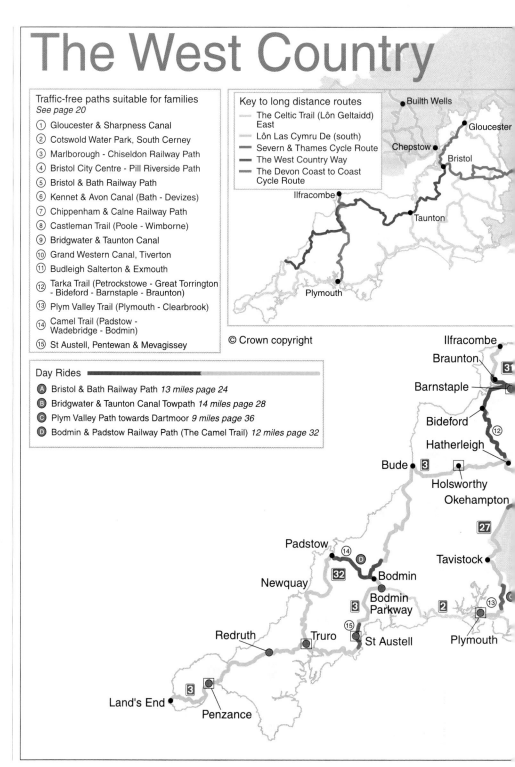

Traffic-free paths suitable for families
See page 20

1. Gloucester & Sharpness Canal
2. Cotswold Water Park, South Cerney
3. Marlborough - Chiseldon Railway Path
4. Bristol City Centre - Pill Riverside Path
5. Bristol & Bath Railway Path
6. Kennet & Avon Canal (Bath - Devizes)
7. Chippenham & Calne Railway Path
8. Castleman Trail (Poole - Wimborne)
9. Bridgwater & Taunton Canal
10. Grand Western Canal, Tiverton
11. Budleigh Salterton & Exmouth
12. Tarka Trail (Petrockstowe - Great Torrington - Bideford - Barnstaple - Braunton)
13. Plym Valley Trail (Plymouth - Clearbrook)
14. Camel Trail (Padstow - Wadebridge - Bodmin)
15. St Austell, Pentewan & Mevagissey

Key to long distance routes
- The Celtic Trail (Lôn Geltaidd) East
- Lôn Las Cymru De (south)
- Severn & Thames Cycle Route
- The West Country Way
- The Devon Coast to Coast Cycle Route

© Crown copyright

Day Rides

- Ⓐ Bristol & Bath Railway Path *13 miles page 24*
- Ⓑ Bridgwater & Taunton Canal Towpath *14 miles page 28*
- Ⓒ Plym Valley Path towards Dartmoor *9 miles page 36*
- Ⓓ Bodmin & Padstow Railway Path (The Camel Trail) *12 miles page 32*

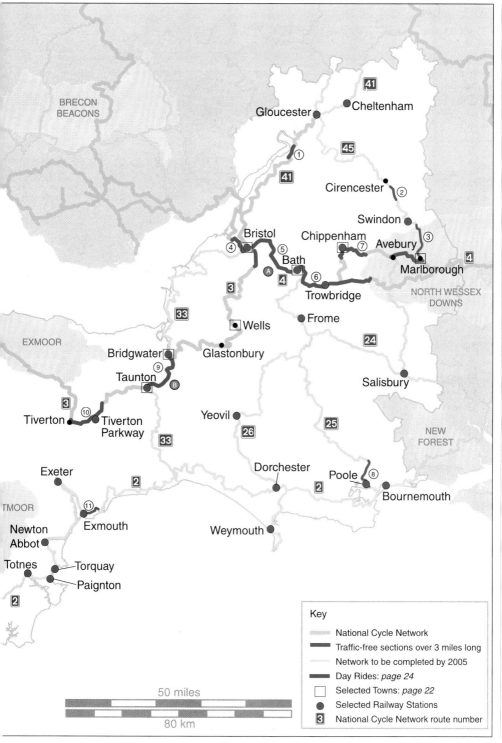

BRECON
BEACONS

Gloucester ● ● Cheltenham ⁴¹

⁴⁵

⁴¹ Cirencester ●②

Swindon ●
Chippenham ③
Bristol ④ ⑤ ⑦ Avebury
Bath ● Marlborough ⁴
④ ⓐ ④ ⑥
Trowbridge NORTH WESSEX
DOWNS
③
③³ Frome ●

EXMOOR ②⁴

Bridgwater ● ⑨ Wells ●
Taunton ● ⓑ Glastonbury Salisbury ●
③ ⑩
Tiverton ● ● Tiverton
Parkway ③³ Yeovil ● ²⁵ NEW
Exeter ● ② ²⁶ FOREST

TMOOR ⑪ Dorchester ● Poole ⑧
Newton Exmouth ② ● Bournemouth
Abbot ● Weymouth ●

Totnes ● ●—Torquay
● Paignton

②

50 miles

80 km

Key

▓▓ National Cycle Network

━━ Traffic-free sections over 3 miles long

── Network to be completed by 2005

━━ Day Rides: *page 24*

☐ Selected Towns: *page 22*

● Selected Railway Stations

③ National Cycle Network route number

17

THE WEST COUNTRY

On the 'first and last' section of the Cornish Way; Marazion, near Penzance, overlooking St. Michael's Mount.

The character of the West Country is largely defined by agriculture, tourism and a very extensive coastline – there is little heavy industry and Bristol and Plymouth are the largest cities. The National Cycle Network passes through many attractive towns and cities such as Bath, Wells, Glastonbury and Salisbury, visits Exmoor and Dartmoor (the two National Parks in the region) and explores much of the coastline of the Southwest Peninsula, reaching the sea at many places including Ilfracombe, Bude, Barnstaple, Padstow, Penzance, Plymouth, Exmouth and Weymouth.

Bristol is the headquarters of Sustrans and is appropriately at a major junction of the National Cycle Network Millennium Routes. Route 4 runs from West Wales across the old Severn Bridge through Bristol, Newbury and Reading to London; Route 41 runs north from Bristol to Gloucester; Route 3, known as the Cornish Way through Cornwall then as the West Country Way, starts at Land's End at the tip of Cornwall, climbs over Exmoor then crosses the Somerset Levels and the Mendips to Bristol. The other Millennium Route in the West Country is the Devon Coast to Coast, connecting Plymouth on the South Coast with Ilfracombe on the North.

The Bristol & Bath Railway Path (featured on pages 24-27) was Sustrans' very first project, started in 1979 and completed in 1986. It now carries over 1.7 million journeys a year.

NATIONAL NETWORK HIGHLIGHTS

Clifton Suspension Bridge

The Clifton Suspension Bridge forms a spectacular gateway to Bristol spanning 214m and crossing nearly 70m above Route 4 on the riverside below. This bridge was designed by the legendary engineer Isambard Kingdom Brunel in 1829 when he was only 23, but not completed until 1864, some five years after his death.

Severn Bridge

The first Severn Bridge takes Route 4 from Bristol to Chepstow and Newport. It opened in 1966, crossing the River Severn with a central span of 987.5m and two side spans of 305m each. The bridge, which has an aerofoil deck, was the first of its kind, and provides a clear deck for cyclists well separated from traffic. Four miles downstream, the second Severn Crossing makes no such provision for either pedestrians or cyclists.

Calne Millennium Bridge

Jack Konynenburg, North Wiltshire District Council's officer has introduced no less than four wonderful new bridges to adorn National Cycle Network Route 4

Avebury

There is no better way of approaching Avebury than on foot or cycle. The route from Chippenham to Marlborough runs right across the full width of the stone circles, along an alignment which has been used for perhaps 3,500 years. In the distance the route climbs to join the Ridgeway which is said to be Britain's oldest "road", thought to have been in use for 6,000 years!

through the Calne and Chippenham area. This modern landmark designed by Mark Lovell comprises a single laminated timber arch balanced against the offset bridge deck. This 'Black Dog' bridge crosses the main A4 and completes a largely traffic-free path along the old branch line to Calne.

Meldon Viaduct

Through the boldness and vision of Devon County Council and Bordon Quarries, the spectacular Meldon Viaduct has been restored and re-used as an unforgettable gateway to Okehampton and Dartmoor.

Land's End Trailblazing Ride

The final day of the celebrated 1996 Trailblazing Ride from Belfast to Land's End via Holyhead, Cardiff, Bristol and Plymouth. Along the way the riders attended numerous receptions where local authorities affirmed their support for the National Cycle Network.

TRAFFIC-FREE CYCLE PATHS SUITABLE FOR FAMILIES

Listed here is a selection of traffic-free routes, often along disused railways, that are more than three miles long and offer ideal cycling for families. Some are covered by the Day Rides, some are shown on the maps below. (Numbers match the map key on p.16)

1. Gloucester & Sharpness Canal, Frampton on Severn
2. Cotswold Water Park, south of Cirencester
3. Marlborough to Chiseldon Railway Path
5. Bristol & Bath Railway Path – see pages 24-27
6. Kennet & Avon Canal from Bath to Devizes
9. Bridgwater & Taunton Canal, Somerset - see pages 28-31
10. Grand Western Canal from Whipcott to Sampford Peverell & Tiverton
11. Budleigh Salterton to Exmouth
13. Plym Valley Path from Laira Bridge, Plymouth to Clearbrook – see pages 36-39
14. Camel Trail from Padstow to Wadebridge & Bodmin – see pages 32-35
15. St Austell, Pentewan & Mevagissey

For further information about traffic-free rides, ask for the Traffic-free Paths Information Sheet from Sustrans Information Service, PO Box 21, Bristol BS99 2HA (0117 929 0888) or visit www.sustrans.org.uk
The Family Cycling Trail Guide (£4.95) contains details of 300 traffic-free rides throughout Britain. Also available from Sustrans.

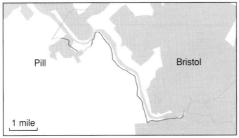

4. Bristol City Centre – Pill Riverside Path
A riverside path running for five miles from Bristol city centre past the CREATE Centre and beneath Brunel's Clifton Suspension Bridge through the Avon Gorge to Ham Green and Pill. A real delight in the changing autumn colours.

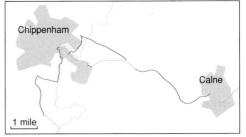

7. Chippenham & Calne Railway Path, Wilts
This six-mile section of the Severn & Thames Cycle Route runs along the course of the old railway that used to link the two towns and crosses the A4 on the unique timber-arched Millennium bridge.

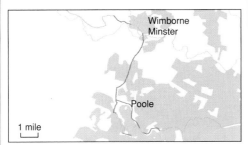

8. Castleman Trail from Upton (near Poole) to Merley (near Wimborne Minster) in Dorset
A woodland railway path between Ringwood and Poole on the course of the old Dorchester to Southampton Railway Line. Two sections of four miles each.

12. Tarka Trail from Petrockstowe to Great Torrington, Bideford, Barnstaple & Braunton, Devon
A magnificent 30-mile railway path from the heart of Devon to the north coast along the estuaries of the Rivers Taw and Torridge, passing through the historic town of Barnstaple.

© Crown copyright

REGIONAL ROUTES AND GOOD CYCLING AREAS

For further information about the leaflets covering all these routes contact Sustrans Information Service, PO Box 21, Bristol BS99 2HA (0117 929 0888) or visit www.sustrans.org.uk

THE BUZZARD CYCLE ROUTE (EAST DEVON) RPR 05
80 miles

Regional Route 52
Links with National Route 2.

A2 size full colour leaflet with basic hand-drawn map of the 80-mile circular route in East Devon, broken down into three stages. Impressionistic colour drawings. A separate leaflet shows two links into Exeter.

WILTSHIRE CYCLEWAY FPR 02
70–160 miles

Regional Routes 20, 21 & 22
Links with National Routes 4, 24, 25, 26, 45.

A2 size full colour leaflet with impressive hand-drawn mapping describing the 160-mile circular route around

Wiltshire. Also features options of six circular routes of between 70 and 160 miles and includes background detail and useful information.

CYCLE ROUND SOUTH SOMERSET FPR 01
80 miles

Regional Route 30
Links with National Route 26.

Revised and updated leaflet describing an 80-mile route on delightful quiet lanes around the lovely ham stone settlements of South Somerset including Castle Cary, South Petherton and Somerton.

AVON CYCLEWAY FPR05
85 miles

Regional Route 10
Links with National Routes 3, 4, 41.

Large full colour map using Stirling Survey mapping shows the course of the 85-mile circular ride around the former County of Avon. On the reverse are details of bike shops, train information, Tourist Information Centres and fascinating features about life in the drystone walls, hedges and verges along the route!

NORTH DORSET CYCLE ROUTE FPR 03
73 miles

Regional route 41
Links with National Route 25.

A3 leaflet in two colours describing the 73-mile route around North Dorset. Hand-drawn map plus town centre insets on one side, basic tourist information on the other side.

Two excellent areas for easy recreational cycling in the West Country are the Somerset Levels and the Severn Vale. Both are flat, with a fine network of lanes carrying little traffic.

TOWNS AND CITIES ON THE NATIONAL CYCLE NETWORK

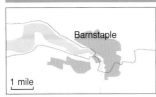

Barnstaple

The town is the gateway to the North Devon coast and represents a key destination on the Tarka Trail and the West Country Way. The extensive network of cycle routes include a good link to the station. The new bridge across the Yeo is part of the regeneration of Barnstaple's waterfront.

Bath

Traffic congestion and pollution have beset this World Heritage Site for many decades. The Bristol & Bath Railway Path and riverside route give walkers and cyclists direct access to the city centre. The National Cycle Network has been integrated into proposals for excluding traffic from the city centre and improvements will continue over coming years. To the east the Kennet & Avon Canal gives traffic-free access to Bathampton, Bradford-on-Avon and Trowbridge.

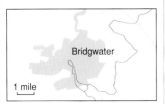

Bridgwater

The M5 makes access to the town difficult but the River Parrett Path and the Bridgwater & Taunton Canal now provide safe routes into this historic port. These routes link with the Somerset Levels. The West Country Way links Bridgwater to Glastonbury and Taunton.

Chippenham

The focus here has been major works to create routes in and out of the town. These include no less than four magnificent bridges, three over the River Avon and one over the busy A4 near Calne.

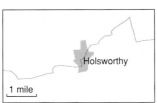

Holsworthy

This market town has campaigned with determination to link up with the West Country Way thus encouraging sustainable tourism to supplement its traditional income from agriculture. The re-opening of the listed Derriton Viaduct establishes Holsworthy as a memorable destination on National Route 3.

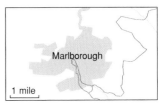

Marlborough

Marlborough is one of a number of historic market towns in Wiltshire where access has been improved through the development of the National Cycle Network. It has become an important destination on the northern leg of National Route 4 (the Severn & Thames Cycle Route). It lies at the head of the Chiseldon Railway Path and is a gateway to the Savernake Forest, the Marlborough Downs and the route to Avebury.

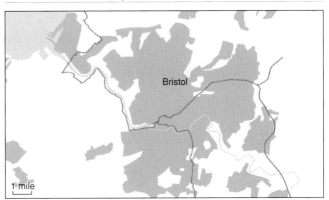

Bristol

The National Cycle Network started with the Bristol & Bath Railway Path, the earliest scheme built by Sustrans and the local cycling group, Cyclebag. The route runs through Castle Park and past Sustrans' offices to reach the @ Bristol Millennium Project. The riverside provides further links into the city including one passing under Brunel's Clifton Suspension Bridge.

© Crown copyright

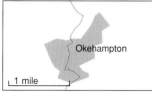

Okehampton

The National Cycle Network has been an integral part of the regeneration of Okehampton as a centre for green tourism, and as a gateway for car-free access to Dartmoor National Park. The Devon Coast to Coast Route (Route 27) combines with the re-opened railway station and the Devon Bike Bus to provide access to Abbeyford Woods to the north and to Prewley Moor and Sourton beyond the magnificent Meldon Viaduct.

Plymouth

One of Sustrans' earliest schemes linked together routes down the Plym Valley and around the edge of the Saltram Estate to reach Laira Bridge. The National Cycle Network has added two links into the city from Laira Bridge. One follows the disused railway lines into Friary Yard and the shopping centre. The other route follows Cattedown Bluffs then crosses Sutton Harbour to reach Plymouth Hoe before continuing to the ferries.

Penzance

The chief achievement of the National Cycle Network in the far west of Cornwall is the proposed construction of a promenade from Penzance to Marazion without which the cyclist is forced onto major roads. The route will continue largely along the waterfront to Newlyn Harbour.

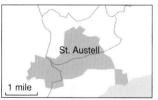

St Austell

St Austell station is an important starting point for joining the National Cycle Routes in Cornwall. It is also a midpoint between the great Eden Domes situated in a former clay pit east of the town, and Heligan Gardens via the Pentewan Tramway Path. To the north, a new railway path leads to the China Clay Museum at Wheal Martyn.

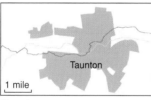

Taunton

The extensive network of cycle routes in Taunton includes National Route 3 (the West Country Way) which serves the town centre and links up with the canal towpath to Bridgwater. East of the town one quickly reaches the Somerset Levels with its maze of quiet lanes offering excellent, easy cycling.

Truro

The county town of Cornwall is a focus of the National Cycle Network in the area. Approaching from the north there is a perfect view under the railway viaduct with the piers of Brunel's earlier timber viaduct framing the twin spires of Truro Cathedral.

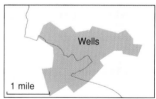

Wells

The route passes alongside the Palace Moat and into the Market Square. This compact city forms an excellent base for touring cyclists as well as a welcome stopping point along the West Country Way to regain strength before the climb up through Wookey Hole to the top of the Mendips.

© Crown copyright

BRISTOL & BATH RAILWAY PATH

Starting less than a mile from Sustrans' Bristol headquarters, the Bristol & Bath Railway Path was one of the charity's earliest successes and has happily and proudly stood the test of time, with each year adding something new to this extraordinarily popular route. It represents a wonderful escape from the urban heart of Bristol into the countryside and on into the centre of Bath. Even the inner city section has a green and rural feeling to it, passing through wooded cuttings with a plethora of wildflowers along the verges in the spring and early summer. The ride takes in a feast of attractions on its course from the centre of Bristol to the centre of Bath:

sculptures of wood, metal and stone (keep an eye out for the upside-down fish and the drinking giant!), the ¼-mile tunnel at Staple Hill, the old train station at Bitton complete with real, working steam engines, several crossings of the meandering, peaceful River Avon, glades of broadleaf woodland carpeted with bluebells in the late spring in Kelston Woods and finally a riverside stretch from the end of the railway path into the heart of the historic city of Bath.

The Bristol & Bath Railway Path has created a linear park into the heart of Bristol.

Starting points

1. Bristol Bridge, Castle Park in the centre of Bristol.
2. The Riverside Path, just off the A4 Upper Bristol Road in Bath.

Distance

16 miles one way, 32 miles return. If you start in Bristol, good turnaround/refreshment points are at Warmley (12 miles round trip), Bitton (17 miles round trip) and Saltford (22 miles round trip).

Grade

Easy.

Surface

Excellent surface throughout, almost all tarmac.

Roads, traffic, suitability for young children

Traffic-free path, ideal for beginners. The signposted approach roads from both Bristol and Bath city centres carry some traffic.

Hills

None.

Refreshments

Lots of choice in Bristol.
Cafes on the railway path at Warmley (seasonal) and at Bitton Station (at the weekend, all year round).
Stationmaster PH, Warmley; Bird in Hand PH, Jolly Sailor PH, Saltford.
Lots of choice in Bath.

Leaflets

CycleCity's *Bristol Cycling Map* is an excellent publication showing the traffic-free paths, signposted cycle routes, advisory routes plus a wealth of other information. It costs £4.95 and is available from Sustrans Information Service, PO Box 21, Bristol BS99 2HA (0117 929 0888) or visit www.sustrans.org.uk

Silhouettes by Katy Hallett set in windows of the ruined Mangotsfield Station.

Nearest railway stations

Bristol Temple Meads, Bath Spa.

The National Cycle Network in the area

Route 4 runs from South Wales to London and uses the whole of the railway path. Routes 4 and 41 together form the Severn & Thames Cycle Route from Gloucester to Newbury. Route 3, the West Country Way and the Cornish Way, heads south west from Bristol to the furthest tip of mainland Britain at Land's End.

Other nearby rides (waymarked or traffic-free)

1. A section of the railway path (between Saltford and Mangotsfield) is used by the Avon Cycleway, an 85-mile signposted route using the network of quiet lanes around Bristol. Leaflet available from Bristol City Council. Tel: 0117 922 2000.

2. The five-mile, traffic-free Pill Riverside Path runs from the Bristol Harbourside along Cumberland Road, then alongside the River Avon to Pill, passing beneath the Clifton Suspension Bridge. There is also a link to this path through Leigh Woods.

3. The Kennet & Avon Canal Towpath from Bath to Devizes is open to cyclists with a pass. Check with British Waterways at Devizes (01380 722859) for the most up-to-date information about passes.

Bath Abbey and Pump Rooms.

DAY RIDE

BRISTOL & BATH RAILWAY PATH

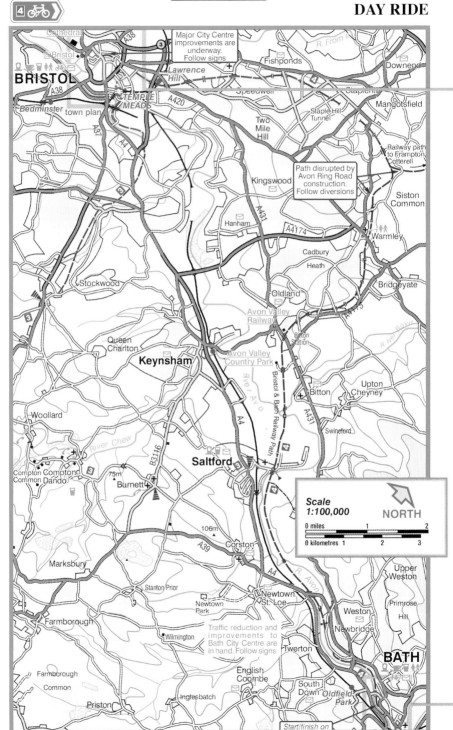

Major City Centre improvements are underway. Follow signs

Path disrupted by Avon Ring Road construction. Follow diversions

Railway path to Frampton Cotterell

Scale 1:100,000

NORTH

0 miles — 1 — 2
0 kilometres 1 — 2 — 3

Traffic reduction and improvements to Bath City Centre are in hand. Follow signs

Start/finish on

© Crown copyright

26

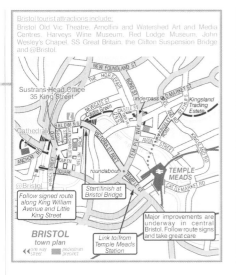

Route instructions (from Bristol to Bath)

Ring Road sculpture by Jim Paulsen.

1. From the traffic lights on the Broadmead side of Bristol Bridge in the centre of Bristol follow signs for the Bristol & Bath Railway Path on the traffic-free path alongside the River Avon across Castle Park.

2. Follow the waymarked route along Castle Street, Tower Hill and Jacob Street. Use the subway beneath Temple Way, go past Gardiner Haskins (Straight Street).

3. Turn right on Russ Street then left at the T-junction with New Kingsley Road. At the T-junction with Midland Road turn right then left onto St Philips Road. The railway path starts after 200 yards.

4. Follow the railway path for 13 miles through Staple Hill Tunnel, the new Ring Road across Siston Common, Warmley, Bitton and Saltford to its end at the Brassmill

Lane Trading Estate on the outskirts of Bath.

5. Continue along Brassmill Lane, bearing right onto the riverside path.

6. For Bath city centre, turn off the riverside path after one mile just after Victoria suspension bridge over the river and follow the waymarked Route 4 via Nelson Villas and James Street West.

Great Pulteney Street, Bath.

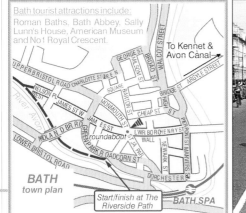

BRIDGWATER & TAUNTON CANAL TOWPATH

This easy ride along the towpath of the Bridgwater & Taunton Canal forms part of a much longer route, as the Cornish Way and West Country Way, National Route 3, runs for 313 miles from Land's End to Bristol. The canal was opened in 1827 as part of a grand scheme to link the Bristol Channel with the English Channel, so avoiding the dangerous passage around Land's End. Sadly, the great link never materialised in full. The Bridgwater & Taunton Canal and the Grand Western Canal near Tiverton (also used on the West Country Way) are all that remain of this ambitious project. As a cyclist along the towpath, enjoy the abundant birdlife – swans, herons and a variety of ducks can all be seen along the canal. There is also a series of stone sculptures of the planets, conceived and built by Pip Youngman in 1997. There are many options to plan your own circular rides using the wonderful network of flat lanes on the Somerset Levels as an alternative to returning along the towpath.

Bridgwater & Taunton Canal.

Starting points

1. Town Bridge, Bridgwater.
2. Bridge Street, Taunton.

Distance

14 miles one way, 28 miles return. For shorter routes (starting from Bridgwater) there are good turnaround points at the Harvest Moon PH in North Newton (10 miles round trip), the Canal Centre and Cafe at Maunsel Lock (14 miles round trip) or the pubs in Creech St Michael (21 miles round trip).

Grade

Easy.

Surface

The towpath has a variable quality gravel surface.

Roads, traffic, suitability for young children

The towpath is suitable for children, provided they know about the dangers of water. There is a three-mile road section in the middle of the ride on quiet lanes south of North Newton.

Hills

No hills along the towpath.

Refreshments

Lots of choice in Bridgwater. Boat & Anchor PH, Huntworth; Harvest Moon PH, North Newton;

A section of the towpath on the Bridgwater & Taunton Canal.

Cafe at the Canal Centre (south of North Newton), open 2.00-6.00; The Bell Inn and The Riverside Tavern, Creech St Michael. Lots of choice in Taunton.

Nearest railway stations

Bridgwater or Taunton.

The National Cycle Network in the area

This ride is part of the West Country Way (Route 3) which runs from Padstow to Bristol. Route 33 is a planned north-south route linking Taunton with the South Coast Route (Route 2) at Axminster and Seaton.

Other nearby rides (waymarked or traffic-free)

There is an excellent network of quiet, flat lanes on the Somerset Levels, to the east of Bridgwater. The South Somerset Cycle Ride is an 80-mile waymarked route around the lovely lanes and ham-stone villages of South Somerset.

The towpath through Creech St. Michael takes you right into the centre of Taunton.

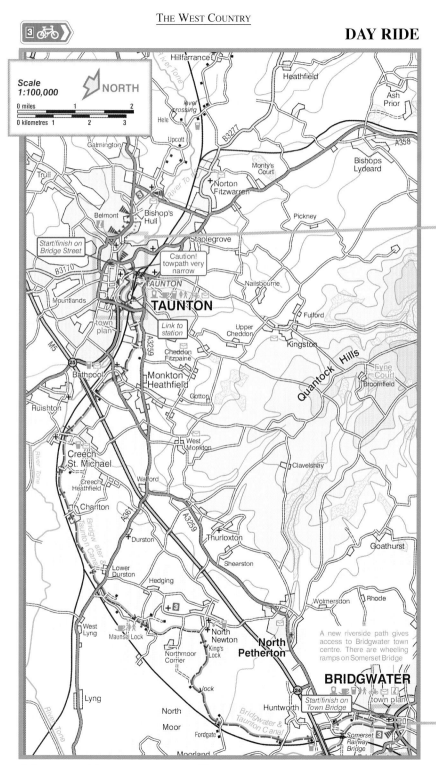

DAY RIDE

BRIDGWATER & TAUNTON CANAL PATH

Scale
1:100,000

NORTH

0 miles 1 2

0 kilometres 1 2 3

Hillfarrance

River Tone

Heathfield

Ash Prior

lever crossing

Hele

B3277

A358

Upcott

Galmington

Monty's Court

Bishops Lydeard

Trull

Norton Fitzwarren

Belmont

Bishop's Hull

Pickney

Start/finish on Bridge Street

Staplegrove

B3170

Caution! towpath very narrow

TAUNTON

Nailsbourne

Fulford

TAUNTON

Mountlands

town plan

Link to station

Upper Cheddon

Kingston

M5

Cheddon Fitzpaine

Quantock Hills

Fyne Court

Bathpool

Monkton Heathfield

Broomfield

Ruishton

Gotton

A3259

West Monkton

Clavelshay

Creech St. Michael

River Tone

Creech Heathfield

Walford

Charlton

A361

A3259

Durston

Thurloxton

Goathurst

Bridgwater & Taunton Canal

Lower Durston

Shearston

Hedging

Wolmersdon

Rhode

West Lyng

Maunsel Lock

North Newton

North Petherton

A new riverside path gives access to Bridgwater town centre. There are wheeling ramps on Somerset Bridge.

Northmoor Corner

King's Lock

BRIDGWATER

lock

town plan

Lyng

North Moor

Huntworth

Start/finish on Town Bridge

Bridgwater & Taunton Canal

Fordgate

Somerset Railway Bridge

River Tone

Moorland

© Crown copyright

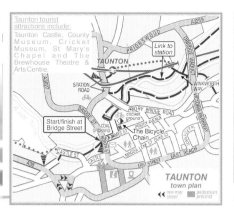

Bridgwater & Taunton Canal.

Route instructions (from Bridgwater to Taunton)

1. From Town Bridge in the centre of Bridgwater, follow Binford Place through Goodland Gardens under the underpass, then left along the Old Taunton Road.

2. Cross the road over the canal and turn left down onto the towpath. Follow in the same direction as the track turns to a tarmac lane and passes beneath the M5. On a sharp right hand bend turn left over the wooden bridge towards the Boat & Anchor pub then turn right along the towpath.

3. Follow the towpath for four miles. Shortly after King's Lock the

track turns to tarmac. Follow the road as it crosses the canal. At the T-junction by the Harvest Moon pub at the end of Church Street in North Newton turn left then shortly turn left again signposted 'Durston, Lyng, Canal Centre'.

4. Ignore the first road to the left (this is a no through road to Coxhill). Go past Maunsel House and take the next road left signposted 'Canal Centre'. Immediately after crossing the bridge over the canal turn right past the cafe/Canal Centre (this would be a good turnaround spot if you are looking for a short return ride).

5. Leave the towpath after ¼-mile and continue in the same direction on a minor lane. **Easy to miss.** After one mile turn right by the bridge over the canal (Outwood Swing Bridge) then left to rejoin towpath.

6. Follow the towpath for 6½ miles, passing through Creech St Michael and beneath the M5 bridge. Shortly after a second tall road bridge the waymarked route leaves the towpath and bears up to the left to a T-junction with a lane. To reach the station, turn right at Obridge under the railway line and first left parallel to the railway.

7. Turn left, then immediately after crossing the river turn right along the riverside path onto track. This turns to tarmac then track again. Immediately after the Somerset Cricket Ground bear left through car park at the 'Route 3' sign.

8. At the mini-roundabout go straight ahead. At the T-junction just past the Bicycle Chain shop turn right along St. James Street to reach Taunton town centre (Bridge Street/North Fore Street).

Approaching Taunton.

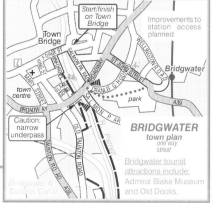

THE CAMEL TRAIL – BODMIN TO PADSTOW

The Camel Trail is the most popular tourist cycle route in the country with over 350,000 visitors a year. This superb ride follows the course of an old railway line from Bodmin along the wooded valley of the River Camel and the sandy shores of the Camel Estuary to Padstow. It also forms part of the West Country Way which runs from Padstow to Bristol. In addition to there-and-back rides along the Camel Trail there are many possible loops using the network of country lanes to explore the coastline east of the estuary at Port Isaac, Polzeath and Rock, or west of Bodmin to Ruthernbridge, Rosenannon and beyond. Bear in mind that this is a hilly part of the country and you are likely to be faced with many short sharp climbs!

Approaching Padstow along the Camel Estuary.

Starting points

1. Bodmin Parkway railway station, five miles south east of Bodmin.
2. Bodmin Jail, town centre.
3. Wadebridge town centre.
4. Padstow harbour.

Distance

The Camel Trail runs for 18 miles from Padstow to Poley's Bridge (situated between St Tudy and Blisland) ie 36 miles there and back. You have a variety of options:
1. The most popular is Wadebridge-Padstow-Wadebridge (12 miles round trip).
2. The longest would be Padstow-Bodmin-Poley's Bridge-Bodmin-Padstow (36 miles).
3. You may wish to devise your own lane routes from the ends of the trail back to Bodmin. Be warned that it is hilly around here!

Grade

The Camel Trail itself is easy, running along the course of an old railway line. The link from Bodmin Parkway to the start of the trail is fairly strenuous.

Surface

Variable gravel surface on the Camel Trail.

Roads, traffic, suitability for young children

The Camel Trail is ideal for young children, with lots to see along the way and superb cycle hire infrastructure in Wadebridge and Padstow which caters for all requirements.
1. You have to go through the centre of Wadebridge on streets but there are so many cyclists that traffic does not pose the normal threats.
2. There is one busy road to cross (the A389) on the Poley's Bridge section.
3. The (hilly) route from Bodmin Parkway to the Camel Trail is mostly on-road, and includes the new Millennium bridge over the A30. Care should be taken crossing the A389 in Bodmin.

Hills

The section between Bodmin and Padstow is flat. There is a gentle 200ft climb from Bodmin north east along the Camel Trail to Poley's

Bridge. The route between Bodmin Parkway station and the start of the Camel Trail is hilly with one particularly steep climb.

Refreshments

Lots of choice in Bodmin, Wadebridge and Padstow. Tea shop near Boscarne Junction Station.

Nearest railway stations

Bodmin Parkway. The Bodmin and Wenford Railway is a tourist line and runs infrequently between Bodmin Parkway, Bodmin and Boscarne Junction.

The National Cycle Network in the area

The Camel Trail is used as part of both the West Country Way and the Cornish Way (Route 3) on its way from Land's End to Bristol. In the future, Route 2 will run from Bodmin to Plymouth.

Other nearby rides (waymarked or traffic-free)

There are waymarked forest trails in Cardinham Woods, east of Bodmin.

Cycle hire is available in Padstow and Wadebridge.

THE CAMEL TRAIL – BODMIN TO PADSTOW

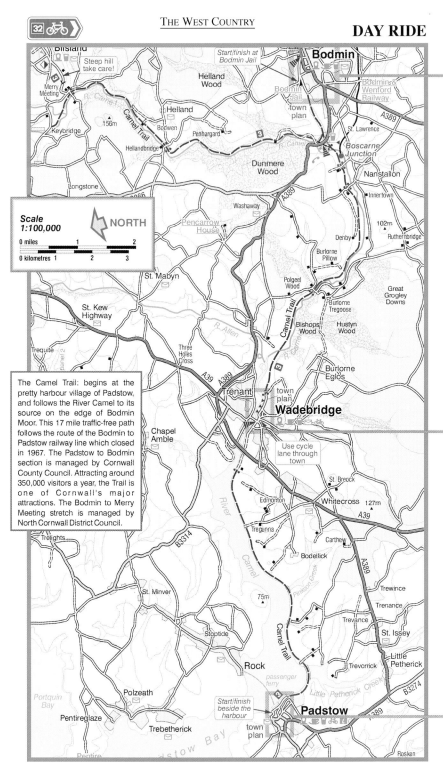

Scale 1:100,000

0 miles — 1 — 2

0 kilometres 1 — 2 — 3

NORTH

The Camel Trail: begins at the pretty harbour village of Padstow, and follows the River Camel to its source on the edge of Bodmin Moor. This 17 mile traffic-free path follows the route of the Bodmin to Padstow railway line which closed in 1967. The Padstow to Bodmin section is managed by Cornwall County Council. Attracting around 350,000 visitors a year, the Trail is one of Cornwall's major attractions. The Bodmin to Merry Meeting stretch is managed by North Cornwall District Council.

© Crown copyright

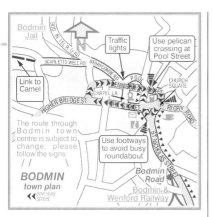

Route instructions (from Bodmin to Wadebridge and on to Padstow)

1. From Bodmin Jail follow the signs for the Camel Trail.

2. After one mile, at a junction of tracks just past a sign for the Borough Arms PH you have a choice:

a) continue straight ahead to Wadebridge (five miles one way) and Padstow (11 miles one way); b) turn sharp right towards Poley's Bridge (seven miles one way).

3. (Route through Wadebridge). Take care with young children on the roads through Wadebridge. Follow the waymarks and rejoin the railway path and follow for a further six miles to the harbour in Padstow.

Overlooking the Camel Estuary.

35

THE PLYM VALLEY PATH TOWARDS DARTMOOR

Starting from the naval city of Plymouth, where Sir Francis Drake played bowls before defeating the Spanish Armada, the Plym Valley Path is the first section of the Devon Coast to Coast Route crossing the county from south to north and finishing at Ilfracombe. The trail runs from the heart of Plymouth alongside the River Plym, passing the magnificent 18th-century mansion Saltram House. The route continues gently uphill through thick woodland, following first the line of the Lee Moor China Clay tramway, then Cann Quarry Canal and finally the course of the old Great Western Railway (built by Isambard Kingdom Brunel) as it crosses a series of viaducts and passes through a curved tunnel. The route described below goes as far as Clearbrook on the edge of Dartmoor. On the return trip to Laira Bridge you are faced with a wonderful descent over several miles to get back to the start.

Plymbridge Woods.

Starting point

Laira Bridge or Saltram House, Plymouth.

Distance

Nine miles from Laira Bridge to Clearbrook, ie 18 miles round trip. It will be much slower climbing up to Clearbrook than coming back downhill!

Grade

Moderate.

Surface

Good gravel track from Laira Bridge to the tunnel. Rougher section from the end of the railway trail up to the Skylark Inn at Clearbrook. Due for improvements soon.

Roads, traffic, suitability for young children

The traffic-free Plym Valley Trail is ideal for children.

The route from the centre of Plymouth to Laira Bridge is on streets. There is a short steep lane section near Bickleigh.

Hills

Steady 500ft climb up from Laira

Bridge to Clearbrook with a steep section on a quiet lane near Bickleigh.

Refreshment

Lots of choice along the seafront in Plymouth.

Skylark PH in Clearbrook.

Nearest railway station

Plymouth.

The National Cycle Network in the area

Plymouth is the starting point of the Devon Coast to Coast (Routes 31, 3 & 27) which runs to Ilfracombe and Bude. Route 2 will run west from

Plym Valley Trail, ideal for a day out.

Exeter via Plymouth to Bodmin.

Other nearby rides (waymarked or traffic-free)

1. There is a waymarked forest route in Bellever Forest on Dartmoor, 11 miles northeast of Tavistock.

2. A section of dismantled railway in Princetown (Dartmoor) has been converted to recreational use.

Route details at Plymbridge Woods.

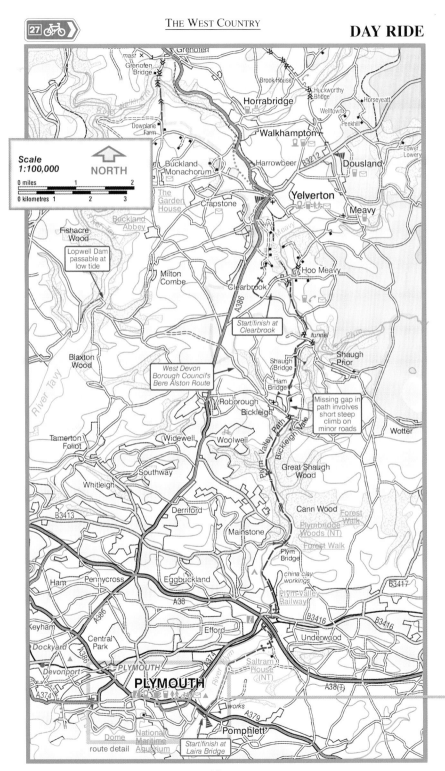

THE PLYM VALLEY PATH TOWARDS DARTMOOR

Scale
1:100,000

NORTH

0 miles   1   2
0 kilometres 1   2   3

Grenofen

mast ×
Grenofen Bridge

Brook House

Huckworthy Bridge

Horseyeatt

Horrabridge

Welltown

Peekhill

Downpine Farm

Walkhampton

Lower Lowery

Buckland Monachorum

Harrowbeer

B3212

Dousland

The Garden House

Crapstone

Yelverton

Meavy

Buckland Abbey

Fishacre Wood

Lopwell Dam passable at low tide

Milton Combe

Clearbrook

Hoo Meavy

A386

Start/finish at Clearbrook

tunnel

Shaugh Prior

Blaxton Wood

West Devon Borough Council's Bere Alston Route

Shaugh Bridge

Ham Bridge

Roborough

Bickleigh

Missing gap in path involves short steep climb on minor roads

Wotter

Tamerton Foliot

Widewell

Woolwell

Great Shaugh Wood

River Tavy

Southway

Whitleigh

Derriford

Cann Wood Forest Walk

B3413

Mainstone

Plymbridge Woods (NT)

Forest Walk

Plym Bridge

B3417

Ham

Pennycross

Eggbuckland

china clay workings

Plym Valley Railway

Keyham

A386

A38

Central Park

Efford

Underwood

B3416

B3416

Dockyard

Devonport

PLYMOUTH

A374

PLYMOUTH

Saltram House (NT)

A38(T)

A374

works

A379

Pomphlett

Dome

National Maritime Aquarium

Start/finish at Laira Bridge

route detail

© Crown copyright

38

Cycle lanes along Plymouth Hoe.

Route instructions (from Laira Bridge, Plymouth to Clearbrook)

1. At the eastern end of Laira Bridge cross the road via traffic lights following signs for Plym Valley. Keep bearing to the left. After ½-mile, opposite a car park to the right, turn left through a wooden gate to continue close to the river.

2. At the fork of tracks beyond the next gate bear left uphill and left again at a T-junction with tarmac. (Remember this point for your return route). The narrow tarmac lane crosses a bridge over the railway. Pass beneath the A38 viaduct. Follow cycle signs for Plym Valley and Tavistock past Coypool Park.

3. After five miles, climbing gently through woodland, where the railway path comes to a T-junction with a lane, turn left steeply uphill then after 200 yds turn first right signposted 'Shaugh Prior'. Shortly after a sharp right-hand bend, turn left onto a continuation of the railway path.

4. After 1½ miles, go through a tunnel. At the end of the track follow red arrows on a steep section to climb up to Clearbrook. Turn left along the road to the Skylark Inn.

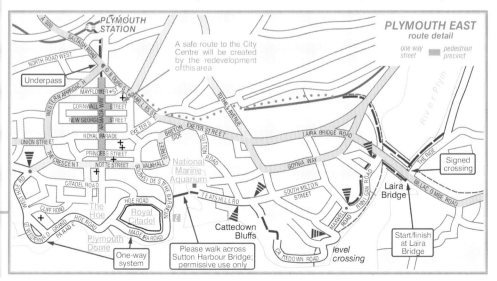

South East

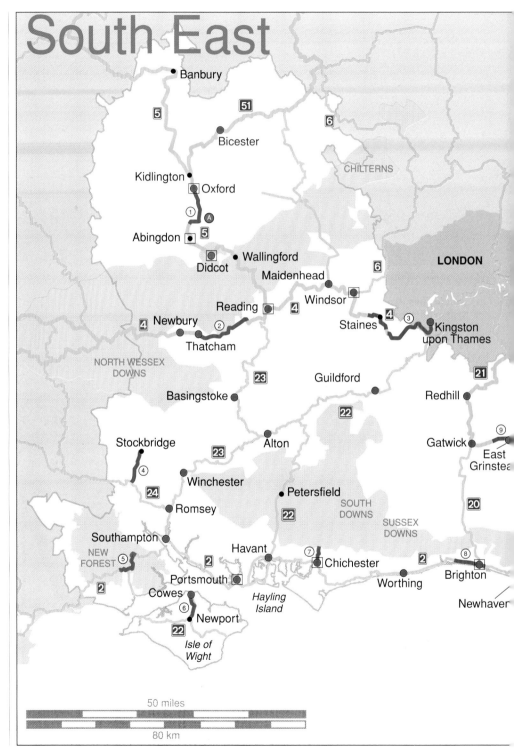

Banbury

5

51

6

Bicester

CHILTERNS

Kidlington
Oxford

① Ⓐ

Abingdon 5

Didcot
Wallingford

Maidenhead

LONDON

Windsor

6

Reading 4

Newbury 4
② Thatcham

4 Staines
③

Kingston
upon Thames

NORTH WESSEX
DOWNS

23

Guildford

21

Basingstoke

22

Redhill

Stockbridge
④

Alton

Gatwick
East
Grinstea

9

23

24

Winchester

Petersfield

SOUTH
DOWNS

20

Romsey

22

SUSSEX
DOWNS

Southampton

Havant

⑦ Chichester

2

Brighton

8

Worthing

NEW
FOREST 5

2

Portsmouth

Cowes

Hayling
Island

Newhaver

⑥ Newport

2

22

Isle of
Wight

50 miles

80 km

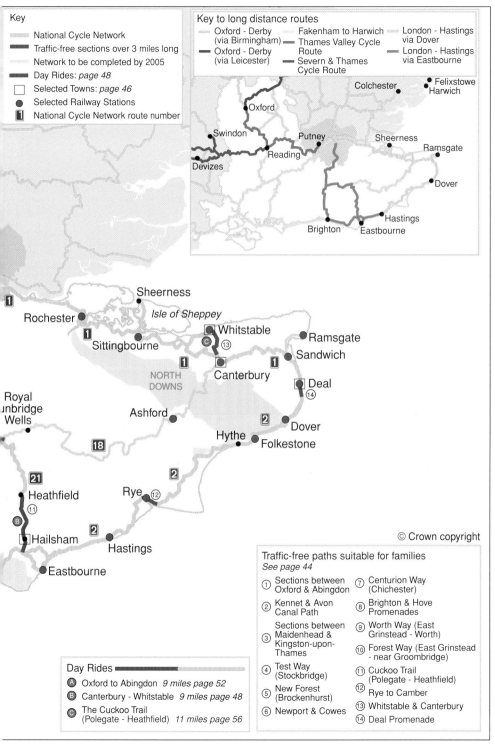

Key

- National Cycle Network
- Traffic-free sections over 3 miles long
- Network to be completed by 2005
- Day Rides: *page 48*
- ☐ Selected Towns: *page 46*
- ● Selected Railway Stations
- 🔟 National Cycle Network route number

Key to long distance routes

- Oxford - Derby (via Birmingham)
- Oxford - Derby (via Leicester)
- Fakenham to Harwich
- Thames Valley Cycle Route
- Severn & Thames Cycle Route
- London - Hastings via Dover
- London - Hastings via Eastbourne

Colchester
Felixstowe
Harwich
Oxford
Swindon
Putney
Sheerness
Ramsgate
Reading
Devizes
Dover
Hastings
Brighton Eastbourne

Sheerness
🔟
Rochester
Isle of Sheppey
🔟 Whitstable
Sittingbourne
ⓒ ⑬ Ramsgate
🔟 🔟 Sandwich
NORTH DOWNS Canterbury
🔟 Deal ⑭
Royal
nbridge
Wells
Ashford
2
Dover
Hythe Folkestone
18
2
21
Heathfield
Rye ⑫
⑪
Ⓑ
2
Hailsham
2
Hastings
Eastbourne

© Crown copyright

Traffic-free paths suitable for families
See page 44

① Sections between Oxford & Abingdon
② Kennet & Avon Canal Path
③ Sections between Maidenhead & Kingston-upon-Thames
④ Test Way (Stockbridge)
⑤ New Forest (Brockenhurst)
⑥ Newport & Cowes
⑦ Centurion Way (Chichester)
⑧ Brighton & Hove Promenades
⑨ Worth Way (East Grinstead - Worth)
⑩ Forest Way (East Grinstead - near Groombridge)
⑪ Cuckoo Trail (Polegate - Heathfield)
⑫ Rye to Camber
⑬ Whitstable & Canterbury
⑭ Deal Promenade

Day Rides

- Ⓐ Oxford to Abingdon *9 miles page 52*
- Ⓑ Canterbury - Whitstable *9 miles page 48*
- Ⓒ The Cuckoo Trail (Polegate - Heathfield) *11 miles page 56*

THE SOUTH EAST

Southeast England is one of the most densely populated areas in Europe with over 17 million people living in or within 60 miles of London. As it is also the most affluent region of Britain, traffic levels are higher here than anywhere else in the country. Sustrans' work is all the more vital in trying to halt the growth of traffic, offering real alternatives to the car for trips to school, work, shopping and leisure.

Four routes leave London, two of which head for the South Coast. The first of these runs east along the Thames Estuary from Greenwich to Gravesend and Faversham, cutting inland to visit the architectural splendours of Canterbury and passing through Kent's 'Garden of England' fruit orchards before rejoining the coast for the journey from Deal to Dover. The other route

Whitstable Harbour.

heads south through the chalk hills of the North Downs, passing through Redhill and crossing the High Weald to East Grinstead to link with the popular traffic-free Cuckoo Trail down to Eastbourne. The coastal route running between Dover and Eastbourne completes the triangle. The third route starts in the centre of London (the Thames Valley Cycle Route) connecting the capital to the dreaming spires of Oxford via the glories of Hampton Court and Windsor and the wooded delights of the Chilterns between Reading and Wallingford. The fourth route heads northwards to reach the Lee valley

NATIONAL CYCLE NETWORK HIGHLIGHTS

Bexhill Promenade

The promenades of the South East offer a wonderful opportunity to cycle beside the sea. Many promenades built in the heyday of rail borne seaside holidays are now much less used by promenaders with the opportunity for introducing traffic-free cycle routes which are an ideal place for the novice and family groups to learn to cycle again.

Didcot Power Station

The power station is known as the Cathedral of the Vale. Its vast cooling towers are visible from miles away in all directions. They are the despair of cyclists because they seem to be at once near yet far. Their scale distort the distances and stretch the time of journeys to Didcot.

Shakespeare Cliffs between Folkestone and Dover

The route here climbs up from sea level at either end to run along the top of these spectacular cliffs with views out to France. Along the way you pass an early wartime listening station in the shape of a shallow parabolic concrete basin.

Portsmouth Harbour Ferry

The ferry to Gosport provides a direct crossing of Portsmouth Harbour for pedestrians and cyclists only. It is one reason why the level of cycling in Gosport is one of the highest in the country.

Milepost at Dover

This milepost at the entrance to Dover ferry announces the start of the National Cycle Network to visitors from the Continent. It is one of 1,000 mileposts marking out the Network which have been funded by The Royal Bank of Scotland, who have supported Sustrans throughout its development of safe and attractive cycle routes.

Canterbury Cathedral

Whatever your beliefs or creed, no cycle route could be called national if it bypassed Canterbury and its ancient and magnificent cathedral. It stands on the site of a Roman church given to the monks by King Ethelbert in 597. This early church was entirely destroyed by fire but was rebuilt. The building we now see was eventually completed in 1495. After the murder of Thomas à Becket in 1170 his shrine was the centre of pilgrimages for centuries. These are fully described by Chaucer in his 'Canterbury Tales'.

TRAFFIC-FREE CYCLE PATHS SUITABLE FOR FAMILIES

Listed here is a selection of traffic-free routes, often along disused railways, that are more than three miles long and offer ideal cycling for families. Some are covered by the Day Rides, some are shown on the maps below. (Numbers match the map key on p.41)

1. Sections between Oxford and Abingdon including the Thames riverside path – see pages 52-55
2. The Kennet & Avon canal towpath between Thatcham and Reading
3. Staines to Kingston upon Thames – see pages 66-71 for the route east of Weybridge
4. Test Way, south of Stockbridge, Hampshire
5. The New Forest
7. The Centurion Way north of Chichester
8. Brighton & Hove Promenades

11. The Cuckoo Trail, a railway path from Polegate to Heathfield – see pages 56-59
13. Canterbury & Whitstable – see pages 48-51
14. Deal Promenade

For further information about traffic-free rides, ask for the Traffic-free Paths Information Sheet from Sustrans Information Service, PO Box 21, Bristol. BS99 2HA (0117 929 0888) or visit www.sustrans.org.uk
The Family Cycling Trail Guide (£4.95) contains details of 300 traffic-free rides throughout Britain. Also available from Sustrans.

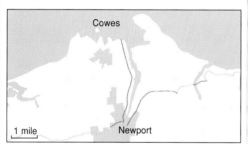

6. Newport to Cowes on the Isle of Wight
A four-mile ride along a dismantled railway between the important sailing centre at Cowes and the island's capital in Newport. The trail runs alongside the Medina River, full of colourful moored yachts.

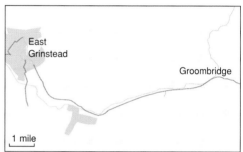

10. Forest Way from East Grinstead to near Groombridge, Sussex
An open ride on a dismantled railway passing through arable land lying between the High Weald to the south and the North Downs to the north. The countryside around Hartfield is the setting of A.A. Milne's *Winnie the Pooh*.

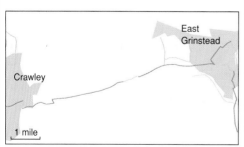

9. Worth Way from East Grinstead to Worth, near Crawley, Sussex
Starting right behind the busy commuter railway station at East Grinstead is a lovely broad wooded trail running west to Worth with its attractive old church.

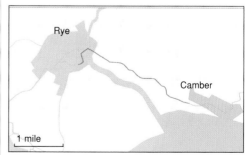

12. Rye to Camber
From the historic Cinque Port of Rye on the Kent/Sussex border, a newly built traffic-free path runs east to the holiday village of Camber, famed for its sandy beach. This provides a gateway to the quiet lane network on Romney Marsh and avoids a long detour on the busy A259.

© Crown copyright

REGIONAL ROUTES AND GOOD CYCLING AREAS

For further information about the leaflets and guidebooks covering all these routes and areas contact Sustrans Information Service, PO Box 21, Bristol BS99 2HA (0117 929 0888) or visit www.sustrans.org.uk

ROUND THE ISLAND CYCLE ROUTE (ISLE OF WIGHT) RPR 08

62 miles

Links with National Route 2 via vehicle and pedestrian ferries. A3 size leaflet printed in two colours showing the course of the 62-mile ride around the Isle of Wight. Route instructions describe the route both clockwise and anti-clockwise

CYCLING IN KENT RPR 03

50 miles

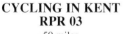

Regional Routes 16,17
Links with National Routes 1, 2, 17 and 18.
This pack includes seven comprehensive leaflets describing the 50-mile 'Cathedral to Coast' route linking Canterbury, Dover and Folkestone; the Dover to Sandwich route; the 'Bluebell Way' from Maidstone to Rochester and the

'Weald on Wheels' linking Ashford to Tenterden and beyond to Tunbridge Wells. Town centre maps showing cycle routes in Ashford and Canterbury are also included. All leaflets feature details of cycle shops, accommodation plus attractions on the routes.

THE RIDGEWAY RB004

One of the oldest 'roads' in Europe, dating back over 5,000 years, the Ridgeway is a broad stone and chalk track which follows the top of the chalk escarpment for 40 miles from near Avebury to the Thames at Goring. It is a long-distance bridleway passing many old earthworks and the White Horse of Uffington. It is best explored on a mountain bike in the summer months. Traffic-free access routes are being developed from Didcot Parkway railway station.

Ordnance Survey Cycle Tours: Berks, Bucks & Oxfordshire contains several rides on the Ridgeway.

THE SOUTH DOWNS RB012

As with the Ridgeway this is a long-distance bridleway which mainly uses stone and chalk tracks on its course from Winchester to Eastbourne. It follows the top of the chalk ridge with dramatic views out over the English Channel to the south and the Sussex Weald to the north. As with the Ridgeway it is best undertaken on mountain bikes, in summer. There are also some tough hills!

Ordnance Survey Cycle Tours: Kent, Surrey & Sussex contains several rides in the South Downs area.

HAMPSHIRE RB008

Between the A3 and the M3 in Hampshire there is a dense network of quiet and gently graded lanes that offer some quintessentially English cycling past thatched cottages with pretty gardens, lovely villages and rich, rolling agricultural land. Good bases might be New Alresford, East Meon or Odiham.

Ordnance Survey Cycle Tours: Dorset, Hampshire & the Isle of Wight contains several rides in Hampshire.

TOWNS AND CITIES ON THE NATIONAL CYCLE NETWORK

Abingdon

Once famous for its MG cars and Morlands Brewery, Abingdon still offers a wide range of attractions and fine riverside views. Although heavily trafficked there is an attractive market square with the classic County Hall (Abingdon was once the county town of Berkshire, although it is now in Oxfordshire). The route towards Oxford uses part of the former railway link into town.

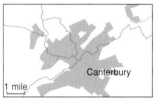

Canterbury

A focus of routes and an excellent example of the success of the Safe Routes to Schools Project (16 schools are involved). The city has a 20 mph traffic zone and a good bike hire centre at the railway station. Canterbury deserves a special mention in this guide because it led the way for Kent to make its contribution to the National Cycle Network. The initiative has created links for cyclists to the Channel ports and opened up the city and much of the rest of the beautiful Kent countryside to exploration by bike.

Chichester

This compact and level city is well-suited to cycling. The Centurion Way, an early Sustrans project, follows the abandoned gravel railway north out of the centre and will ultimately be extended to connect with the South Downs Way. At its south end the Centurion Way links to the South Coast Cycle Route which runs past the station, the cathedral and the remains of the palace of the Roman Governor in England, in Fishbourne.

Deal

The obvious route for novice cyclists through this seaside town runs along the promenade in front of Deal and Walmer Castles. The latter is the traditional home of the Lord Warden of the Cinque Ports. The route passes the quaint old pier and close to the famous Royal St George's Golf Club.

Didcot

The dominant image of Didcot is of the massive power station cooling towers, known locally as the Cathedral of the Vale. But with easy access to the Thames Valley Cycle Route in both directions and off-road connections to the Ridgeway, Didcot station could become the gateway to the countryside for those arriving by train from all over the country.

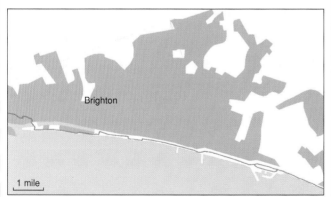

Brighton & Hove

The key South Coast Cycle Route runs along the seafront via the well-established promenade cycle tracks. East of the Palace Pier the route runs along the spectacular Undercliff Walk to reach Saltdean, where it will connect with a link to the ferry port at Newhaven. A Regional Route north east of the town has been developed which runs past the universities at Falmer to Lewes.

© Crown copyright

Hailsham

The Cuckoo Trail (see pages 56-59) is an excellent example of the development of a high quality railway path. Completed in 1993, the path was developed by Sustrans for Wealden District Council and East Sussex County Council and has become the focus for development of cycling in the area, with a particular emphasis on tourism. The path runs right through the centre of Hailsham, passing the Community Centre and linking to the Council Offices and Leisure Centre.

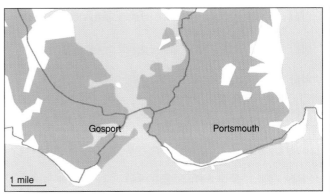

Portsmouth and Gosport

The towns are level and ideal for cycling. Either side of the city, ferries to Gosport and Hayling Island specifically provide for cyclists, whilst the National Routes follow largely traffic-free corridors around the periphery of the promontory. Gosport has the highest level of cycling of any town in the South of England. The route to Fareham follows the course of the former railway which is planned to become the route of a rapid transport system. The National Cycle Network around Portsmouth Harbour is a classic example of a route which is both attractive for novices and useful for local journeys.

Oxford

The City of Dreaming Spires is teeming with cyclists. The National Routes follow existing urban cycling routes for the most part, leaving the city to the north via the towpath of the Oxford Canal and by the riverside path along the Thames to the south. The latter provides a charming way into the heart of this university town.

Reading

Riverside National Routes 4 and 5 meet at the convergence of the Thames and the Kennet forming a tranquil route around the town. The new Oracle shopping centre spans the Kennet and incorporates a key section of the National Cycle Network through the town centre. A link from National Route 4 connects to the new Reading Stadium to the south. A very pleasant link to the east following the Thames towpath passes through Sonning village where the main route can be rejoined along traffic-calmed roads.

Whitstable

A small seaside town with rows of wooden summer huts along the beach, a working harbour and small, intimate streets. Whitstable was the destination of the world's first regular passenger railway (from Canterbury) the course of which the cycle route partly follows. Notice also the unusual path surface of cockle shells on the outskirts of the town, scoured from Whitstable Harbour and reflecting the path's name – the Crab & Winkle Way.

Windsor & Eton

The Thames, Eton College, Windsor Castle and both town centres are all within yards of the National Route. From the centre of Windsor the route passes the Leisure Centre following quiet residential roads to Windsor Great Park. An attractive two-mile traffic-free path through the park leads to Ranger's Gate and a quiet network of park roads.

© Crown copyright

CANTERBURY & WHITSTABLE CYCLE PATH

A short ride encapsulating all that is best about the National Cycle Network – a route starting from the centre of a beautiful, historic city, passing along traffic-calmed roads and specially-built cyclepaths into the countryside, following the course of a dismantled railway through broadleaf and conifer woodland to an attractive seaside town. Canterbury has been a place of pilgrimage for many centuries. The streets around the cathedral are a real delight. The cathedral area is best explored on foot and there is, in any case, a restriction on cycling here between 10.30AM and 4.00PM. The route climbs steadily out of the city with wonderful views opening up behind you. After passing close to the university the route soon joins a traffic-free section that runs for over four miles past fruit farms and through woodland to South Street on the edge of Whitstable. Cyclepaths and traffic-calmed streets lead right into the heart of this fine coastal town.

Canterbury beside the Great Stour.

48

Starting points
1. Westgate, Canterbury.
2. Whitstable town centre.

Distance
(a) Canterbury to Whitstable – nine miles one way, 18 miles return.
(b) Canterbury to Fordwich – three miles one way, six miles return.

Grade
Easy.

Surface
Streets at the start and finish, a fine stone-based path between the university and South Street, on the edge of Whitstable.

Roads, traffic, suitability for young children
The route through Canterbury and Whitstable uses traffic-calmed streets or cycle paths. The central section is on a newly-built traffic-free path through woodland, partially using the old railway line.

Hills
There is a gentle 200ft climb out of Canterbury and an undulating middle section before dropping down to the coast at Whitstable.

Refreshments
Lots of choice in Canterbury.
Lots of choice in Whitstable.

Leaflets
Canterbury Cycle Routes is an A3 leaflet showing cycle routes in Canterbury. Available from Canterbury City Council, Council Offices, Military Road, Canterbury, Kent CT1 1YW (01227 763763).

Nearby railway stations for longer linear ride
Starting from Whitstable you could follow Route 1 west to Faversham and Sittingbourne or east to Sandwich, Deal and Dover and catch the train back.

1999 Workcamp at Canterbury and Fordwich.

Canterbury to Fordwich
Another option from the centre of Canterbury is to follow the newly-built path out to the east to Fordwich where you join a delightful network of lanes meadering across rich agricultural country eastwards to Sandwich and the coast.

The National Cycle Network in the area
Canterbury lies at a crossroads of the Network. The east-west route from London to Dover is already in place (Route 1). To the south Routes 16 and 17 will go to Ashford and Hythe respectively. To the north Route 15 will run along the North Kent Coast to Ramsgate.

Other nearby rides (waymarked or traffic-free)
The Cathedral to Coast Ride is a waymarked 50-mile circular route linking Canterbury, Folkestone and Dover. It is made up of two Sustrans Regional Routes: Route 16 (Canterbury-Dover) and Route 17 (Dover-Folkestone-Canterbury). A leaflet is available from Kent Tourism, Kent County Council, Springfield, Maidstone, Kent ME14 2LL (01622 696165).

Route 1 - Canterbury to Whitstable through the University of Kent.

CANTERBURY & WHITSTABLE CYCLE PATH

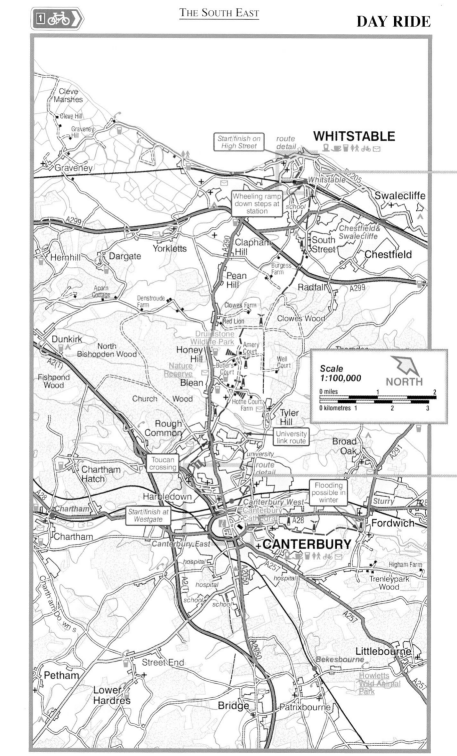

WHITSTABLE

Start/finish on High Street

route detail

Swalecliffe

Wheeling ramp down steps at station

Chestfield & Swalecliffe

Chestfield

Cleve Marshes

Cleve Hill

Graveney Hill

Graveney

Hernhill

Dargate

Yorkletts

Clapham Hill

South Street

Burgess Farm

Pean Hill

Radfall

Acorn Cottage

Denstroude Farm

Clowes Farm

Red Lion

Clowes Wood

Dunkirk

North Bishopden Wood

Druidstone Wildlife Park

Honey Hill

Amery Court

Well Court

Thornden

Nature Reserve

Butler's Court

Fishpond Wood

Blean

Church Wood

Hothe Court Farm

Tyler Hill

Rough Common

University link route

Broad Oak

Chartham Hatch

Toucan crossing

university route detail

Harbledown

Start/finish at Westgate

Canterbury West

Flooding possible in winter

Sturry

Chartham

Canterbury Cathedral

CANTERBURY

Fordwich

Chartham

Canterbury East

hospital

Higham Farm

hospital

hospital

Trenleypark Wood

school

school

Charth am Do wn s

Petham

Street End

Bekesbourne

Littlebourne

Lower Hardres

Bridge

Patrixbourne

Howletts Wild Animal Park

Scale 1:100,000

NORTH

0 miles   1   2

0 kilometres 1   2   3

© Crown copyright

WHITSTABLE
route detail

Whitstable tourist attractions
include: The Oyster & Fisheries
Exhibition and Whitstable
Museum & Gallery

The seafront between Whitstable and Seasalter.

Route instructions – Canterbury to Whitstable

1. From Westgate, at the junction of Pound Lane and St Peter's Street in the centre of Canterbury, use the cycle island to cross the main road and follow the route waymarked 'Route 1, Whitstable' along Westgate Green and Whitehall Rd.

2. Follow the 'Route 1, Whitstable'

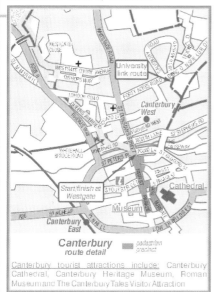

Canterbury
route detail

Canterbury tourist attractions include: Canterbury
Cathedral, Canterbury Heritage Museum, Roman
Museum and The Canterbury Tales Visitor Attraction

waymarks carefully through a series of junctions. The route runs eastwards, parallel with the A2050 then turns north through a more rural setting and climbs steadily. Look behind you and to your right for fine views of Canterbury and the cathedral.

3. Go past a tall white water tower. Use the toucan crossing to cross the busy Whitstable Road (A290) onto the shared-use pavement. Opposite Kent College turn right onto a limestone path. The first sculpture on the route can be found near here. Keep straight on, pass a car park onto a track and continue northwards.

4. Descend to cross a stream, climb again passing fruit orchards and farms. Follow the obvious track into woodland turning right

at the first crossroads then left at a T-junction of forestry tracks. (To your left is a picnic site at the pond which was used to cool the winding gear on the old Canterbury & Whitstable Line).

5. After ¾-mile bear left away from the wide forestry track, descend to cross the bridge over the new A299 and follow the farm track to the road near Brooklands Farm, South Street.

6. Turn left on the road for 300 yds then immediately after passing Millstrood Road to the left bear left onto the red tarmac cycle path signposted 'Station, Town Centre Cycle Route'. At the end of the cycle path turn left then right downhill through the residential road with sea views ahead.

7. Follow the waymarked route past the station entrance into the heart of Whitstable. It is well worth visiting the harbour. (Follow: All Saints Close, railway station, Stream Walk, Albert Street, town centre and harbour).

SOUTH FROM OXFORD TO ABINGDON

The key to linking the architectural glories of Oxford with the surrounding countryside whilst avoiding the busy roads that surround the city is to use the paths alongside its waterways. As these paths are inevitably busy, the National Route is signed via a network of minor road and cycleway links, leaving the canal and riverside for informal use. The route south to Abingdon follows the South Oxford Cycle Route through traffic-calmed streets as far as the ring road, briefly runs alongside the river before joining a specially built path parallel with the railway line. Traffic-free paths take you across parkland into the very heart of the attractive, historic town of Abingdon.

Oxford, City of dreaming spires.

Starting point
George Street in the centre of Oxford.

Distance:
8 miles one way, 16 miles return.

Grade
Easy.

Surface
Mixture of roads, tarmac cycle paths and stone-based paths.

Roads, traffic, suitability for young children
The busy roads are all crossed via toucan crossings.
The riverside path by the Thames and the path alongside the railway are ideal for children.

Hills
None.

Refreshments
Lots of choice in Oxford.
Lots of choice in Abingdon.

Leaflets
1. CycleCity produce an excellent map of Oxford showing the traffic-free paths, the signposted routes and the advisory routes. It is available for £4.95 from Sustrans Information Service, PO Box 21, Bristol. BS99 2HA (0117 929 0888) or visit www.sustrans.org.uk

2. *Cycle into Oxford* is a comprehensive guide to cycle routes in and around Oxford. Available from Oxford City Council, Department of Environmental Services, Clarendon House, Cornmarket Street, Oxford OX1 3HD. (01865 252405)

3. *Abingdon Town Cycle Map*. Large fold-out two colour leaflet showing existing and proposed cycle routes in the town. On the reverse are sections containing tourist information plus an inset

1999 Summer Workcamp beside the River Thames at Kennington.

showing the National Route between Oxford and Didcot.
Contact: Abingdon Town Council, Stratton Lodge, 52 Bath Street, Abingdon OX14 3QH (01235 522 642).

Nearest railway stations
Oxford, Radley, Didcot.

The National Cycle Network in the area
1. Oxford is on Route 5 which runs from Birmingham to Reading (where it links with Route 4 from Wales to London).
2. Route 51 heads north from Oxford and uses a new bridge to cross the A40 before reaching Kidlington where it continues north east to Bicester, Milton Keynes and Cambridge.

Other nearby rides (waymarked or traffic-free)
1. The Ridgeway Path is a broad chalk and stone track offering good off-road riding for hybrid and mountain bikes in the summer months. It runs from West Kennett (on the A4 west of Marlborough) to Goring on Thames, north west of Reading. The route can be followed beyond Goring towards Chinnor on the Icknield Way and Swan's Way.

2. The Oxfordshire Cycleway is a 200-mile waymarked ride around the County of Oxfordshire. Contact: Countryside Service, Department of Leisure & Arts, Oxfordshire County Council, Library Service HQ, Holton, Oxford OX9 1QQ.

The River Thames path beside Iffley Lock.

SOUTH FROM OXFORD TO ABINGDON

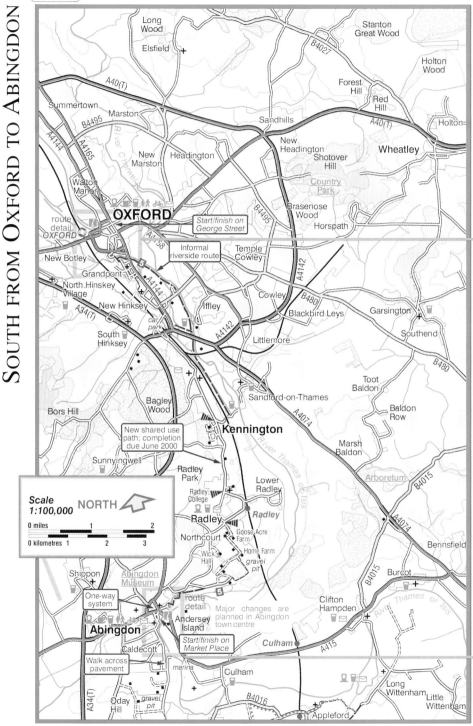

Long Wood
Elsfield
Stanton Great Wood
Holton Wood
A40(T)
B4027
Summertown
Marston
B4495
A4144
A4165
River Cherwell
Forest Hill
Red Hill
A40(T)
Holton=
Sandhills
New Marston
Headington
New Headington
Shotover Hill
Wheatley
Walton Manor
Country Park
OXFORD
Brasenose Wood
Horspath
route detail OXFORD
Start/finish on George Street
B4495
New Botley
A4158
Informal riverside route
Temple Cowley
A4142
Grandpont
North Hinskey Village
New Hinksey
5
A4144
Iffley
Cowley
B480
Blackbird Leys
Garsington
A34(T)
car park
A4142
South Hinksey
Littlemore
Southend
B480
Bagley Wood
Sandford-on-Thames
Toot Baldon
Baldon Row
Bors Hill
New shared use path; completion due June 2000
Kennington
A4074
Marsh Baldon
Sunnyingwell
Radley Park
Lower Radley
River Thames or Isis
Arboretum
B4015

Scale 1:100,000
NORTH

| 0 miles | 1 | 2 |
| 0 kilometres | 1 | 2 | 3 |

Radley College
Radley
A4074
Northcourt
Goose Acre Farm
Home Farm
gravel pit
Wick Hall
Berinsfield
Shippon
Abingdon Museum
B4015
Burcot
One-way system
route detail
Major changes are planned in Abingdon town centre
Clifton Hampden
Thames or Isis
A4074
Andersey Island
Abingdon
Start/finish on Market Place
Culham
A415
Caldecott
Walk across pavement
marina
Culham
Long Wittenham
Little Wittenham
A34(T)
Oday Hill
gravel pit
B4016
Appleford

© Crown copyright

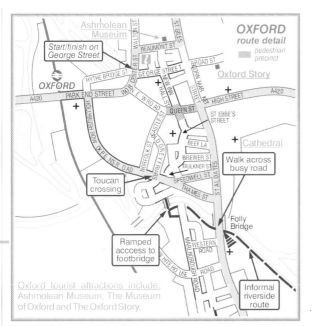

Oxford.

Route instructions from Oxford to Abingdon

1. From George Street in the centre of Oxford turn left onto New Inn Hall Street and follow signs for the 'South Oxford Cycle Route'.

2. Use the traffic lights to cross the busy Oxpens Road then cross the

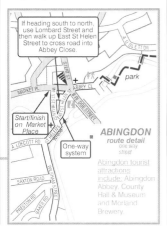

river via a metal bridge* following signs for the 'South Oxford Cycle Route' or 'Kennington'. Follow a series of quiet residential roads and cyclepath links.

* *An alternative informal route runs along the riverside path (keep the water to your left) from here to the Oxford Southern Bypass.*

3. Use the toucan crossings to cross to the east side of the busy Abingdon Road. Follow for ½-mile then immediately before the bridge over the main river use the ramp on the left to access the towpath. Turn right under the bridge and follow the riverside route to the meadows.

4. Bear right away from the river onto the newly-built path alongside the railway. At the T-junction with Sandford Lane turn right following waymarking.

5. At the T-junction with Kennington Road turn left and use the cycle lane marked on the road. Follow this to Radley village.

6. Shortly after passing Radley College turn left signposted 'Route 5', follow the road through the village and past Radley railway station. After ½-mile turn left onto Thrupp Lane signposted 'Route 5'.

7. Follow the road round a sharp right-hand bend, a sharp left-hand bend then a second right-hand bend. Shortly, turn left onto a wide stone track. At the bottom of the gentle descent turn right along the line of the old railway.

8. The track emerges onto another new track across Barton Fields and crosses a steep footbridge before turning right along Abbey Meadows and into the park on the eastern edge of Abingdon.

9. Turn right across the bridge and through the car park. Follow this road until you see an arch on the left. This leads directly to the centre of Abingdon. **Take care at this busy junction.**

CUCKOO TRAIL – POLEGATE TO HEATHFIELD

The Cuckoo Trail is one of the most popular family cycle rides in the South East. It gained its name from the Sussex tradition that the first cuckoo of spring was released at Heathfield Fair. Built on the bed of a dismantled railway it offers superb traffic-free cycling through a mixture of broadleaf woodland, open grassland, arable farmland and pasture. As you head back down towards Polegate there are views of the rolling chalk hills of the South Downs ahead of you.

Along the way are metal sculptures by Hamish Black, an arch in the form of a Chinese Pagoda roof, a claw-like hand and plenty of carved wooden seats with a variety of motifs, made by the sculptor, Steve Geliot, from local oaks blown down in the Great Storm of 1987. The verges are thick with wildflowers such as willowherb and vetch. There is a gentle climb up from Polegate to Heathfield so that you can look forward to a gravity-assisted return journey! In several places bridges have been dismantled and houses have been built on the course of the railway requiring you to cross minor roads and use short sections of estate roads through Hailsham and Horam to regain the railway path.

One of a series of carved oak seats by Steve Geliot.

Starting point

Polegate railway station, four miles north of Eastbourne near the junction of the A22 and A27.

Distance

11 miles one way, 22 miles return. The route can easily be shortened. Bear in mind that there is a 400ft climb from Polegate up to Heathfield so it is easier heading south than north!

Grade

Easy.

Surface

Tarmac and fine gravel path.

Roads, traffic, suitability for young children

The Cuckoo Trail is traffic-free and ideal for children. There are short sections on road at the start from the railway station in Polegate and through Hailsham in the middle of the ride. There are several quiet lanes to cross. The one busy road that needs to be crossed has a toucan crossing.

Hills

There is a gentle 400ft climb over 11 miles from Polegate up to Heathfield.

Refreshments

Lots of choice in Polegate, Hailsham and Heathfield. Tea shop on the trail at the Old Loom Mill Craft Centre (two miles north of Polegate, just before crossing the B2104).

Leaflets

An A3 leaflet describing the Cuckoo Trail is available from Boship Tourist Information Centre, Lower Dicker, Hailsham, East Sussex BN27 4DT (01323 442667).

Nearest railway station

Polegate.

Rio Summit 1992 Sculpture by P. Millmore.

The National Cycle Network in the area

The Cuckoo Trail forms part of Route 21 which runs south from London through Reigate and East Grinstead to Eastbourne. From Eastbourne the South Coast Cycle Route (Route 2) runs east through Pevensey Castle to Bexhill and west to Newhaven and Brighton.

Other nearby rides (waymarked or traffic-free)

The Forest Way and Worth Way are two railway paths starting in East Grinstead. There is a round reservoir route at Bewl Water (southeast of Tunbridge Wells) and a waymarked route in Friston Forest, to the west of Eastbourne. The South Downs Way is suitable for fit cyclists on mountain bikes during the summer months.

Jet of the Gladiators opening the Cuckoo Trail near Heathfield.

CUCKOO TRAIL – POLEGATE TO HEATHFIELD

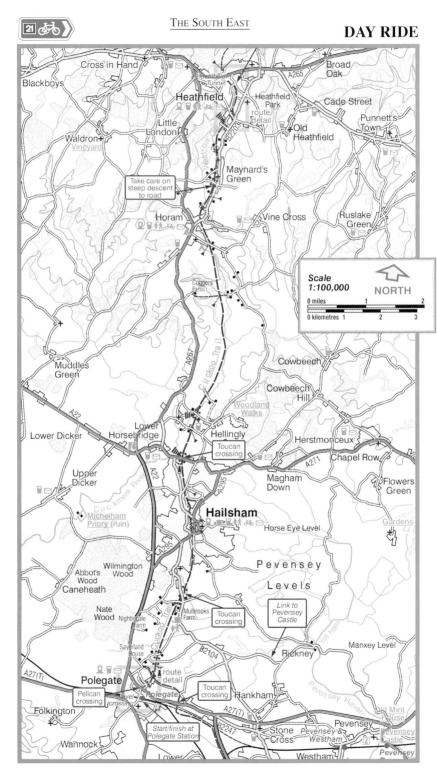

Scale
1:100,000   ⬆ NORTH

0 miles | 1 | 2
0 kilometres | 1 | 2 | 3

Route instructions from Polegate to Heathfield

1. Make your way from Polegate railway station to the start of the Cuckoo Trail following the signposts. Take care on this section as you have to follow the main street through Polegate then cross a busy road via a toucan crossing.

2. Follow the railway path for three miles into Hailsham. At this point the route follows estate roads so look out for 'Cuckoo Trail (bikes)' signs.

3. Rejoin the railway path and follow for five miles through to Horam. There is a second, short section on estate roads.

4. The trail ends after a further three miles in Heathfield. In this final section there are several roads to cross, mainly quiet lanes, but care should be taken none the less if you are with young children.

North of Hellingly on a winter's day.

Decoration on underpass at Hailsham with a motif recalling local rope works by Aaron Davies.

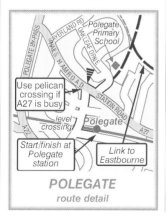

59

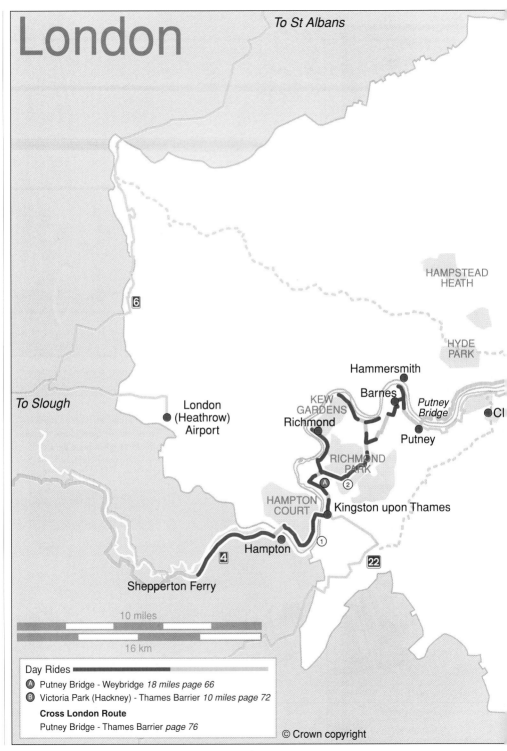

London

To St Albans

To Slough

HAMPSTEAD
HEATH

HYDE
PARK

Hammersmith

Barnes

KEW
GARDENS

Putney
Bridge

Cl

London
(Heathrow)
Airport

Richmond

Putney

RICHMOND
PARK

Ⓐ
②

HAMPTON
COURT

Kingston upon Thames

①

Hampton

④

22

Shepperton Ferry

10 miles

16 km

Day Rides
Ⓐ Putney Bridge - Weybridge *18 miles page 66*
Ⓑ Victoria Park (Hackney) - Thames Barrier *10 miles page 72*
Cross London Route
Putney Bridge - Thames Barrier *page 76*

© Crown copyright

60

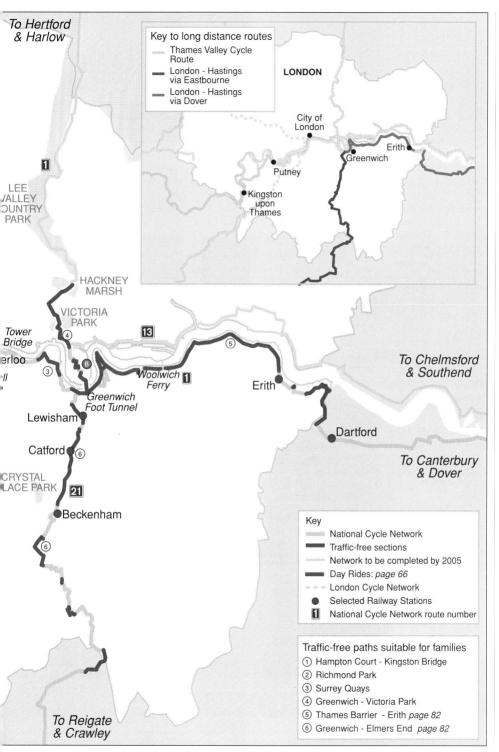

To Hertford & Harlow

Key to long distance routes
- Thames Valley Cycle Route
- London - Hastings via Eastbourne
- London - Hastings via Dover

LONDON

City of London

Erith

Greenwich

Putney

Kingston upon Thames

LEE VALLEY COUNTRY PARK

HACKNEY MARSH

VICTORIA PARK

Tower Bridge

13

erloo

③

Ⓑ

Woolwich Ferry **1**

Erith

To Chelmsford & Southend

④

⑤

Greenwich Foot Tunnel

Lewisham

Dartford

Catford ⑥

To Canterbury & Dover

CRYSTAL PALACE PARK

21

Beckenham

⑥

Key
- National Cycle Network
- Traffic-free sections
- Network to be completed by 2005
- Day Rides: *page 66*
- London Cycle Network
- ● Selected Railway Stations
- **1** National Cycle Network route number

To Reigate & Crawley

Traffic-free paths suitable for families
① Hampton Court - Kingston Bridge
② Richmond Park
③ Surrey Quays
④ Greenwich - Victoria Park
⑤ Thames Barrier - Erith *page 82*
⑥ Greenwich - Elmers End *page 82*

LONDON

London is the largest and busiest city in Britain so, not surprisingly, the creation of the National Cycle Network in the capital has thrown up enormous challenges to all those who have been involved in the project. Considerable effort and resources have been invested to create continuous, quality routes leading into and through London, enabling people to see and experience the city as never before.

Many main road crossings, traffic-calming measures and other features have been installed across London to improve safety and access for walkers and cyclists. These will not only make cycling more popular in London but will also ensure that one of the best ways of viewing Britain's capital city is by bike. For example, major improvements for cyclists have been installed at Blackfriars Bridge, Millbank, Westminster Bridge and Lambeth Bridge. Sustrans is also working with landowners and developers to create underpasses beneath other major Thames bridges. A number of dedicated

bridges have been built that provide vital links, including the new bridge over the River Lee in Hackney Marsh, and over the mouth of the River Wandle in Wandsworth.

As the Network continues to grow in London it is proposed to develop a series of additional family-friendly routes that will link together the main parks and open spaces, helping people to start cycling again.

Five routes in the National Cycle Network meet in London, crossing the Thames at Greenwich:

East from Greenwich, the Thames Cycle Route (Route 1) winds around the Dome peninsula, following a shared-use riverside promenade which will be opened after the Millennium Exhibition. From there, the route remains close to the riverbank passing the spectacular Thames Barrier, then runs along new promenades at Woolwich and Thamesmead. It continues along the riverbank to Erith where it turns south inland to Dartford and follows the northern edge of Kent.

West from Greenwich the Thames Cycle Route becomes Route 4, using the riverbank and adjacent quiet streets with breathtaking views of Tower Bridge and the City. Passing through the heart of the capital on the south bank of the Thames, Route 4 crosses over Lambeth Bridge to the north side and continues to follow the river through Chelsea before crossing back at Putney where it joins the riverside towpath. Futher upstream, the main route leaves the river to cross Richmond Park and rejoin the Thames at Teddington Lock.

There are also several 'spur' routes, which use short sections of riverside path and are suitable for families with small children. These spurs offer links to the major centres of Richmond, Kew and Hammersmith. Back on the main route at Kingston, the cyclist travels past the majestic buildings of Hampton Court, continuing along a delightful long stretch of towpath through to Weybridge and Staines before a final loop through Windsor Great Park to Windsor town centre.

Houses of Parliament.

Right: Canary Wharf.

South of Greenwich the Waterlink Way (Route 21) follows the valley through Lewisham, Bromley and Croydon. Several new pedestrian/ cycle bridges have been specially constructed over the Ravensbourne River, joined by many new sections of cycle and walking routes following the riverbank and parkland. Route 21 continues south to Hastings, picking up the popular Cuckoo Trail at Heathfield.

North of Greenwich, the Network makes use of the Greenwich Foot Tunnel to join the Lee Valley Link, which, as Route 1, eventually leads all the way to Inverness! Within London itself, the route passes to the west of Canary Wharf then links together several excellent sections of riverside promenade, towpath and parkland. Innovative features include the superb 'Green Bridge', a wide, tree-lined grass bridge over the A11, joining the two halves of Mile End Park. Route 1 then meanders alongside waterways and through wetlands to the Lee Valley Regional Park, with all its recreational opportunities. It continues north to Waltham Abbey then runs east to join to the Harwich to Hull Route.

North East a route will go through Dagenham and Thurrock to Southend.

THE LONDON CYCLE NETWORK

The National Cycle Network in London is complemented by the London Cycle Network (LCN), which is taking shape around the capital. Started in 1995 and due for completion in 2005, the London Cycle Network will comprise 1900

Woolwich Riverside with Thames Barrage and Dome in the background.

miles (3,000 kms) of routes and provide direct access to all major centres of employment, education and leisure in addition to all of London's railway stations. By early 2000, well over 800 miles had been completed. Look out for the blue and white signs with the route number and the distinctive 'London Cycle Network' logo.

LONDON CYCLING CAMPAIGN

With over 8,000 members, the London Cycling Campaign (LCC) is the largest urban cycling campaign in the world. Created in 1979, LCC has campaigned ceaselessly to implement a network of safe cycle routes in London and to raise awareness of cycling in the capital. Its campaign for a 'Thousand Mile Network' gave rise to the London Cycle Network which in 1995 gained government funding. The London Cycling Campaign has local groups in each of the 33 London Boroughs. They work locally with councils to improve conditions for cyclists and also organize rides and events. Membership benefits include discounts in many London bike shops and a regular magazine. To join telephone 0207 928 7220.

The route runs past the Tate Gallery from where it is a short ride to the Tate Bankside.

NATIONAL CYCLE NETWORK HIGHLIGHTS

Tower Bridge
The riverside is the best place from which to view the City of London, The Tower, St. Paul's, and Tower Bridge.

Hampton Court
This Palace is one of the most magnificent sights along the river, all the more memorable on account of the open riverside approach from both directions.

The London Eye
Travelling along the Thames Cycle Route, the Tate Gallery, the London Eye, South Bank, Tate Bankside, the New Thames Footbridge, the Globe Theatre and Greenwich, all fall within an easy cycling distance.

The Millennium Dome
Now that the Millennium Dome is open, the riverside promenade will be opened up right around the peninsula.

Greenwich Foot Tunnel
The Cutty Sark frames the Greenwich entrance to the foot tunnel under the Thames leading to the Isle of Dogs and Canary Wharf. This is one of only three under-river tunnels used in the whole Network (the others being under the River Tyne and under the River Clyde).

Mile End Park
A11 - bridge is a highlight of the Park and of this section of National Route 1. The bridge causes a thread of landscaping over the busy road below to create the illusion of an uninterrupted park.

PUTNEY BRIDGE TO WEYBRIDGE

For anyone who believes that there is no escape for cyclists from London's traffic, this ride is the answer: enjoy cycling along the green corridor that lies right on the doorstep of the capital. Putney Bridge marks the eastern end of a long stretch of the Thames riverside path which can be explored by bike. The National Cycle Network itself bears away from the river after a mile or so crossing Richmond Park (where you have the option of completing a totally traffic-free circuit of the park) before rejoining the river, threading its way through Kingston upon Thames and passing the majestic buildings of Hampton Court. The Thames is followed closely for the next six miles, passing Sunbury Lock and finishing at Weybridge. This route is part of the Thames Valley Cycle Route and if you wish you could follow the ride beyond Weybridge to Windsor, Reading and Oxford.

Upstream from Hampton Court the route follows along the bank of the River Thames all the way to Shepperton Ferry.

Starting points
1. The south side of Putney Bridge.
2. The riverside path (by the pedestrian ferry) in Weybridge.

Distance
18 miles one way, 36 miles return. For a shorter trip, starting from Putney Bridge, there are good turnaround points at Richmond Park (12 miles round trip), Kingston upon Thames (18 miles round trip) or Hampton Court (24 miles round trip).

Grade
Easy.

Surface
Mixture of tarmac and good quality gravel paths.

Roads, traffic, suitability for young children
The route is a mixture of quiet streets and cyclepaths. The best traffic-free section alongside the river runs west from Kingston

Bridge, crosses to the other side at Hampton Court then continues to Weybridge (a total of 9 miles one way, 18 miles return).

Hills
Richmond Hill.

Refreshments
All along the way.

Leaflets
1. *The London Cycling Campaign's Cyclists' Route Map for London* shows a vast amount of detail for both the leisure cyclist and the commuter in the capital. It costs £4.95 and is available from London Cycling Campaign, 3 Stamford Street, London SE1 9NT (0207 928 7220). Also available from Sustrans.

2. *Cycling the Thames*. The Thames Landscape Strategy produces a pack of 10 laminated cards describing 10 rides of 5-12 miles in length between Weybridge and

Hammersmith. Available for £3.50 from Thames Landscape Strategy, c/o Holly Lodge, Richmond Park, Richmond TW10 5HS (0208 940 0654). Also available from Sustrans.

Nearest railway stations
Putney, Barnes, Kingston upon Thames, Hampton Court.

The National Cycle Network in the area
The ride described here is the first section of the Thames Valley Cycle Route which runs from Putney Bridge to Oxford (Route 4 to Reading then Route 5 from Reading to Oxford). East from Putney Bridge a route runs right through the heart of London to Greenwich and the Dome.

Other nearby rides (waymarked or traffic-free)
There is a traffic-free circular ride around Richmond Park.

Route instructions
1. From the south side of Putney Bridge push your bike along the pavement of Richmond Road for 100yds then bear right downhill onto the one way street (with cycle contraflow) alongside the river.

2. Follow this to the end and continue in the same direction, as tarmac turns to gravel track. After one mile, with Fulham Football Club ground opposite you on the other side of the Thames, turn left through gates onto a tarmac track leading away from the river.

3. The track joins the sports centre access road. Continue in the same direction. Just before the crossroads with the main road bear left onto a path through the park parallel with Rocks Lane.

4. Use the toucan crossing to cross onto Ranelagh Avenue then take the first track to the left (opposite no.10). Please dismount and push your bike across Barnes Common. Cross Mill Hill Road with care before continuing through the open scrubland and woodland.

5. At the junction with Rocks Lane, bear right onto the quiet road towards Barnes railway station. Immediately after passing the station on your left, bear left alongside the railings on a gravel track.

6. At the T-junction with the road, bear left to go over two level crossings. Just before the traffic lights (at the main road) bear right onto a gravel track and use the toucan crossing to cross over onto

the green cycle path opposite running along Priory Lane.

7. After ¾-mile, at the end of the green painted cycle lane, turn right onto Bank Lane, then shortly first left onto Roehampton Gate. At the T-junction, turn right through the gate into Richmond Park onto a cycle lane parallel with the busy road.

8. Just before the crossroads by a white signpost, turn left at the cycle crossing to join the road towards White Lodge. Immediately after passing a car park to the right, turn right towards Isabella Plantation.

9. At the crossroads, use the cycle crossing and carry on down Ham Gate Avenue. Exit Richmond Park. At the crossroads use the toucan

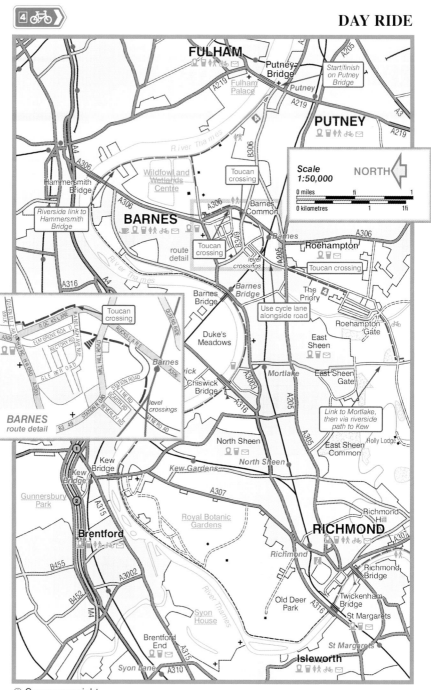

DAY RIDE

© Crown copyright

Old Deer Park
North Sheen
East Sheen
The Priory
East Sheen Gate
Roehampton Gate
East Sheen Common
RICHMOND
Richmond
Link to Mortlake, then via riverside path to Kew
Holly Lodge
White Lodge
Twickenham Bridge
Richmond Hill
Richmond Bridge
Richmond Gate
St Margarets
Pen Ponds
car park
Robin Hood Gate
Pedestrian and cycle ferry telephone 0181 892 9620 for times
Marble Hill
R i c h m o n d
P a r k
Twickenham
Petersham
Pembroke Lodge
Eel Pie Island
Ham House (NT)
Sudbrook Park
Isabella Plantation
Link via riverside path to Richmond
Ham
Toucan crossing
Ham Gate
Ham Common

Scale
1:50,000
NORTH

0 miles   fi   1
0 kilometres   1   1fi

Strawberry Hill
route detail
KINGSTON UPON THAMES
Teddington Lock
weir
HAM
route detail
TEDDINGTON
Norbiton
LO CARO RD
LAWRENCE ROAD
BROUGHTON CLOSE
RIVERSIDE DRIVE
HARDWICK RD
DUKES AVENUE
WICK MEADFIELD
BEAUFORT ROAD
B358
A310
Norbiton
A2043
Toucan crossing
track
Hampton Wick
Kingston
Hampton Wick
Kingston Bridge
Berrylands
footbridge
Teddington Weir
Segregated cycle track available upon bridge completion due 2001
B u s h y
P a r k
SURBITON
Hampton Court Park
Hampton Court

© Crown copyright

69

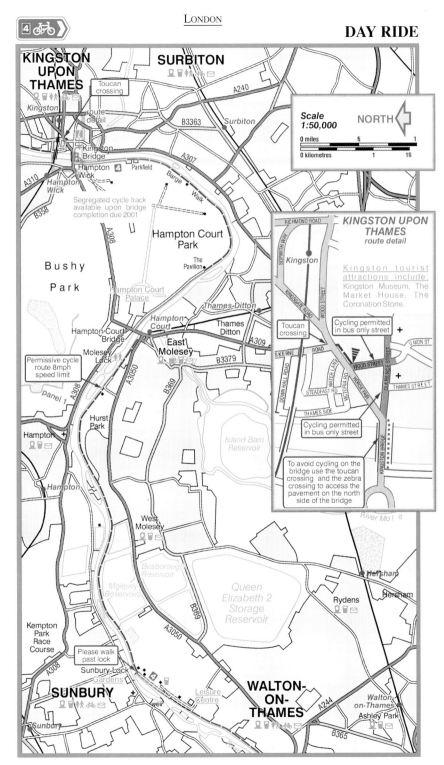

KINGSTON UPON THAMES

Toucan crossing

Kingston

route detail

Kingston Bridge

Hampton Wick
Parkfield

Hampton Wick

A310

A358

SURBITON

A240

B3363
Surbiton

A307

Barge
Walk

Segregated cycle track available upon bridge completion due 2001

A308

Hampton Court Park

The Pavilion

B u s h y

P a r k

Hampton Court Palace

Thames-Ditton

Hampton Court
Bridge

Hampton Court

Thames Ditton

A309

Molesey Lock

East Molesey

B3379

Permissive cycle route 8mph speed limit

Panel 1

A308

A3050

B369

Hurst Park

Hampton

Island Barn Reservoir

Hampton

West Molesey

Besborough Reservoir

Molesey Reservoirs

Queen Elizabeth 2 Storage Reservoir

Rydens

Kempton Park Race Course

A3050

B369

Please walk past lock

Sunbury Lock Gardens

A308

SUNBURY

Sunbury

weir

Leisure Centre

WALTON-ON-THAMES

A244

Walton-on-Thames

Ashley Park

B365

Hersham

Hersham

River Mole

Scale 1:50,000

NORTH

0 miles   fi   1

0 kilometres   1   1fi

KINGSTON UPON THAMES
route detail

RICHMOND ROAD

SOPWITH WAY

WOOD STREET

KINGSGATE ROAD

Kingston

Kingston tourist attractions include: Kingston Museum, The Market House, The Coronation Stone.

Toucan crossing

Cycling permitted in bus only street

UNION ST

S KERNE

ROAD

DOWN HALL ROAD

WATER LANE

STEADFAST RD

VICTORIA RD

HORSE FAIR

WOOD STREET

CLARENCE STREET

THAMES STREET

THAMES SIDE

Cycling permitted in bus only street

KINGSTON BRIDGE

To avoid cycling on the bridge use the toucan crossing and the zebra crossing to access the pavement on the north side of the bridge

© Crown copyright

70

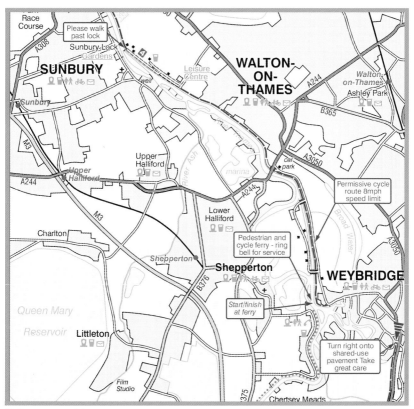

© Crown copyright

crossing and go straight ahead onto the road through Ham Common. Follow 'Teddington Cycle Route' signs.

10. Continue in the same direction, then at the T-junction at the end of Lock Road turn right then left after 50 yds onto a shared-use path. Go straight ahead at two crossroads, following the cycle paths between houses and into the woods near the river. At T-junction with the riverside path, turn left.

11. At the T-junction with the road, bear right then after 400 yds leave the road and bear right again back onto the riverside path.

12. (Route through Kingston.) At the end of the riverside path, bear left down Hall Road. At the junction, cross over the busy road to a shared-use path outside Bentalls, using the toucan crossings. Follow the path to the right, leading into Wood Street (between Bentalls and John Lewis). Turn right into Clarence Street and continue onto the bridge.

13. Cross the road via the toucan crossing and push your bike on the pavement to cross Kingston Bridge (or take great care if you use the road) then turn left onto Barge Walk via the pedestrian crossing. (A two way cycle path will be built on the south side of Kingston Bridge in 2001.)

14. Follow the riverside path past Hampton Court. At the bridge turn right and use the pelican crossing to cross the road. Use the segregated cycle path on the pavement to cross the bridge over the river, and turn right to rejoin the riverside path for six miles to Weybridge.

15. In Weybridge you have a choice of visiting the pubs just beyond the car park, catching the ferry across the river to the pubs on the other side or returning back towards Putney. Weybridge railway station is about 1½ miles south of this point. Alternatively, if you cross to the other side of the river via the ferry, you could catch a train from Shepperton station. The most convenient railway station is Hampton Court.

VICTORIA PARK TO THE THAMES BARRIER

Linking together many of the most outstanding features of east London, this ride provides a fascinating way to explore an area not normally associated with sightseeing in the capital. There are myriad unexpected visual treats to be enjoyed from the traffic-free paths through Victoria Park, along the Regent's Canal (Grand Union Canal), across Mile End Park and down to the Thames at Limehouse Reach. The huge pyramid-topped white tower of Canary Wharf dominates much of the early part of the ride. After walking through the Greenwich Foot Tunnel to emerge at the Cutty Sark the route turns east in front of the Naval College. The route crosses the Greenwich Peninsula to end at the silver shell structures of the Thames Barrier, built to protect London from flooding in the event of an unlucky combination of storms and high tides.

Starting points

1. St Mark's Gate, Victoria Park, Hackney.
2. The Thames Barrier, Woolwich.

Distance

10 miles one way, 20 miles return.

Grade

Easy.

Surface

All tarmac.

Roads, traffic, suitability for young children

Although there are short traffic-free sections, the route is largely on traffic-calmed streets through the East End of London, so it is not really suitable for young children. If you are with older children (10+), the best time to do this ride is early on a Sunday morning.

Hills

None.

Refreshments

Lots of choice all along the way.

Leaflets

The London Cycling Campaign's Cyclists' Route Map for London shows a vast amount of detail for both the leisure cyclist and the commuter. It costs £4.95 and is available from the London Cycling Campaign, 3 Stamford Street, London SE1 9NT (0207 928 7220). Also available from Sustrans.

Nearest railway stations

Hackney Wick, Greenwich.

The National Cycle Network in the area

1. To the north of Victoria Park Route 1 continues up the Lee Valley corridor on broad gravel tracks, either alongside or parallel with the canal known as the Lee & Stort Navigation.
2. To the east of the Thames Barrier Route 1 continues along the Thames estuary as far as Gravesend where it heads inland through Kent then on to Canterbury and Dover.
3. Route 21 links London with the South Coast via the Waterlink Way running down through Deptford, Catford and Lewisham towards Croydon and Redhill.

Other nearby rides (waymarked or traffic-free)

As mentioned above, there are miles and miles of attractive traffic-free cycling in the Lee Valley Park.

Route instructions

Complicated routes through urban areas need a long and difficult set of instructions. Instead we have shown the route highlighted on street mapping so that if you ever miss a turning and lose sight of the National Cycle Network signposting and waymarks you can refer to the detailed mapping to find your way back to the route.

In broad terms you are linking the following: Victoria Park (Hackney), the Regent's Canal (Grand Union Canal), Mile End Park, Limehouse Basin, Cascades Tower, Millwall Inner Dock, Mudchute, the Greenwich Foot Tunnel, the Cutty Sark and the Thames Barrier.

Green Bridge linking Mile End Park route.

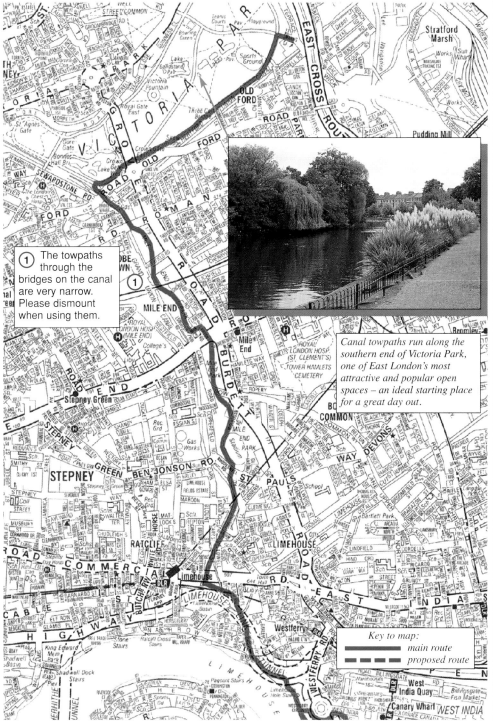

① The towpaths through the bridges on the canal are very narrow. Please dismount when using them.

Canal towpaths run along the southern end of Victoria Park, one of East London's most attractive and popular open spaces – an ideal starting place for a great day out.

Key to map:
━━━━━ main route
━ ━ ━ proposed route

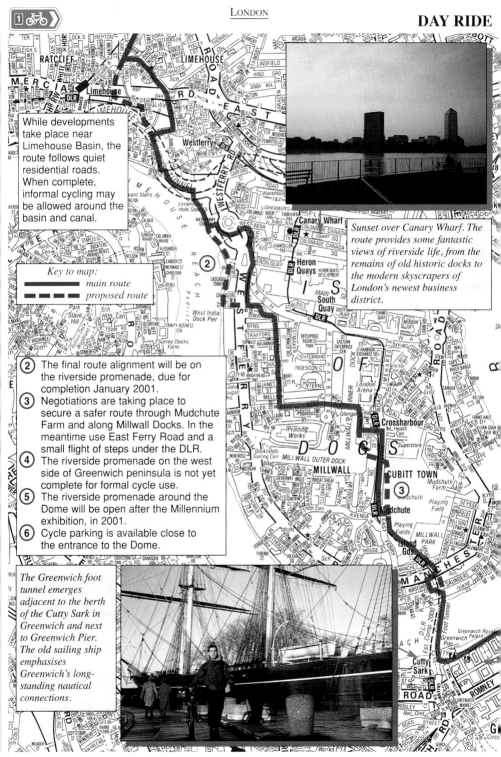

While developments take place near Limehouse Basin, the route follows quiet residential roads. When complete, informal cycling may be allowed around the basin and canal.

Sunset over Canary Wharf. The route provides some fantastic views of riverside life, from the remains of old historic docks to the modern skyscrapers of London's newest business district.

Key to map:
━━━━━━ main route
▬ ▬ ▬ ▬ proposed route

② The final route alignment will be on the riverside promenade, due for completion January 2001.

③ Negotiations are taking place to secure a safer route through Mudchute Farm and along Millwall Docks. In the meantime use East Ferry Road and a small flight of steps under the DLR.

④ The riverside promenade on the west side of Greenwich peninsula is not yet complete for formal cycle use.

⑤ The riverside promenade around the Dome will be open after the Millennium exhibition, in 2001.

⑥ Cycle parking is available close to the entrance to the Dome.

The Greenwich foot tunnel emerges adjacent to the berth of the Cutty Sark in Greenwich and next to Greenwich Pier. The old sailing ship emphasises Greenwich's long-standing nautical connections.

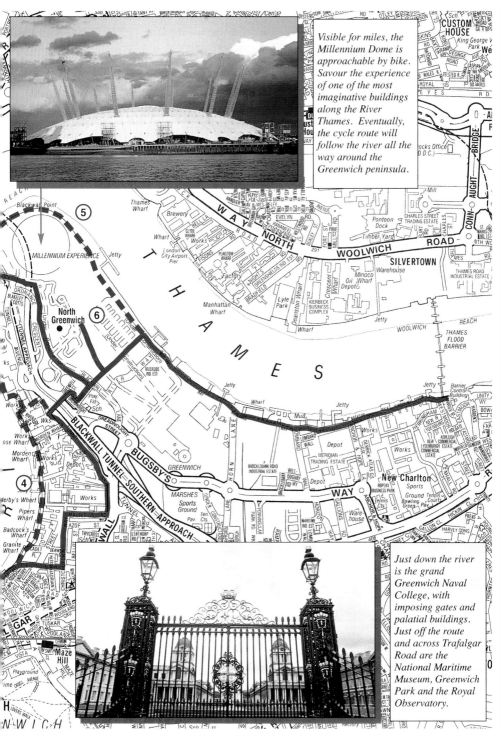

Visible for miles, the Millennium Dome is approachable by bike. Savour the experience of one of the most imaginative buildings along the River Thames. Eventually, the cycle route will follow the river all the way around the Greenwich peninsula.

Just down the river is the grand Greenwich Naval College, with imposing gates and palatial buildings. Just off the route and across Trafalgar Road are the National Maritime Museum, Greenwich Park and the Royal Observatory.

PUTNEY BRIDGE TO THE THAMES BARRIER

The route of the National Cycle Network through Central London broadly follows the line of the Thames, although for the majority of this section the route is slightly set back from the river on traffic-calmed streets. The ideal time to do this ride would be on a fine Sunday morning. There is far less traffic around so not only are the roads quieter but any impromptu outside refreshment stop at a cafe or pub is likely to be more pleasant. There are so many attractions along the way that one of the best sorts of ride would link together museums and cafes, palaces and pubs, galleries and riverside views.

Coming from the west the National Cycle Network has closely followed the Thames for several miles on the south side of the river. At Putney Bridge you cross to the north side as far as Lambeth Bridge, at first following back streets then using a shared-use pavement along Cheyne Walk and Chelsea Embankment with wonderful views across the river to Battersea Park (and the power station!). You may choose to drop into the Chelsea Physic Garden, where the country's earliest rock garden is made of building stone from the old Tower of London and Icelandic lava.

1. Negotiations are continuing to develop a riverside route from Hurlingham Park to Chelsea Wharf. It is hoped that this longer-term alignment will be implemented over the next five years.
2. An additional southern route is being developed from Putney Bridge to Lambeth Bridge, which will be constructed by 2005.
3. Segregated two-way cycle lanes along the Embankment will be constructed by Dec 2000.
4. Traffic calming along Lupus St will be implemented by Dec 2000.

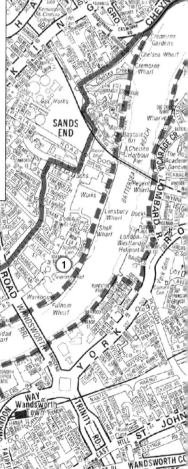

Key to map:
━━━━━ main route
■ ■ ■ ■ proposed route

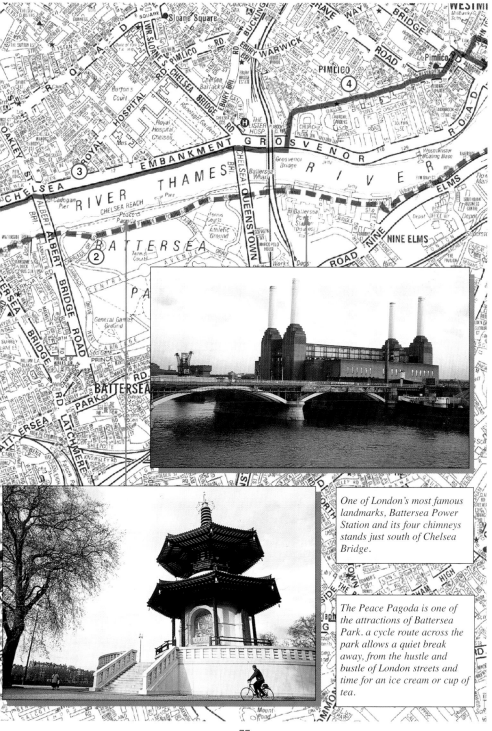

One of London's most famous landmarks, Battersea Power Station and its four chimneys stands just south of Chelsea Bridge.

The Peace Pagoda is one of the attractions of Battersea Park. a cycle route across the park allows a quiet break away, from the hustle and bustle of London streets and time for an ice cream or cup of tea.

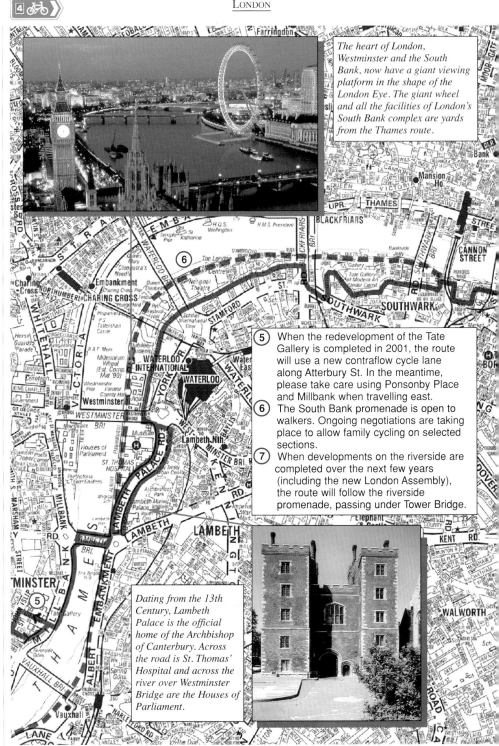

The heart of London, Westminster and the South Bank, now have a giant viewing platform in the shape of the London Eye. The giant wheel and all the facilities of London's South Bank complex are yards from the Thames route.

5 When the redevelopment of the Tate Gallery is completed in 2001, the route will use a new contraflow cycle lane along Atterbury St. In the meantime, please take care using Ponsonby Place and Millbank when travelling east.

6 The South Bank promenade is open to walkers. Ongoing negotiations are taking place to allow family cycling on selected sections.

7 When developments on the riverside are completed over the next few years (including the new London Assembly), the route will follow the riverside promenade, passing under Tower Bridge.

Dating from the 13th Century, Lambeth Palace is the official home of the Archbishop of Canterbury. Across the road is St. Thomas' Hospital and across the river over Westminster Bridge are the Houses of Parliament.

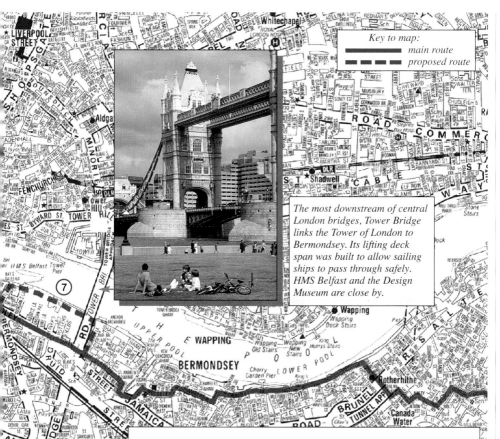

Key to map:
━━━ main route
━ ━ ━ proposed route

The most downstream of central London bridges, Tower Bridge links the Tower of London to Bermondsey. Its lifting deck span was built to allow sailing ships to pass through safely. HMS Belfast and the Design Museum are close by.

On towards Lambeth Bridge you pass the Tate Gallery with its magnificent Historic British and 20th Century Collections. Once Lambeth Bridge is crossed, back to the South Bank, the National Cycle Network stays on the south side of the river to Greenwich, the main crossroads of the Network in London. If your interests lie in the past then parts of Lambeth Palace, the official home of the Archbishop of Canterbury, date back to the 13th century. If your tastes are more aligned to the present, the Museum of the Moving Image is an interactive guide to the moving image from Chinese puppets to video production. Between the two, the Jubilee Gardens would make a fine stop to appreciate views of the Thames.

Running east towards Southwark the route runs right past the Shakespeare Globe Theatre, a replica theatre to replace the 16th-century original, where Shakespeare's plays were first performed. On past Southwark Cathedral you come to the London Dungeon, a gruesome medieval horror museum with displays including a headless Mary, Queen of Scots!

Beyond Tower Bridge, the last bridge over the Thames before Dartford, you briefly rejoin the river through Bermondsey before cutting inland through the Russia Dock Woodland and Ecological Park.

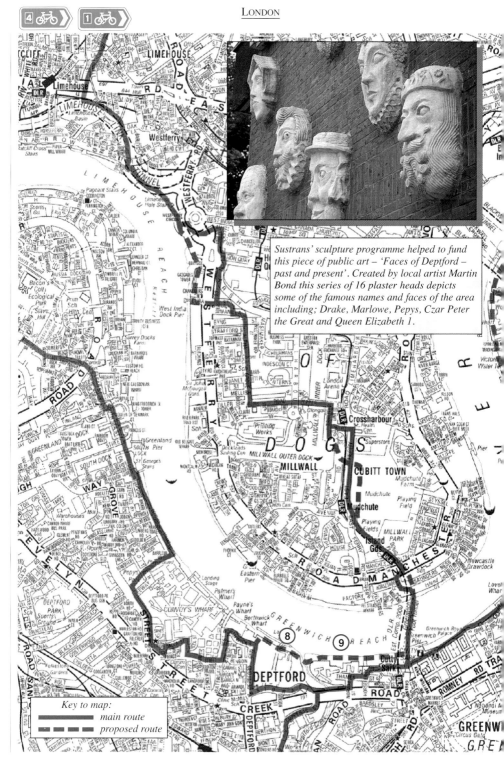

Sustrans' sculpture programme helped to fund this piece of public art – 'Faces of Deptford – past and present'. Created by local artist Martin Bond this series of 16 plaster heads depicts some of the famous names and faces of the area including; Drake, Marlowe, Pepys, Czar Peter the Great and Queen Elizabeth 1.

Key to map:
main route
proposed route

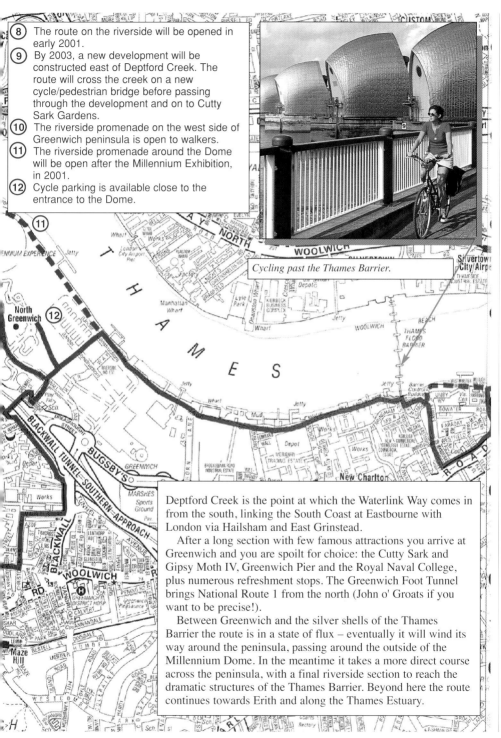

8 The route on the riverside will be opened in early 2001.

9 By 2003, a new development will be constructed east of Deptford Creek. The route will cross the creek on a new cycle/pedestrian bridge before passing through the development and on to Cutty Sark Gardens.

10 The riverside promenade on the west side of Greenwich peninsula is open to walkers.

11 The riverside promenade around the Dome will be open after the Millennium Exhibition, in 2001.

12 Cycle parking is available close to the entrance to the Dome.

Cycling past the Thames Barrier.

Deptford Creek is the point at which the Waterlink Way comes in from the south, linking the South Coast at Eastbourne with London via Hailsham and East Grinstead.

After a long section with few famous attractions you arrive at Greenwich and you are spoilt for choice: the Cutty Sark and Gipsy Moth IV, Greenwich Pier and the Royal Naval College, plus numerous refreshment stops. The Greenwich Foot Tunnel brings National Route 1 from the north (John o' Groats if you want to be precise!).

Between Greenwich and the silver shells of the Thames Barrier the route is in a state of flux – eventually it will wind its way around the peninsula, passing around the outside of the Millennium Dome. In the meantime it takes a more direct course across the peninsula, with a final riverside section to reach the dramatic structures of the Thames Barrier. Beyond here the route continues towards Erith and along the Thames Estuary.

GREENWICH TO THE THAMES BARRIER

THAMES BARRIER TO ERITH

East of the Thames Barrier, the character of the river changes dramatically as it broadens out across the flood plains on its way to the sea. The Thames Cycle Route follows the river all the way to Erith, inviting you to discover this magnificent, but rarely appreciated, part of the Thames.

Developments are taking place on the first section of the riverside, where the route will eventually go. From the Woolwich Ferry, the ride takes you along beautiful new riverside promenades in front of the Old Woolwich Dockyard, (recently converted into a sculpture park), and the Old Royal Arsenal site which supplied the battalions of Britain for much of the 19th and 20th centuries. Pop in to the Royal Artillery Museum on the site, to find out more. From here, the route launches out along the majestic sweep of Gallions Reach before connecting with the promenade at Thamesmead Town. Just past the Crossness Sewage Works where the magnificent Victorian Pumping Station is well worth a visit. The remainder of the ride makes its way through the interesting working wharfs of Bexley before leading you into Erith where you can catch a train back to London or Kent. Alternatively, carry on through Erith to enjoy the wildlife and wetlands of Crayford Marshes before turning south to Dartford.

GREENWICH TO ELMERS END – Waterlink Way

Starting on the banks of the Thames at Greenwich, under the bow of the Cutty Sark, the Waterlink Way makes its way south through Lewisham, Bromley and Croydon. It follows the valley of the little-known Ravensbourne River, journeying through the pretty suburbia of London. Many new bridges and underpasses have been built for the route (as part of the new Docklands Light Railway works). There's even a suspended walkway through a tunnel over a river! The route takes you through many delightful parklands, both new and rejuvenated, making at least half of the ride traffic-free. At Catford, the route picks up the Pool River and follows it into Bromley. From park to park you hop before entering the borough of Croydon at Elmers End. Here, you can pick up a train back to London or head on south into South Norwood Country Park.

REGIONAL ROUTES AND GOOD CYCLING AREAS

For further information about the leaflets and guidebooks covering all these routes/areas contact Sustrans Information Service, PO Box 21, Bristol BS99 2HA (0117 929 0888) or visit www.sustrans.org.uk

THAMES VALLEY CYCLE ROUTE NN5A

National Route Map shows the course of the 97-mile route from Putney Bridge to Weybridge, Windsor, Reading and Oxford. Price £5.99

CYCLISTS ROUTE MAP: CENTRAL LONDON RPL03

Published by the London Cycling Campaign, this map shows the streets of London within the square formed by Wimbledon (SE), Willesden (NW), Stratford (NE) and Beckenham (SE). Coloured highlights show implemented cycle routes, advisory cycle routes and leisure routes. On the reverse are details of cycle shops and useful contacts. Maps for West and North West London are also available at the same price of £4.95.

NATIONAL CYCLE NETWORK IN LONDON MAP LN001

Shows the Thames Cycle Route from Hampton Court to Dartford, detailing adjoining London Cycle Network routes and giving suggestions for pleasant day rides in and around the capital.

LONDON CYCLE GUIDE RBH09

This spiral-bound, 144-page, full colour book describes 25 rides of 4-24 miles in and around London. Over 125 miles of traffic-free trails are included. The book uses a mixture of colour street mapping and Ordnance Survey Landranger mapping together with detailed route instructions and other essential information for leisure rides inside the M25. Price £8.99.

CYCLING WITHOUT TRAFFIC – THE SOUTHEAST RBA01

A friendly, easy-to-use guide covering London and the South East, describing in detail 30 traffic-free rides in the region. The rides are a mixture of railway paths, waymarked forestry routes, round

reservoir routes, canal towpaths and country parks. The book is illustrated with full colour photography and hand-drawn mapping. Each route has details of distance, grade, surfacing, road crossings, refreshments, useful maps and nearby places of interest. Includes Grand Union Canal, Lee Navigation, Thames Towpath, Richmond Park, Wimbledon Common and Epping Forest. There is now a second volume covering 30 more rides in the area. Price £10.99.

CYCLING THE THAMES RPL37

The Thames Landscape Strategy produces a pack of laminated cards describing 10 rides of 5-12 miles from Weybridge to Hammersmith. Available for £3.50 from Thames Landscape Strategy, c/o Holly Lodge, Richmond Park, Richmond TW10 5HS (0208 940 0654).

THE OFFICIAL LONDON CYCLE NETWORK MAP

The map covers the entire LCN and is useful as a journey planner. Available free from the London Cycle Network Project Team (0208 547 5907).

East of England

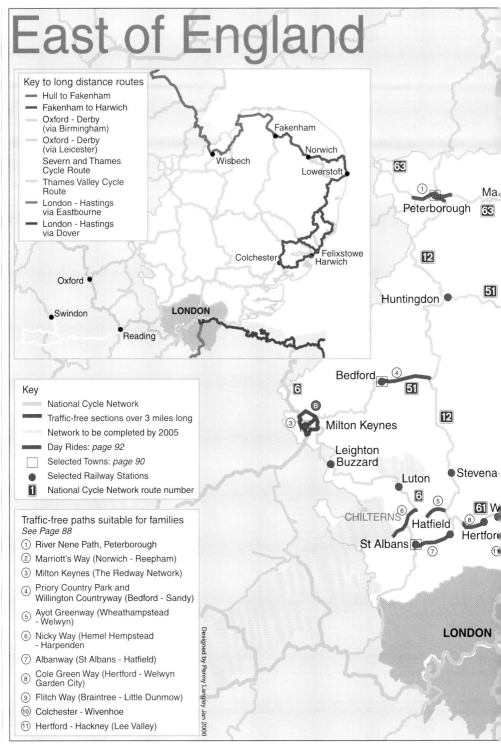

Key to long distance routes
- Hull to Fakenham
- Fakenham to Harwich
- Oxford - Derby (via Birmingham)
- Oxford - Derby (via Leicester)
- Severn and Thames Cycle Route
- Thames Valley Cycle Route
- London - Hastings via Eastbourne
- London - Hastings via Dover

Fakenham
Norwich
Wisbech
Lowerstoft
Colchester
Felixstowe
Harwich

Oxford
Swindon
LONDON
Reading

Peterborough
Huntingdon
Bedford
Milton Keynes
Leighton Buzzard
Luton
Stevena
CHILTERNS
Hatfield
St Albans
Hertfor
Ma

Key
- National Cycle Network
- Traffic-free sections over 3 miles long
- Network to be completed by 2005
- Day Rides: *page 92*
- ☐ Selected Towns: *page 90*
- ● Selected Railway Stations
- [1] National Cycle Network route number

Traffic-free paths suitable for families
See Page 88
1. River Nene Path, Peterborough
2. Marriott's Way (Norwich - Reepham)
3. Milton Keynes (The Redway Network)
4. Priory Country Park and Willington Countryway (Bedford - Sandy)
5. Ayot Greenway (Wheathampstead - Welwyn)
6. Nicky Way (Hemel Hempstead - Harpenden
7. Albanway (St Albans - Hatfield)
8. Cole Green Way (Hertford - Welwyn Garden City)
9. Flitch Way (Braintree - Little Dunmow)
10. Colchester - Wivenhoe
11. Hertford - Hackney (Lee Valley)

LONDON

Designed by Penny Langley Jan 2000

84

Hunstanton

NORFOLK COAST

1

KING'S
LYNN Ⓐ

Fakenham ▪

King's Lynn

1

Wisbech

② **1**

Norwich

Great
Yarmouth

Lowestoft

13

THE
BRECKS

1

Ely

Thetford

Bury
St Edmunds

51

1

Cambridge

51 Wickham Market ●

SUFFOLK
COAST &
HEATHS

13

Ipswich

Ⓒ

Orford

11

DEDHAM
VALE

Felixstowe

16 Braintree Colchester

Harwich

Bishop
Stortford

⑨

1 ⑩

1

1 Chelmsford

ow

13

© Crown copyright

Basildon

Southend
-on-sea

13

Day Rides ▬▬▬▬▬▬▬▬▬▬▬▬

Ⓐ King's Lynn to Shepherd's Port *15 miles page 96*

Ⓑ Milton Keynes *9 miles page 100*

Ⓒ Wickham Market to Orford *14 miles page 92*

50 miles

80 km

85

EAST OF ENGLAND

Beck's Green, Suffolk.

This is the flattest region in the whole Network – the highest point between London and the Norfolk Coast is just north of Stevenage, where the land rises to a mighty 555 ft. The highest point between Cambridge and the Wash is a mere 20 ft! The Hull to Harwich Route runs right down through the East of England and, with its easy gradients, is one of Sustrans' most popular routes for people returning to the saddle after a few years' absence.

The area is defined by intensive agriculture, particularly in the fens. The rainfall is the lowest of any region in the country, giving cyclists a greater chance of a dry ride than anywhere else.

The Hull to Harwich long-distance route has been a shining example of what can be achieved when the will power and resources of the local authorities and the Regional Tourist Board are collectively mobilised to throw their weight behind the National Cycle Network. The 369-mile route was opened seven years ahead of schedule.

NATIONAL CYCLE NETWORK HIGHLIGHTS

Cambridge

Cycling is a way of life in Cambridge, both amongst the locals and the students. Just join the throng - they are bound to take you somewhere interesting! Arriving by train, a packed crush of bikes greets you from the station entrance, whilst to the north, Britain's only covered and heated cycle bridge takes you over the railway and away from the city centre.

Shanks Millennium Bridge, River Nene, Peterborough

This new bridge, part of the Peterborough Millennium Green Wheel Project, will be made from recycled steel collected at the city's recycling plant. Linking the northern and southern parts of the Green Wheel, a cycle route around the city with "spokes" into the centre, it will also form part of the National Cycle Network, providing a much more direct and attractive alternative to the busy roads between Peterborough and Whittlesey.

Kesgrave School

This chance picture taken whilst surveying National Route 1 between Ipswich and Woodbridge, led us to Kesgrave School, which was later featured in the Safe Routes to School project. Thanks to this traffic-free green lane and some decent links, the High School enjoys the highest level of cycling in Britain with 60% of its pupils cycling each day. Consequently its pupils are relatively fit and the school successful in sports of all kinds!

Harwich and Felixstowe Ferry

This ferry has had a chequered history and its future is in doubt, despite the fact that a 10-minute ferry trip saves a journey of nearly 35 miles via Ipswich. The ferry trip is an experience in its own right, with the estuary dominated by massive container ships. The ferry has solved difficulties with docking at Felixstowe enabling the service to restart. The service may change, so check the latest developments and use it!

Castle Rising and Sandringham Path

This new path beside the busy A149 Hunstanton Road near King's Lynn shows how the Network with local authority support can achieve vital local routes. Negotiations with the Royal Estates by Norfolk County Council allowed this path to be constructed. It links quiet minor roads and avoids the main road. Without this work King's Lynn was effectively isolated from its countryside to all but the most experienced cyclists. Quality details of this sort determine popularity.

Milton Keynes

Of all the British new towns Milton Keynes has the most extensive system of cycle paths, including over 200km of redways (red tarmac shared use paths), plus gravel surfaced leisure paths, giving cyclists the chance to pass through parks and villages that are now part of Milton Keynes. The cycle network deserves to be better known but competes with an equally modern road system which leaves little advantage for the cyclist.

TRAFFIC-FREE CYCLE PATHS SUITABLE FOR FAMILIES

Listed here is a selection of traffic-free routes, often along disused railways, that are more than three miles long and offer ideal cycling for families. Some are covered by the Day Rides, some are shown on the diagrammatic maps below. (Numbers match the map key on p.84)

1. The River Nene riverside path through Peterborough
3. The Redway Network in Milton Keynes offers many miles of attractive recreational cycling alongside canals and through parkland (see pages 100-103)
4. Priory Country Park and Willington Countryway from Bedford to Sandy, Bedfordshire
5. Ayot Greenway from Wheathampstead to Welwyn, Hertfordshire
6. Nicky Line from Hemel Hempstead to Harpenden, Hertfordshire
8. Cole Green Way from Hertford to Welwyn Garden City, Hertfordshire
11. Hertford to Hackney along the Lee Valley Corridor. Superb towpath along this waterway close to London

For further information about traffic-free rides, ask for the Traffic-free Information Sheet from Sustrans Information Service, PO Box 21, Bristol. BS99 2HA (0117 929 0888) or visit www.sustrans.org.uk

The Family Cycling Trail Guide (£4.95) contains details of 300 traffic-free rides throughout Britain. Also available from Sustrans.

2. Marriott's Way, Norfolk

This railway path is largely rural in nature and offers a wonderful way to see the Norfolk countryside. As you approach Norwich city centre you pass industrial sites between glimpses of the River Wensum. Soon after crossing the river the path emerges on the edge of the city centre.

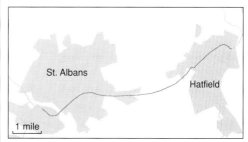

7. Albanway

The former Hatfield to St Albans branch line of the Great Northern Railway now helps to link two of the major attractions of Hertfordshire – Hatfield House and St Albans. The route is also particularly useful for students, many of whom live in St Albans and study in Hatfield.

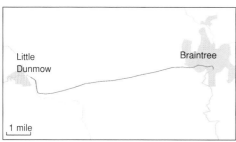

9. Flitch Way (Braintree to Little Dunmow)

You will not find a railway path with better access by train anywhere in the UK. Braintree Station is close to the start of the Flitch Way. This seven-mile route along the former Braintree to Bishop's Stortford railway is a fine way to see the Essex countryside.

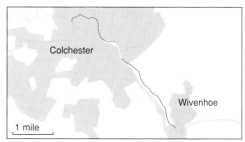

10. Colchester - Wivenhoe

This riverside path, squeezed between the river and the railway, gives great views of the River Colne. The path runs from the centre of Colchester to Wivenhoe Station but it is well worthwhile starting in Colchester's Dutch Quarter and finishing at Wivenhoe's attractive quay.

© Crown copyright

REGIONAL ROUTES AND GOOD CYCLING AREAS

For further information about leaflets covering these routes contact Sustrans Information Service, PO Box 21, Bristol BS99 2HA (0117 929 0888) or visit www.sustrans.org.uk

NORFOLK COAST CYCLEWAY RPR10

60 miles

Regional Route 30

Links with National Route 1. A3 leaflet using Stirling Survey 1:100,000 mapping shows the course of the 60-mile linear route that runs from King's Lynn to Cromer along the North Norfolk Coast. The leaflet carries details of bike shops, cycle hire, Tourist Information Centres and train information.

THE SUFFOLK COASTAL ROUTE RPL16

75 miles

Regional Route 41

Links with National Route 1. A2 full colour leaflet describing the waymarked circular route linking Felixstowe, Woodbridge, Framlingham and Orford passing through the lovely countryside of South Suffolk. The leaflet also contains details of accommodation, pubs, cycle shops and other useful publications. Further information from: The Cycling Officer, Suffolk County Council, Environment & Transport Dept., St Edmund House, County Hall, Ipswich IP4 1LZ (01473 230000).

THE HEART OF SUFFOLK ROUTE

100 miles

Regional route 40

Links with National Route 1. A Millennium Project to create a series of linking circular routes in the south of Suffolk covering the county from Sudbury and Long Melford in the west to the tip of the Shotley Peninsula in the east. Further information from the Tourism Officer, Babergh District Council, Corks Lane, Hadleigh, Ipswich IP7 6SJ (01473 825846).

PETERBOROUGH GREEN WHEEL

A network of cycleways, footpaths and bridleways that provide safe, continuous routes around the city and 'spokes' linking the Wheel to residential areas and the city centre. The Green Wheel celebrates over 2000 years of Peterborough's social, cultural, economic and environmental history through a series of sculptures and colourful interpretation boards along the route. For further information contact: Peterborough Environment City Trust, High Street, Fletton, Peterborough PE2 8DT (01733 760883).

89

TOWNS AND CITIES ON THE NATIONAL CYCLE NETWORK

Bedford

Bedford was a cycling showcase in the late 1970s. It seemed then that the town was a leading light in developing routes for cyclists. The National Route picks up some remnants of these early schemes, along the riverside and the disused Bedford-Sandy railway.

Colchester & Wivenhoe

The riverside route between the two towns was an early example of the formal use of a river flood defence bank. It has been used by the Environment Agency as an example of good practice. Colchester has led the way on the Safe Routes to Schools Project.

Harlow

As a New Town, Harlow was provided with some cycling infrastructure but it falls far short of the level of provision in Milton Keynes or Peterborough. A lot remains to be done to encourage cycling but efforts are now being made to build missing links on the town's cycle network. The spread-out nature of the town means that there is generally plenty of space for new paths but a lot of work is needed to develop links beyond the town itself.

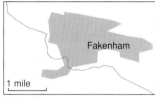

Cambridge

Any book about cycling has to include this university city, closely associated with the bicycle and now "Silicon Fen." The high level of cycling helps to keep this busy city moving, despite the narrow, congested streets and the National Routes shown here pick up some of the best opportunities along the River Cam and past the colleges in the city centre.

Fakenham

As with so many towns set in fine countryside, it is the roads on the fringe which set the most testing problems and pose the most obstacles to the novice cyclist. The route to Little Walsingham and Holkham on the Norfolk Coast solves this with simple road crossing details. To the south east the river and disused railway form a potentially attractive route to Great Ryburgh. Further south there are some delightful lanes near the junction of routes 1 & 13.

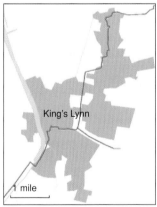

King's Lynn

The route passes through the heart of this medieval mercantile town. This is the railhead from London and from here you are on the threshold of some of the best cycling country in Britain – the Fens and Norfolk.

Chelmsford

The well-established riverside route has recently been extended to Chelmer Village and the National Cycle Network provides links to the countryside.

An example of the excellent cycle routes in Colchester.

© Crown copyright

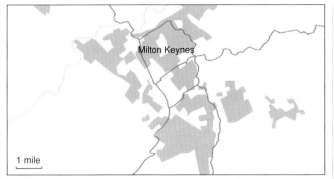

Norwich

The route through the centre of the city passes between the cathedral and the castle; take care not to miss either and ensure you give yourself plenty of time to wander around the narrow streets in the heart of the city. Beyond the centre, Norwich's industrial heritage is evident in the route along the River Wensum and along the Marriott's Way, a disused railway.

Milton Keynes

The town has over 150 miles of purpose-built cycle routes permeating almost the whole of the urban area. The National Cycle Network makes use of these and allows you to enjoy a day trip around the town. Long negotiations and major construction work have also created links south east to Winslow (on the way to Oxford) and north towards Northampton. The city has an extensive collection of sculpture in the open air.

St Albans

In Roman times St Albans was known as Verulamium and Verulamium Park lies at the heart of the modern town. The railway path to Hatfield forms the basis of the National Cycle Network looping around the north of London. The railway path to Hatfield and the route to Watford form the basis of the National Cycle Network looping around the north of London.

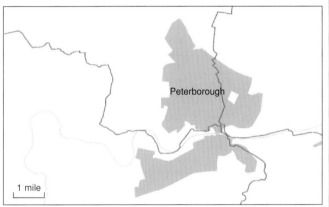

Peterborough

Extensive cycle routes were developed as Peterborough grew rapidly with New Town status. Its own Millennium Green Wheel Project has sought to link these schemes together and to give ready access to the countryside. The National Routes mesh with this and focus on the city's cathedral.

Chelmsford.

© Crown copyright

WICKHAM MARKET TO ORFORD

The gentle countryside of the Suffolk Coast provides ideal cycling for people wishing to progress from traffic-free cycle paths to the enjoyment of the wonderful network of country lanes that criss-cross Britain. These Suffolk roads carry very little traffic, the gradients are easy, the visibility is good and in Campsey Ash you have a railway station right in the middle of the countryside. This means there are no city streets to negotiate before setting out on your trip. You will cross the fertile farmland and plantations of pines to the delights of the Maltings at Snape and the wonderful village of Orford with its castle, quayside, pubs and tea rooms. There are various options to turn this into a circular ride by using a mixture of B roads and forest roads or by catching the ferry across Butley River. (Devise your own routes using Ordnance Survey Landranger maps 156 and 169.)

Orford Castle.

Starting point

Wickham Market railway station,
20 miles northeast of Ipswich. The
station is not in Wickham Market
itself but at the nearby village of
Campsey Ash.

Distance

14 miles one way, 28 miles return.
For a shorter ride, turn around at
Snape Maltings (10-mile round
trip).

Grade

Easy.

Surface

All tarmac.

Roads, traffic, suitability for young children

The whole route is on road, mainly
on very quiet country lanes. There
are a couple of short sections on B
roads. There are nearby traffic-free
trails in Rendlesham and Tunstall
Forests.

Hills

None to mention.

Refreshments

Ship PH, Blaxhall.
Tea room, Plough & Sail PH, Snape
Maltings.
Jolly Sailor PH, Crown & Castle.
PH, Kings Head PH, Old
Warehouse Cafe, Orford.

Nearby railway stations for longer linear rides

Route 1 could be followed north to
Halesworth (21 miles) or Beccles
(32 miles). Alternatively head south
to Felixstowe (32 miles).

The National Cycle Network in the area

The ride is part of the Hull to
Harwich Cycle Route (Route 1)
which runs north to Beccles and
Norwich. There are two options on
its course south to Harwich, either
inland via Ipswich and Colchester

Views towards Orford Castle.

or along the coast via Felixstowe.
The latter route uses three ferries
and it is advisable to ring in
advance to check the timetable:
1. Butley Ferry (south of Orford):
01394 410096 (Bryan Rogers).
2. Bawdsey to Felixstowe Ferry:
0780 347 6621 or 01394 270106
(Odd Time Ferries).
3. Felixstowe to Harwich: 0589
371138.
4. Felixstowe Tourist Information
Centre: 01394 276770.

Other nearby rides (waymarked or traffic-free)

1. The Three Forest Ride is a 25-
mile ride linking the Forestry

Commission holdings in
Rendlesham, Tunstall and Dunwich
(a few miles to the north). It links
traffic-free forest trails via quiet
lanes. A leaflet is available from
Forest Enterprise, Tangham,
Woodbridge IP12 1PE.

2. The Suffolk Coastal Cycle Route
is a waymarked 75-mile route.
Leaflet available from Suffolk
County Council, Economic
Development Unit, St Edmund
House, County Hall, Ipswich IP4
1LZ (01473 230000).

Snape Maltings, home of the
Aldeburgh Festival.

WICKHAM MARKET TO ORFORD

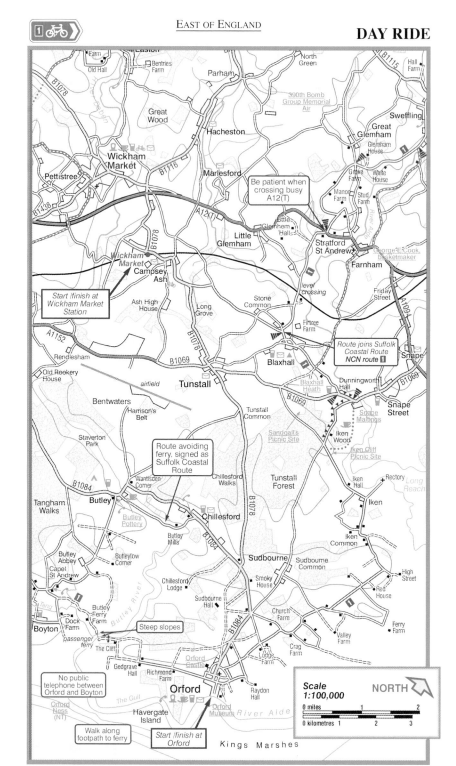

© Crown copyright

Route instructions – Campsey Ash to Orford

1. Exit Wickham Market railway station (at Campsey Ash) and turn right. Ignore the first left to Marlesford on a sharp right-hand bend. On the next sharp right-hand bend after ¾-mile bear left signposted 'Blaxhall, Snape'.

2. At the crossroads with Red House Farm ahead, turn right. At the next crossroads (with a church to your left) go straight ahead.

3. Three closely-spaced junctions! At a crossroads by a Give Way sign go straight ahead signposted 'Snape'. At the T-junction turn left (same sign). At the next crossroads turn right (same sign).

4. At the T-junction with the B1069 turn left then take the first road to the right signposted 'Iken, Orford'

(or to visit Snape Maltings continue straight ahead for 200yds).

5. After one mile take the first left. Follow signs for Orford for five miles.

6. **Easy to miss**. Ignore turnings to left and right. Shortly after passing two left turns signposted 'High House Farm' and 'Crag Farm' (this second left turn is by a large red-brick, thatched house) take the third left, signposted 'Orford 1½'.

7. After one mile, at a crossroads shortly after an electricity sub-station turn left. Shortly, at a junction by a triangle of grass with a no through road to Raydon Hall ahead, turn right.

8. At the crossroads in the centre of Orford, turn left for Orford Quay, turn right for the castle and pubs or go straight ahead for the Ore Estuary.

Snape Maltings now house a concert hall, shops and cafes.

KING'S LYNN TO SHEPHERD'S PORT

This ride is a short section of the popular long-distance Hull to Harwich Cycle Route running down the east side of the country. The whole route was opened several years earlier than planned because of the enthusiasm and support of the local authorities and the East of England Tourist Board. King's Lynn lies on the course of the River Ouse which drains much of the fertile dark earth of the Fens.

The lively port and market town is a major hub in Norfolk and boasts many fine old buildings. The ride leaves the railway station on a traffic-free path through parkland before joining the course of an old railway to arrive at the outskirts of the town. After crossing the broadleaf woodlands of Ling Common you come to the attractive village of Castle Rising with its magnificent castle and defences and old almshouses dating from the 17th century. The route continues through more woodlands and banks of rhododendrons surrounding Sandringham, country home of the Royal Family. The rhododendrons are at their best for about six weeks from mid-April to the end of May. If you have not stopped for tea at the Visitor Centre at Sandringham you are likely to be tempted by the various pubs and coffee houses in Snettisham, which also has one of the finest churches in Norfolk. If the tide is in, or if you are birdwatching, it is worth pushing on to the coast at Shepherd's Port, but be aware that when the tide is out you will be confronted by a vast expanse of mud!

North of Sandringham on the road to Snettisham.

Starting point
King's Lynn railway station.

Distance
15 miles one way, 30 miles return. The ride could be shortened by making the turnaround point either the attractions and refreshment stops at Castle Rising (12 miles round trip) or Sandringham Country Park (19 miles round trip).

Grade
Easy.

Surface
All tarmac with the exception of an (optional) short stretch through Sandringham Estate on good quality gravel track.

Roads, traffic, suitability for young children
The first section, from the railway station, across the parkland and onto the dismantled railway is all traffic-free. Beyond the end of the railway path the route uses quiet lanes as much as possible. The busy main roads are all crossed via central islands.

Hills
Gently undulating.

Refreshments:
Lots of choice in King's Lynn.
House on the Green PH, North Wootton.
Tea rooms at the Post Office, Black Horse PH, Castle Rising.
Tea rooms at Sandringam Visitor Centre.
Rose & Crown PH, Queen Victoria PH, Compasses PH, Old Bank Coffeehouse, Snettisham.

Railway stations for longer rides
It is 74 miles along Route 1 from King's Lynn to Norwich or 100 miles north to Lincoln.

The National Cycle Network in the area
The ride described is part of the Hull to Harwich Cycle Route (Route 1).
1. East from Hunstanton, Route 1 turns inland through Ringstead and Burnham Market to Fakenham.
2. West from King's Lynn, Route 1 crosses the Fens to Wisbech and Boston.
3. Route 11 will run south from King's Lynn through Downham Market to Ely Cathedral and Cambridge

St. John's Walk, King's Lynn, leads direct to the station and town centre.

Other nearby rides (waymarked or traffic-free)
The Norfolk Coast Cycleway is a 60-mile linear route that runs from King's Lynn to Cromer along the North Norfolk Coast.

The absence of traffic on the old road from Castle Rising to Sandringham leaves space for fishing.

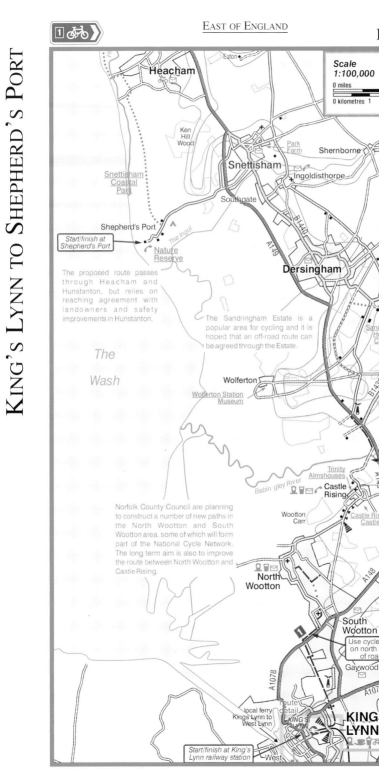

KING'S LYNN TO SHEPHERD'S PORT

Scale 1:100,000

NORTH

0 miles 1 2
0 kilometres 1 2 3

Heacham

Eaton

Ken Hill Wood

Park Farm

Shernborne

Snettisham

Ingoldisthorpe

Snettisham Coastal Park

Southgate

Shepherd's Port

Start/finish at Shepherd's Port

The Ingol

Nature Reserve

Dersingham

Sandringham

Sandringham House & Country Park

West Newton

The proposed route passes through Heacham and Hunstanton, but relies on reaching agreement with landowners and safety improvements in Hunstanton.

The Sandringham Estate is a popular area for cycling and it is hoped that an off-road route can be agreed through the Estate.

The Wash

Wolferton

Wolferton Station Museum

Foot, cycle and horse access only

Trinity Almshouses

Babingley River

Castle Rising

Norfolk County Council are planning to construct a number of new paths in the North Wootton and South Wootton area, some of which will form part of the National Cycle Network. The long term aim is also to improve the route between North Wootton and Castle Rising.

Wootton Carr

Castle Rising Castle

North Wootton

South Wootton

Use cyclepath on north side of road

Gaywood River

Gaywood

local ferry Kings Lynn to West Lynn

route detail

KING'S LYNN

Start/finish at King's Lynn railway station

West

© Crown copyright

Route Instructions – King's Lynn to Sandringham and the coast

1. Exit King's Lynn railway station and turn left onto the pavement/cycle path, soon turning left again at the church to pass through the park along a tree-lined avenue. Cross the road at the end of the park, turn left over the railway lines then immediately right, following signs for 'Sandringham Railway Path'.

2. Shortly bear left, go past a school on the left. At the next road (Gaywood Road) cross via toucan crossing, past the Leisure Centre.

3. At the T-junction with the main road (A1078) turn right on the cycle path alongside the road (signposted 'Woottons, Castle Rising, Sandringham') then shortly cross the road via traffic island – (**TAKE CARE**) to continue in the same direction. Take the first road to the left (Hall Lane) then turn right along a new path beside the church to join Church Lane (a continuation of Hall Lane).

4. At the T-junction with Nursery Lane turn left, passing Meadow Road on your left. Turn into Avon Road on your right, then turn left along the edge of some grazing land on to a new path, which links to paths which take you through parkland. Head north keeping to the left and following signs to North Wootton and Castle Rising until you reach All Saints Drive. Turn right into All Saints Road then right into Manor Road and left into Ling Common Road.

5. At the T-junction at the end of Ling Common Road turn left signposted 'Castle Rising. Route 1'.

A busier road. Immediately after the Black Horse pub in Castle Rising turn left past the church onto a no through road signposted 'Route 1'.

6. Lovely old road, now shut to traffic. At the T-junction with the main road (A149) turn left onto the new cycle track. Ignore the first right on the B1439. After ¼-mile take the next right signposted 'Route 1'. **TAKE CARE** crossing this road via traffic island

7. At cross roads go straight ahead. At the T-junction after ¾-mile bear right. Go past the Sandringham Visitor Centre (tea rooms).

8. At the T-junction with the B1140 turn right signposted 'King's Lynn' then left signposted 'Sandringham Sawmill. Route 1'.

9. At the first crossroads (your priority) go straight ahead. At the next crossroads (Give Way) go straight ahead onto Mill Road.

10. **Easy to miss**. After 1½ miles, having climbed up and over a gentle hill, take the second of two closely spaced right turns. At the next crossroads turn left* (leaving the waymarked Route 1). Aim for the distant Snettisham church spire which you pass after ½ mile.

Another option from Snettisham is to continue along Route 1 to Sedgeford then turn left on the B1454 to visit Norfolk Lavender at Heacham.

11. At the T-junction at the end of Old Church Road turn right then left onto Alma Road. At the next T-junction (with the main A149) turn left then right (**TAKE CARE**) onto Common Road. After ½-mile, at the end of Common Road, bear right and follow this no through road for two miles, passing various caravan sites, out to the coast.

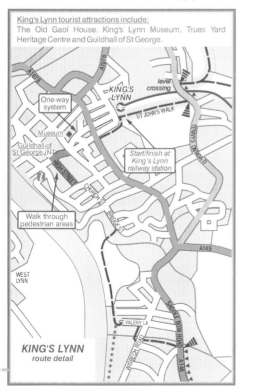

King's Lynn tourist attractions include: The Old Gaol House. King's Lynn Museum. Trues Yard Heritage Centre and Guildhall of St George.

KING'S LYNN
route detail

A CIRCUIT OF MILTON KEYNES

If you have never cycled in Milton Keynes you will be astonished when you explore the place for the first time. There are a wealth of choices for the cyclist, including attractive gravel-finished paths through parks, red tarmac paths that form the famous Redway Network and many quiet roads. These will enable you to explore the city visiting lakes, canals, the Buddhist pagoda, adventure playgrounds, all the while diving in and out of stretches of broadleaf woodland. Every now and then you will come across an attractive village that is now part of urban Milton Keynes, but which still maintains its village character. The city was designed as a whole series of individual communities, and central Milton Keynes is unlike any other city centre in the country, with its wide boulevards, unusual architecture and impressive sculptures. Milton Keynes boasts probably the best collection of public art in the country.

This ride uses parts of the National Cycle Network through Milton Keynes with two links, to give a circular route through the city. The route takes in paths beside the Grand Union Canal, Campbell Park, the beautiful old stone buildings of Great Linford, a section of dismantled railway through a thickly wooded cutting and a leisure route along the Loughton Valley passing through a curious little tunnel. Last but not least there is a chance to see the famous concrete cows of Milton Keynes and the giant Head Sculpture (which forms the junction of the National Cycle Routes in Milton Keynes). It is hoped that during 2000 the links will be signed as links to the National Network giving a signed circular route.

'Circle Dance' by Claire Wilks. Steel frame sculpture on the Grand Union Canal.

Starting points
Central Railway Station, Milton Keynes.

Distance
9-mile circuit.

Grade
Easy.

Surface
Red tarmac or gravel paths throughout.

Roads, traffic, suitability for young children
All busy roads are crossed via underpasses or bridges. Several quiet estate roads are crossed and some quiet roads are used.

The National Route runs past the station (in the foreground) and through the shopping centre of Milton Keynes with wide underpasses at every main road junction.

Hills
The route follows the valleys, avoiding most of the hills in Milton Keynes.

Refreshments
Lots of choice in the square by the railway station and elsewhere in central Milton Keynes.
Pub and shop in Woughton on the Green (just off the route).
Tea shop at Bradwell Abbey.
Nags Head PH, Great Linford.

Leaflets
The *Milton Keynes Redway Map* shows the full extent of the cycleway network and is indispensable when exploring the city. Available from: Commission for New Towns, Saxon Court, 502 Avebury Boulevard, Saxon Gate East, Central Milton Keynes MK9 3HS (01908 227229).

Nearest railway stations
Milton Keynes Central, Wolverton.

The National Cycle Network in the area
Milton Keynes is at a crossroads of the National Cycle Network. Route 6 passes through Milton Keynes on its way south from Leicester and Northampton to St Albans and Slough.
Route 51 runs from Oxford to Bedford, Cambridge and the coast. The circular route could be adapted by following Route 6 to Castlethorpe, an attractive village on the way to Northampton. For the more ambitious, Route 51 would take you out into the Buckinghamshire countryside to Winslow an attractive town with a famous tea shop. If you prefer to stay within Milton Keynes, Willen Lake and Caldecotte Lake are on the course of the second phase of the National Cycle Network (to Bedford) and are attractive destinations.

Other nearby rides (waymarked or traffic-free)
There is a comprehensive network of traffic-free paths and quiet roads with plenty of adventure playgrounds and picnic spots along the way. Use the Redway Map (see 'Leaflets' above) to explore the area

Cycle route around Willen Lake.

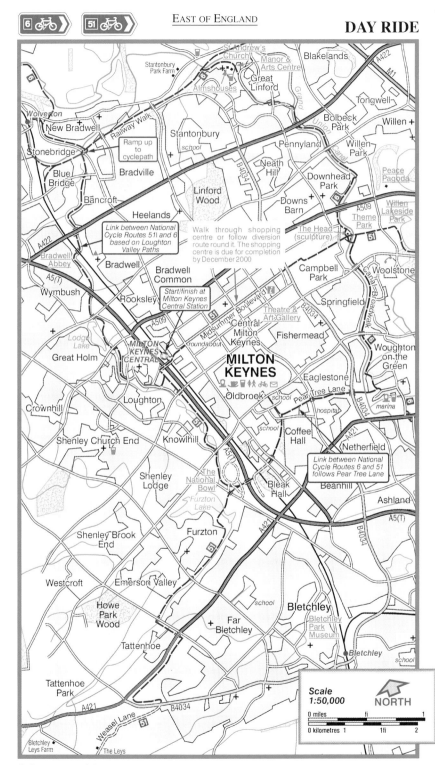

A CIRCUIT OF MILTON KEYNES

MILTON KEYNES

Link between National Cycle Routes 51 and 6 based on Loughton Valley Paths

Walk through shopping centre or follow diversion route round it. The shopping centre is due for completion by December 2000

Start/finish at Milton Keynes Central Station

Link between National Cycle Routes 6 and 51 follows Pear Tree Lane

Scale
1:50,000

NORTH

0 miles   fi   1

0 kilometres 1   1fi   2

© Crown copyright

Route instructions

1. With your back to Milton Keynes railway station, cross over the first road then turn right then right again at the end of the glass-fronted building. Cross the bridge over the railway lines then at the T-junction turn left signposted 'Loughton, Knowlhill, Milton Keynes Bowl'.

2. Follow signs for Route 51 and Milton Keynes Bowl. Go round the outside of the Bowl past Gates 3 and 2. At the T-junction with V4 turn left signposted 'Bletchley, Route 51'.

3. At Gate 1 bear left then at the T-junction turn left (leaving Route 51) signposted 'Bleakhall, Coffee Hall'. Cross the A5 and the railway line then pass beneath a second main road. At a fork of paths bear right (there are signs for Woughton Campus a little way along the left-hand fork).

4. Gentle descent. At the crossroads go straight ahead onto 'Public Bridleway'. Cross the canal and follow the signs for 'The Green, Woughton Ouzel Valley Park'.

5. Shortly after the red-brick houses on the left, turn left alongside black railings on a tarmac path. Continue in the same direction. At the canal turn right signposted 'Woolstones, Newlands, Campbell Park'. Follow the Canal Broadwalk for 1½ miles.

6. After passing under two closely-spaced road bridges turn next left over the canal and into Campbell Park. Take the second path to the right towards and past the Head Sculpture. Rejoin the canal, now on your right.

7. Cross the canal at Bridge 80A, rejoin the Broadwalk, with the canal now on your left. At the red-brick hump-backed bridge no. 79, turn left over the bridge and follow the path away from the canal. After 300 yds turn right then left. Go past a few old houses and turn right opposite a sign for Harpers Lane.

8. Continue in the same direction along Great Linford High Street, past a telephone box and the Nag's Head pub. Go through gates into the park and bear left following Route 6 signs past lovely old buildings, a church and a stone circle.

9. Rejoin the canal then shortly bear left uphill onto the railway path. Follow for almost two miles.

10. Emerge from the wooded railway cutting and continue straight ahead, crossing the bridge over V6 signposted 'Wolverton, Stony Stratford, Stacey Bush'. Immediately after crossing the bridge turn right and follow the path downhill and round to the right to pass beneath the bridge. The path soon runs parallel with the stream to your right. Pass beneath a curious wooden bridge.

11. The path joins the Redway near to the famous concrete cows. Bear right signposted 'Bradwell Village, Bradwell Abbey, Lodge Lake, Loughton Village'.

12. Continue in the same direction over crossroads. At a T-junction turn right to go over a narrow bridge inside a tunnel! At the end of the tunnel turn sharp left 'Lodge Lake, Loughton Village'.

13. Follow close to the stream, passing beneath two large bridges. At a T-junction turn left then right signposted 'Loughton Village, Tear Drop Lake'.

14. At the T-junction at the end of the lake turn left (same sign). Follow the path to Linceslade Grove, keeping to the right. Cross the road on the raised crossing and turn left onto the Redway. At the end of the bridge turn right and continue beside the stream.

15. At the T-junction turn right then left onto The Green. At the junction with Bradwell Road go straight ahead onto Leys Road then at the end turn left onto the Redway. Continue up Common Lane towards the railway station. Turn left then right over the A5 and the railway to take you back to Station Square.

'Head' in Campbell Park by Allen Jones.

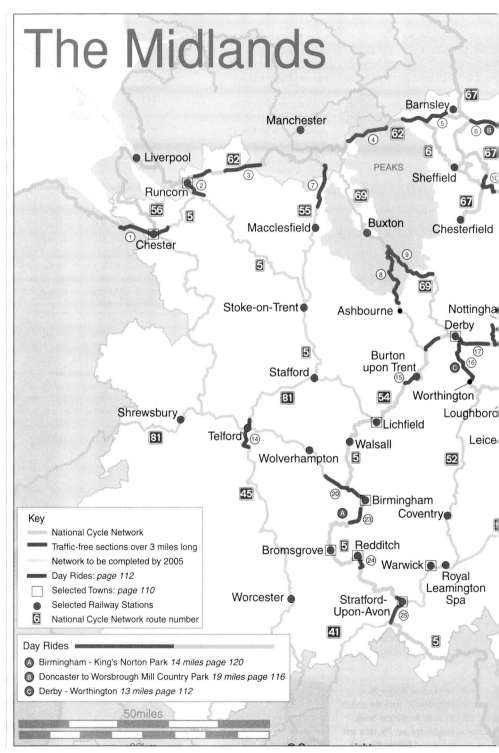

The Midlands

Barnsley **67**

Manchester **62** **5** **6** **B**

Liverpool **62** **6** **67**

PEAKS

Sheffield

Runcorn **2** **3** **7** **69**

56 **5** **55**

Macclesfield **Buxton** Chesterfield

5 **9**

Chester **8** **69**

Stoke-on-Trent Ashbourne Nottingham

Derby

Burton **5** upon Trent **17**

Stafford **16**

81 **54** **C** **15**

Worthington

Shrewsbury Loughborough

81 Telford **14** Lichfield Leice

Walsall

Wolverhampton **5** **52**

45 **20** Birmingham

A **23** Coventry

Bromsgrove **5** Redditch

24 Warwick

Worcester Stratford- Royal

Upon-Avon **25** Leamington

Spa

41 **5**

Key

- National Cycle Network
- Traffic-free sections over 3 miles long
- Network to be completed by 2005
- Day Rides: *page 112*
- Selected Towns: *page 110*
- Selected Railway Stations
- **6** National Cycle Network route number

Day Rides

- **A** Birmingham - King's Norton Park *14 miles page 120*
- **B** Doncaster to Worsbrough Mill Country Park *19 miles page 116*
- **C** Derby - Worthington *13 miles page 112*

50miles

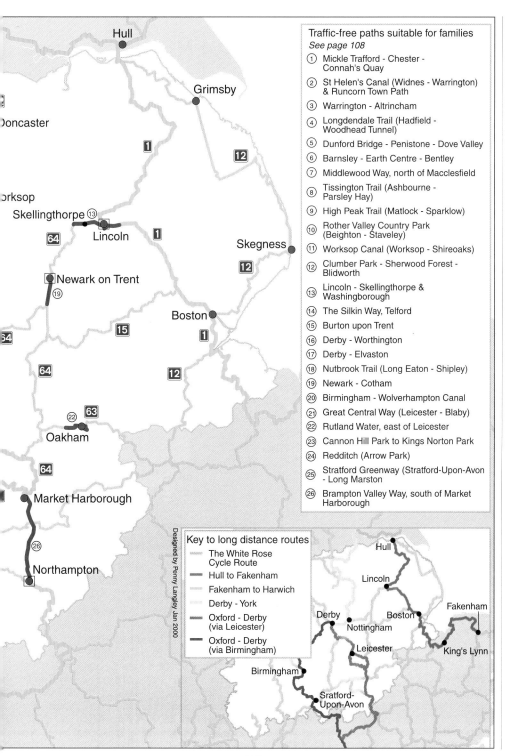

Hull

Grimsby

Doncaster

[1]

[12]

Worksop

Skellingthorpe (13)

[64] Lincoln [1]

Skegness

[12]

Newark on Trent

(19)

Boston

[15] [1]

[64] [12]

(22) [63]

Oakham

[64]

Market Harborough

(26)

Northampton

Traffic-free paths suitable for families
See page 108

(1) Mickle Trafford - Chester - Connah's Quay
(2) St Helen's Canal (Widnes - Warrington) & Runcorn Town Path
(3) Warrington - Altrincham
(4) Longdendale Trail (Hadfield - Woodhead Tunnel)
(5) Dunford Bridge - Penistone - Dove Valley
(6) Barnsley - Earth Centre - Bentley
(7) Middlewood Way, north of Macclesfield
(8) Tissington Trail (Ashbourne - Parsley Hay)
(9) High Peak Trail (Matlock - Sparklow)
(10) Rother Valley Country Park (Beighton - Staveley)
(11) Worksop Canal (Worksop - Shireoaks)
(12) Clumber Park - Sherwood Forest - Blidworth
(13) Lincoln - Skellingthorpe & Washingborough
(14) The Silkin Way, Telford
(15) Burton upon Trent
(16) Derby - Worthington
(17) Derby - Elvaston
(18) Nutbrook Trail (Long Eaton - Shipley)
(19) Newark - Cotham
(20) Birmingham - Wolverhampton Canal
(21) Great Central Way (Leicester - Blaby)
(22) Rutland Water, east of Leicester
(23) Cannon Hill Park to Kings Norton Park
(24) Redditch (Arrow Park)
(25) Stratford Greenway (Stratford-Upon-Avon - Long Marston)
(26) Brampton Valley Way, south of Market Harborough

Designed by Penny Langley Jan 2000

Key to long distance routes

The White Rose Cycle Route
Hull to Fakenham
Fakenham to Harwich
Derby - York
Oxford - Derby (via Leicester)
Oxford - Derby (via Birmingham)

Hull

Lincoln

Derby
Boston
Fakenham
Nottingham
King's Lynn
Leicester
Birmingham
Sratford-Upon-Avon

105

THE MIDLANDS

Birmingham and Wolverhampton Mainline Canal near the city centre.

With the exception of the Peak District in the centre of the region and the Welsh Marches to the west, the Midlands offers relatively gentle cycling with the land rarely rising above 600ft. The area described is bounded to the north by the Trans Pennine Trail, a coast to coast route from Southport/Liverpool in the west to Hull and the North Sea in the east.

Further south, the area is dominated by the vast conurbation of Birmingham and Wolverhampton (the West Midlands) and the smaller cities of Coventry, Stoke, Nottingham, Derby, Leicester and Sheffield. With the exception of Coventry and Stoke, all these cities of the Midlands are linked by the Dover to Inverness National Cycle Route, which divides into two strands at Kidlington, just north of Oxford, and becomes

one again at Derby. The western route passes through Stratford and Birmingham, the eastern route through the amazing cycling infrastructure in Milton Keynes then north through Northampton and Leicester. The Midlands is blessed with the highest density of traffic-free trails in the country with hundreds of miles of railway paths, round reservoir routes and many canal towpaths. Trails include the popular Tissington and High Peak trails in the Peak District, Rutland Water and routes through Clumber Park and Sherwood Forest, and the extraordinary network of canal paths in the West Midlands.

NATIONAL CYCLE NETWORK HIGHLIGHTS

Clumber Park

A wide expanse of parkland, farmland and woodland, part of Nottinghamshire's famed 'Dukeries' and with a superb serpentine lake at its heart. There are many interesting features across the estate, including a classical bridge, temples, lodges and gate piers. Clumber House was demolished in 1938, but the fine Gothic Revival chapel survives.

The Ironbridge at Coalbrookdale

The Ironbridge at Coalbrookdale was one of the world's first iron bridges. It was opened in 1779 and spans 30.5 m (100 ft) across the River Severn to link the developing industry on both sides of the valley.

Trent Viaduct, Melbourne

The Grade II listed Trent Viaduct, Melbourne was built in 1869 by the Midland Railway Company. Its cast iron parapet was recast to match when the viaduct was incorporated into the cycling route. This crossing of the Trent takes cyclists south and avoids the narrow Swarkestone causeway which by contrast was the turning point for Bonnie Prince Charlie's forces in their advance on London.

Birmingham Centenary Square

Centenary Square is evidence of Birmingham's desire to improve its image and is part of a strategic policy designed to attract people back to the city to live and work. It is a site where art is integral rather than superimposed, a place for quiet reflection as well as a square for programmed concerts and other entertainment. The high profile given to art work is tangible proof to tourist and conference visitors that Birmingham has a new-found confidence that comes from including the visual life of the environment in its overall investment programme.

Telford Aqueduct, Smethwick

The Birmingham Main Line Canal was built between 1825 and 1838 under the direction of Thomas Telford. It cut seven miles off the distance between Birmingham and Wolverhampton. The Aqueduct took a branch off the older Smeaton Canal over the newer one, whose direct route involved massive earthworks. The cycle route follows the towpath.

Sandwell Valley Country Park

The conversion of this subway under the M5 motorway provided the crucial link between the Main Line Canal, The Midland Metro Cycle Route and Sandwell Valley Country Park – a thread of open green spaces, lakes, rivers and canals, which stretches all the way to the outskirts of Walsall. It is details of this kind which link routes together and make the whole Network possible.

TRAFFIC-FREE CYCLE PATHS SUITABLE FOR FAMILIES

These traffic-free routes are shown on the map on p.104

1. Mickle Trafford through Chester to Connah's Quay on a railway path
2. St Helen's Canal (Sankey Valley Park) from Widnes to Sankey Bridges
3. Warrington and Lymm to Altrincham via railway path
4. Longdendale Trail, a railway path from Hadfield to the Woodhead Tunnel (east of Manchester)
5. Dunford Bridge to Penistone and Barnsley (Upper Don and Dove Valley Trail) along railway paths
7. Middlewood Way railway path (Marple to Macclesfield, south of Manchester)
9. High Peak Trail, another very popular Peak District railway path (from Matlock to Sparklow), linking with the Tissington Trail
10. Staveley to Beighton railway path and Rother Valley Country Park, south east of Sheffield
11. Worksop Canal west of Worksop
12. Clumber Park and Sherwood Forest, south east of Worksop
13. Lincoln to Skellingthorpe and Washingborough
14. The Silkin Way, a railway path south from the Town Park in Telford
15. Burton-upon-Trent
16. Derby to Worthington – a mixture of riverside, canal towpath and railway path (see pages 112-115). The riverside path can also be followed east to Elvaston Castle
17. Nutbrook Trail, a canal towpath and railway path linking Long Eaton and Shipley Country Park
18. Newark to Bottesford railway path
19. Coalville
20. Birmingham to Wolverhampton Main Line Canal towpath
22. Rutland Water, east of Leicester – the most popular round reservoir route in the country
23. Cannon Hill Park (Birmingham) to Kings Norton
24. Arrow Park, Redditch

8. Tissington Trail

One of the most popular traffic-free rides in the country, the trail climbs 700ft over 13 miles from Ashbourne up to Parsley Hay passing through magnificent Peak District scenery. There are excellent cycle hire facilities.

21. Routes through Leicester

Leicester promotes itself as Environment City and it has made big strides in providing attractive and safe cycle routes passing right through the city centre along the riverside, including the Great Central Way to Blaby.

25. Stratford Greenway from Stratford-upon-Avon to Long Marston

This five-mile railway path runs from near the centre of town, past the Racecourse into open countryside via the old railway bridge over the River Avon. The route links to the Stratford-upon-Avon Canal towpath to Wilmcote.

256. Brampton Valley Way from Market Harborough to Northampton

A well-maintained 14-mile railway path passing a collection of old steam locomotives at Chapel Brampton and using two tunnels to link Market Harborough with the northern edge of Northampton.

© Crown copyright

REGIONAL ROUTES AND GOOD CYCLING AREAS

For further information about leaflets covering these routes contact Sustrans Information Service, PO Box 21, Bristol BS99 2HA (0117 929 0888) or visit www.sustrans.org.uk

THE NORTHERN WARWICKSHIRE CYCLEWAY RPR09

35 miles

Regional Route 11
Links with National Route 5. Full colour A2 leaflet with hand-drawn mapping and detailed route instructions describing a 35-mile road route around the gently rolling hills of North Warwickshire.

THE PEAK DISTRICT RB016

Few parts of the country offer so many traffic-free trails in such a small area. There are dismantled railways, round reservoir routes and country parks plus a fine network of quiet lanes through the magnificent dry-stone walled scenery of the National Park.

Ordnance Survey Cycle Tours: The Peak District contains 23 (mainly road) rides in the area.

Cycling Without Traffic: the Midlands & the Peak District has details of 29 traffic-free routes, with more than a dozen in or close to the Peaks.

NORTH WALES AND THE MARCHES RB013

GLOUCESTERSHIRE AND HEREFORD & WORCESTERSHIRE RB011

The beautiful unspoilt country through Shropshire, Herefordshire and Worcestershire provides excellent cycling with more energetic challenges the further west you go.

Two *Ordnance Survey Cycle Tours* titles contain rides in the area: *North Wales & the Marches* describes four rides in Shropshire; *Gloucestershire, Herefordshire & Worcestershire* covers the southern half of the Welsh Marches.

HEART OF ENGLAND (LEICESTERSHIRE, WARWICKSHIRE, NORTHAMPTONSHIRE)

With the exception of Warwick and Stratford-upon-Avon this area in the Heart of England is little visited by tourists and yet it offers excellent cycling along gently undulating lanes through some attractive stone-built villages.

TOWNS AND CITIES ON THE NATIONAL CYCLE NETWORK

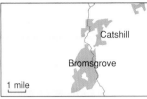

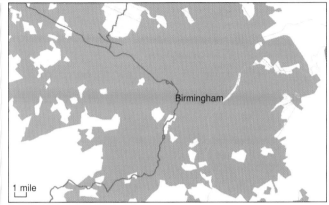

Bromsgrove

The National Cycle Network will link the centre of Bromsgrove with Catshill, thus offering a more attractive alternative to the two busy roads which connect them. In the centre of Bromsgrove itself the National Route passes North Bromsgove High School, North East Worcestershire College and the Dolphin Leisure Centre. Bromsgrove is linked to Redditch via five miles of country lanes.

Chester

The Mickle Trafford railway corridor provides the core of the National Cycle Network and a cross-city link. The route north to Liverpool serves schools and goes past Chester Zoo to join up with the canal towpath before connecting to minor roads up the Wirral. To the south of the Mickle Trafford Line the route goes through the middle of the city to pick up minor roads to Shrewsbury. The National Cycle Network in Chester will be the spine around which many local routes can develop.

Birmingham

To the south of the city, the Rea Valley Route extends to King's Norton and the aim is to continue to Longbridge. In the city centre itself, high profile cycle facilities (such as contraflow cycle lanes) have been installed on busy roads like Hurst Street. To the north west, the Birmingham to Wolverhampton Canal towpath has benefited from top grade resurfacing as far as the city boundary. Other informal cycle routes follow the extensive and excellent canal towpaths which thread through the area to give an interesting view of the City.

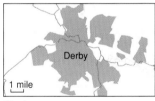

Derby

The abandoned and filled-in Derby Canal forms the basis of an early Sustrans project from the south of the city and connects with a fine riverside route from Elvaston Park to Abbey Fields.

Leamington Spa & Warwick

The excellent cycleway through these prosperous, handsome heritage towns links railway stations to provide a congestion-beating school and commuter route. As National Route 52 it will extend eastwards through Victorian spa-scapes and south-westwards via medieval Warwick to provide a unique showcase of English urban style over the last 500 years.

Leicester

The city pioneered the use of coloured banding to mark routes through the city, and this is now commonly adopted to weave routes through complex urban areas. The routes shown on the map follow the river corridor, the Great Central Way, and detailed works in the city centre.

© Crown copyright

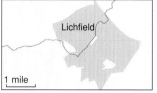

Lichfield

The National Cycle Network follows the Netherstowe Cycle Route to the east of the town centre – opening up a formerly unavailable route to Netherstowe Secondary School from the Eastern Avenue area. The route continues into the historic city centre with fine views of the three-spired cathedral. A new toucan crossing of the A51 links Leamonsley to the city centre and provides a valuable safe route to school.

Lincoln

Whether approaching Lincoln from the east or the west along the National Cycle Network, it is Lincoln's magnificent cathedral that dominates the skyline, standing at the top of Steep Hill, above the Witham valley. Railway paths take you to the edge of the city, where you follow the Roman Fossdyke Canal into the modern campus of the University of Lincolnshire.

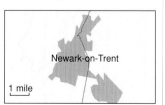

Newark-on-Trent

A traffic-free path along the former Bottesford railway leads into this bustling market town. The cobbled Market Square is the site for weekly markets, whilst a few minutes away Newark Castle forms the backdrop for the Sealed Knot's re-enactment of action during the Civil War.

Northampton

The Northampton area includes a number of disused railways, such as the popular Brampton Valley Way. Linking these disused railways with the railway station and the attractive Guildhall in the town centre has taken many years and the completion of the routes by the millennium owes a great deal to the National Cycle Network.

Nottingham

Nottingham is the home of Raleigh Cycles and the city has a long history of providing cycle routes and the National Network has linked these together, extended them and in places improved their quality.

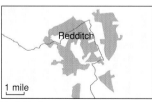

Redditch

The spine path through Arrow Valley Park has been upgraded and a link is being created to Halfords' headquarters. The spine path is linked to the town centre via a traffic-calmed road with cycle lanes. To the west, the Musketts Way footpath has been upgraded providing a link from the Web Heath area to the centre. To the south of Redditch a link to Studley is built along an old railway line. The route passes a hospital, the Leys High School and the leisure centre.

Runcorn

Runcorn is a New Town with a number of excellent cycle routes running through it, and the National Cycle Network aims to extend these. One particular problem is how to cross the River Mersey on the Runcorn Bridge to the north. Plans are in hand to improve access at either end along the pavements. Elsewhere the Network is aiming to create quality links from Runcorn to its surrounding countryside.

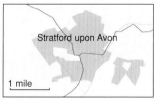

Stratford-upon-Avon

The Stratford Greenway railway path from Long Marston has been extended right into the heart of town. Stratford College has benefited from the creation of a new route from the south as a result of footpath widening. The Stratford Canal towpath forms the basis of the route from the town centre to Wilmcote, and then via country roads to Redditch.

© Crown copyright

DERBY TO WORTHINGTON

The 13-mile ride out of Derby to the small, pretty village of Worthington is in many ways a perfect blueprint for what Sustrans would like to achieve throughout the country. An attractive traffic-free path starts in the heart of the city near where people live, work and shop. The route passes right by schools and colleges, crosses busy roads safely via toucan crossings, and uses a mixture of specially-built cycle paths, railway paths and canal towpaths to reach deep into the countryside along a green corridor, occasionally wooded and frequently punctuated with magnificent Millennium Mileposts and stone sculptures. It is a route that serves schoolchildren, commuters and leisure cyclists alike, whether they are novice cyclists, young families or more experienced cyclists looking for an attractive route out of the city to link with the network of country lanes. The Trent Viaduct is crossed near Melbourne – this is Grade 2 Listed, built in 1869 and was repaired by Sustrans in the late 1980s. The second half of the ride has views of the limestone bluff of Breedon on the Hill, topped by a Norman church. The village of Worthington boasts an attractive church with a small wooden spire, an octagonal red-brick lock-up dating back to the 18th century, and a pub.

The Melbourne Railway Path.

112

Starting points
1. Derby railway station.
2. The Riverside Path in the centre of Derby (Bass's Recreation Ground).

Distance
13 miles one way, 26 miles return.

Grade
Easy.

Surface
Almost all on fine quality stone paths.

Roads, traffic, suitability for young children
Once onto the Riverside Path the route is excellent for young children. All the busy roads are crossed via bridges, subways or with toucan crossings.

There is a one-mile road section to visit Melbourne and a shorter (quieter) road section to visit Worthington.

Hills
No hills.

Refreshments
Lots of choice in Derby.
Lots of choice in Melbourne.
Malt Shovel PH in Worthington.

Leaflets
1. The Derby Cycling Group publishes an excellent cycling map of Derby, available from Sustrans Information Service, PO Box 21, Bristol. BS99 2HA (0117 929 0888) or visit www.sustrans.org.uk

2. Derby City Council produces a free leaflet *Recreational Routes in and around Derby* showing many of the traffic-free trails in the area. Available from Derby City Council, Planning and Technical Services Dept., Roman House, Friar Gate, Derby DE1 1XB (01332 255021).

Derby town centre with the River Derwent Weir.

Nearest railway station
Derby.

The National Cycle Network in the area
Derby is at a major junction of the National Cycle Network:
Route 6 runs north from Milton Keynes through Northampton and Leicester to Derby, then on through Nottingham to join the Trans Pennine Trail in Sheffield and Barnsley.
Route 54 runs south west from Derby through Burton-upon-Trent and Lichfield to Birmingham. From Etwall, five miles along this route, you can pick up the Pennine Cycleway (Route 69) which is open via Ashbourne and the Tissington Trail to Buxton and eventually reaches Berwick-on-Tweed.

Other nearby rides (waymarked or traffic-free)
1. The Riverside Path alongside the River Derwent runs east to Elvaston Castle Country Park where there is a circuit of the park.
2. To the north of Derby city centre (Exeter Bridge) the path continues alongside the Derwent past the Industrial Museum towards Chester Green and Darley.

DERBY TO WORTHINGTON

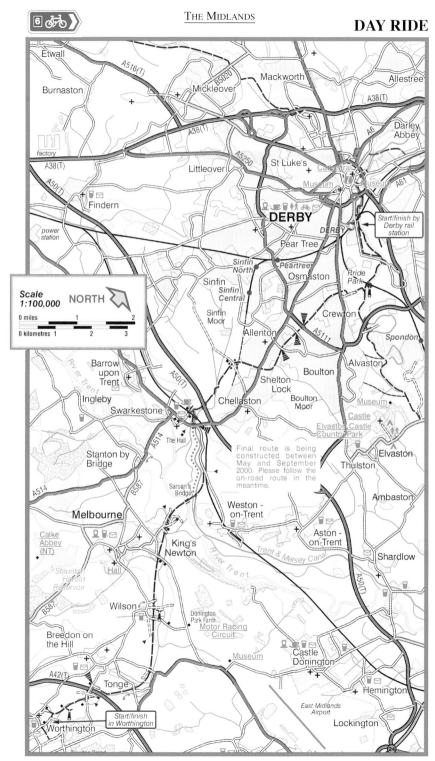

© Crown copyright

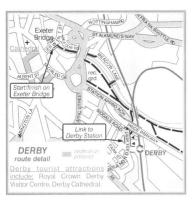

Route instructions – Derby to Worthington

1. Exit Derby railway station and turn right. Either ride along the road (with care) or walk your bike along the pavement for 300 yds. Use the traffic lights just before the flyover to cross the road to the right and go beneath the bridge towards the Riverside Path.

If starting from the centre of Derby (Bass's Recreation Ground) follow the River Derwent east out of the city (ie keep the river on your left). Rejoin at Instruction 2.

2. Go past Pride Park (the stadium for Derby County Football Club), pass beneath a railway bridge then take the second of two closely spaced paths to the right.

3. Go past a lake then take the next right past the college buildings. Keep bearing left to pass beneath a bridge.

4(a). After one mile, cross three roads in quick succession, the first and the third using toucan crossings.

4(b). After a further mile, near the end of the built-up area, at a crossroads with a minor lane go straight ahead signposted 'Swarkestone Lock'. ('Sinfin' is signposted to the right).

5. Pass beneath the A50, cross a bridge over the canal then turn left onto the towpath signposted 'Melbourne'.

6(a). After two miles, just before the large bridge over the river, bear right and join the railway path.

6(b). After one mile, for Melbourne, cross the bridge over the river, pass beneath the power lines then fork right by the small, wooden Ranger's Hut. At the T-junction with the lane turn right. At the crossroads at the end of Trent Lane go straight ahead onto Jawbone Lane. At the T-junction at the end of Jawbone Lane, turn left then immediately right and follow this road into the heart of Melbourne.

Near Worthington.

7. For Worthington, stay on the main railway path. After 4 miles the path veers right and runs parallel with the A42. Cross the bridge over the dual carriageway then bear left to rejoin the railway path.

8. After 1½ miles the trail ends. If you wish to visit Worthington with its attractive church, octagonal lock-up and pub, turn left onto the minor lane, then at the crossroads at the end of Breedon Lane turn left onto Church Street signposted 'Griffydam, Osgathorpe'. Follow this road through the village for ¾-mile past the octagonal red-brick lock-up to the Malt Shovel pub.

DONCASTER TO THE EARTH CENTRE AND BARNSLEY

The Trans Pennine Trail crosses the country from coast to coast, starting in Southport and passing through Liverpool and South Manchester before crossing the Pennines to Barnsley, Doncaster, Hull and the North Sea coast. It links together many traffic-free stretches along dismantled railways, riverside paths, canal towpaths and across land regenerated after the demise of the area's heavy industries. The section described below goes right past the Earth Centre, a 400-acre ecology park which is situated on reclaimed derelict land.

The River Don is crossed to the west of Doncaster over a viaduct high above the water, from where the railway path northwards passes Cusworth Park Museum, on the route to York. The river is then followed westwards on a delightful woodland stretch, passing the locks on the river at the Boat Inn in Sprotbrough before climbing to the northern end of the magnificent Conisborough viaduct. This was the last major viaduct built for the railways in Britain. Leave yourself time to visit the Earth Centre before continuing westwards through the newly-built wetlands area to the north of Wath upon Dearne and joining the course of the old dismantled railway (the Dove Valley Trail) which will take you all the way to Worsbrough Mill Country Park (or into Barnsley).

The Trans Pennine Trail runs beside the River Don here viewed from Conisbrough Viaduct.

Starting points
Worsbrough Mill Country Park, south of Barnsley.
Doncaster Railway Station.
The Earth Centre, Conisbrough.

Distance
18 miles one way, 36 miles return. For shorter rides starting from Doncaster there are good turnaround points at the Boat Inn, Sprotbrough (6 miles round trip), The Earth Centre (13 miles round trip), the Harlington Inn (17 miles round trip).

Grade
Easy.

Surface
Tarmac and stone-based track.

Roads, traffic, suitability for young children
The route is mainly traffic-free and ideal for children. There are short road sections at the start in

Doncaster and the end at Worsbrough Mill. There are also two short stretches on roads in the middle section, through Harlington and through Bolton upon Dearne.

Hills
One or two short climbs but no major hills.

Refreshments
Boat Inn, Sprotbrough.
Refreshments at the Earth Centre (although you will need to pay the entrance fee). Ring 01709 513933 to check opening times and admission changes.
Harlington Inn, Harlington.

Nearest railway stations
Doncaster, Conisbrough, Barnsley.

The National Cycle Network in the area
Barnsley is at a crossroads of the National Cycle Network: the Trans Pennine Trail (Route 62) runs from

Cyclists head west along the paved path beside the River Don.

Southport to Liverpool then east through Manchester, Barnsley and Hull to the North Sea Coast. Route 6 goes south from Barnsley to Sheffield, Worksop and Nottingham. Route 67 links Barnsley to Leeds.

Other nearby rides (waymarked or traffic-free)
Many sections of the Trans Pennine Trail are traffic-free: from Worsbrough via Penistone and Dunford Bridge to Hadfield (near Glossop, on the western side of the Pennines) the trail is almost all traffic-free. On the southern link there is a long traffic-free stretch from the Rother Valley Park down into Chesterfield.

There is a waymarked Forestry Commission trail in Wharncliffe Woods, north west of Sheffield.

117

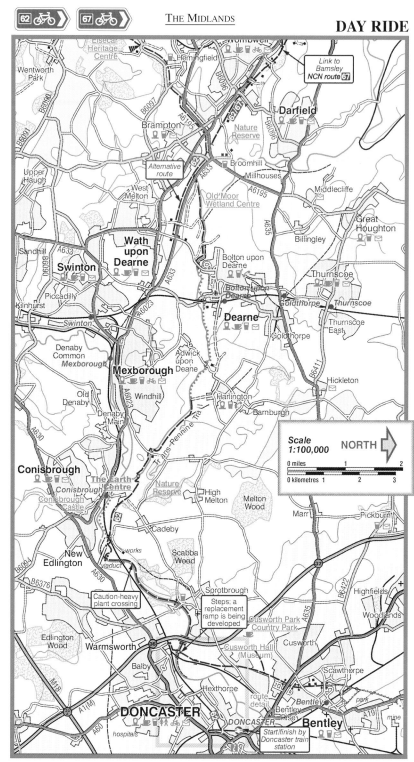

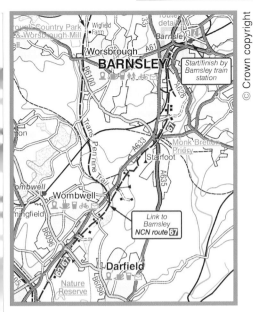

The Earth Centre.

Route instructions from Doncaster to Worsbrough Mill and Barnsley

1. With your back to Doncaster railway station, bear right on the red-brick path alongside the station car park then go through the adjoining car park. At the offset crossroads go straight ahead onto West Street then right at the T-junction with St Sepulchre Gate.

2. Continue in the same direction, past St James' Church, over the railway bridge and follow the road to the right then left. At the Rising Sun PH turn right onto Flowit St.

3. At the T-junction with Shady Side turn right then right again onto Bramworth Road. After 50 yds, as the road swings right, turn left through a small gateway onto tarmac path. Shortly, take the third of three right turns, keeping the children's playground to your right.

4. Cross a bridge over the railway line, turn right along the road then first right signposted 'Warmsworth Cycle Route'. After almost one mile cross the bridge over the disused railway and turn right signposted 'Trans Pennine Trail' (opposite Church Lane). Follow this to its end as tarmac turns to track, cross a bridge over the railway and follow the track round to the right.

5. Go past a cemetery, through a barrier then sharply right steeply downhill to cross the viaduct. Descend via the steps to the left (there are plans for a ramp). Follow the riverside path for three miles, passing beneath the A1 road bridge, alongside the locks and the Boat Inn at Sprotbrough.

6. Continue along the broad stone track climbing to join the road near the right-hand of the viaduct ahead. Continue past the Earth Centre.

7. At the road cross straight ahead then turn right over wooden bridge and join a railway path. Follow this for 1½ miles. Opposite a footbridge over the river turn right onto a track.

8. This turns to tarmac. At the T-junction (at the end of Mill Road) turn left. Go past the Harlington Inn. At the T-junction at the end of Doncaster Road turn left signposted 'Adwick, Mexborough' then after ¼-mile, on a sharp left-hand bend turn right onto a track.

9. There are some rough sections on this stretch. The track turns to tarmac. At the T-junction (at the end of Station Road) just past the railway station, turn left then right just after the church. At the mini-roundabout turn left.

10. Shortly after crossing the bridge, turn right onto a track through the newly created wetlands area, following Trans Pennine Trail signs.

11. Join the railway path, follow for three miles. At major fork of tracks bear left* and cross in quick succession two bridges over roads. After ½-mile at a fork of tracks bear right onto the lower track, towards a pylon.

* or bear right here and follow the signposted route into Barnsley.

12. Continue in the same direction for a further 3 miles. At the crossroads by the Ship PH and a sign for Wigfield Farm, leave the Trans Pennine Trail (which continues straight ahead towards Oxspring, Penistone and Dunford Bridge) turn left for 300 yds then right into Worsbrough Mill Country Park.

119

BIRMINGHAM TO KING'S NORTON PARK

Chamberlain Square and Victoria Square in the very heart of Birmingham are a glorious tribute to the dynamic approach that has created attractive open spaces for pedestrians and cyclists in the centre of a major city. Fine old and modern buildings stand side by side, and the whole area is enhanced by a series of huge sculptures. This ride starts from this place of vision and links with the traffic-free Rea Valley Route via a series of contraflow cycle lanes and other facilities which make life easier for the city centre cyclist. A minaret at the end of Gooch Street is testimony to the high proportion of Muslims living in this multi-cultural city and stands as a contrast to the fine ornate façade of Edward Road Baptist

Church which you soon pass. Cannon Hill Park is an oasis of green with bright displays of flowers and marks the start of the traffic-free Rea Valley Route which is followed for four miles (for one section joining the excellent towpath of the Worcester & Birmingham Canal). The route ends at King's Norton Park where there is a playground for children. The route continues along the line of the river valley to Northfield and Longbridge, and eventually works its way out of the city southwards to Stratford-upon-Avon.

The junction of the Worcester & Birmingham Canal with the Mainline Canal at the Convention Centre.

Starting point

Tourist Information Centre, Chamberlain Square, Central Birmingham.

Distance

Seven miles one way, 14 miles return.

Grade

Easy.

Surface

Mixture of road, tarmac cyclepath and stone-based tracks.

Roads, traffic, suitability for young children

The ride uses some traffic-calmed streets in Central Birmingham, although some streets are still busy. Once out of the centre, all the busy roads are crossed via toucan crossings. The section along the Rea Valley Route through Cannon Hill Park and along the Worcester & Birmingham Canal is traffic-free and ideal for children.

Hills

None.

Refreshments

Lots of choice in Birmingham city centre.
Cafe/tea room in Cannon Hill Park.

Leaflets

CycleCity's Birmingham Cycling Map – City Centre and Suburbs is an excellent publication showing the traffic-free paths, signposted cycle routes, advisory routes and a wealth of other information. It costs £4.95 and is available from Sustrans Information Service, PO Box 21, Bristol BS99 2HA (0117 929 0888), or visit www.sustrans.org.uk

Nearest railway stations

Birmingham New Street in the centre of the city.
King's Norton.

The carriage drive through Cannon Hill Park is now open for cyclists.

The National Cycle Network in the area

Birmingham is at a crossroads of the National Cycle Network:
Route 5 comes north from Reading through Oxford, Banbury, Stratford and Bromsgrove (and is followed in this ride into the centre of Birmingham). It continues north east via Lichfield and Burton-on-Trent to Derby.
Route 81 follows the Main Line Canal to Wolverhampton and will eventually strike into the heart of Mid Wales.
Route 44 is a long-term plan to link Birmingham to Chepstow through Worcestershire, Herefordshire and the Forest of Dean.

Other nearby rides (waymarked or traffic-free)

1. Although, as we are forever being told, Birmingham has more miles of canal than Venice, from a cyclist's point of view the towpath network is not formalised, but there is much to explore including the Worcester & Birmingham Canal towpath which is used for part of this route. For the most up-to-date information contact British Waterways: 01902 409010.
2. Sutton Park is a large park just north of Birmingham where motor traffic has been banned.
3. The Kingswinford Railway Path runs for 10 miles from Pensnett (west of Dudley) to Wolverhampton.
4. National Cycle Route 5 follows the Birmingham & Wolverhampton Canal from the centre of Birmingham to Sandwell Valley Country Park.

A good example of the high quality city centre towpath rebuilt by British Waterways.

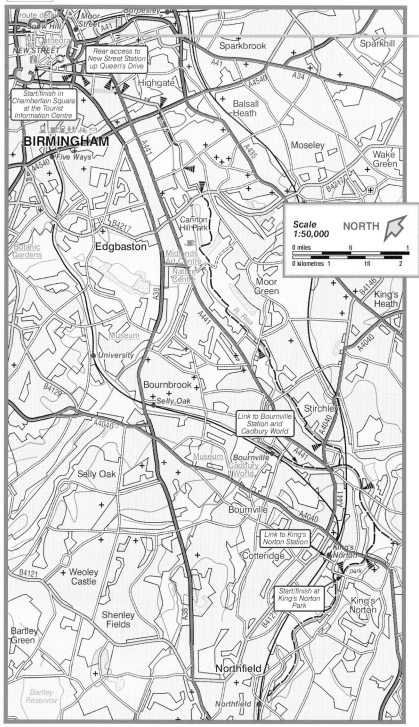

BIRMINGHAM TO KING'S NORTON PARK

© Crown copyright

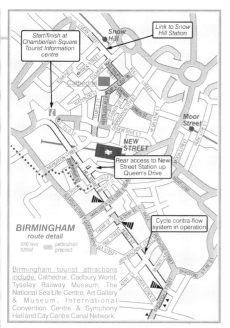

BIRMINGHAM
route detail

one way street ▪ pedestrian precinct

Birmingham tourist attractions include: Cathedral, Cadbury World, Tyseley Railway Museum, The National Sea Life Centre, Art Gallery & Museum, International Convention Centre & Symphony Hall and City Centre Canal Network.

Route instructions from Birmingham to King's Norton Park

1. With your back to the Tourist Information Centre, go to the left of the Iron Man down Pinfold Street, left into Stephenson Street – follow round to the right into Navigation Street. Left at the traffic lights into Hill Street.

2. Go straight ahead at the traffic lights. Continue downhill. Go straight ahead on the bus/cycle lane as the traffic bears left. Go straight ahead at the traffic lights at the crossroads with Smallbrook Queensway dual carriageway.

3. Move into the cycle lane in the centre of the road to cross to the pedestrian area in front of the Hippodrome Theatre. Go straight ahead onto Hurst Street. At the traffic lights go straight ahead into a contraflow lane continuing down Hurst Street.

4. Use the cycle facility to turn right at the traffic lights onto the cycle lane in Sherlock Street. Shortly, turn left into Gooch Street.

5. At the Post Office and shops follow Gooch Street around to the right. At the traffic lights get into the cycle lane and cross straight ahead (onto Longmore Street). Just after the lights move right and cross to the cycle track on the grassed open space alongside the road.

6. At the crossroads with Edward Road at the end of Cheddar Road, go straight ahead onto Harbury Road. At the T-junction with Willows Crescent (you can just see Edgbaston Cricket Ground to your right) turn left then shortly right onto Cannon Hill Road.

7. At the crossroads with the busy Edgbaston Road use the toucan crossing to go straight ahead through the gates into the delights of Cannon Hill Park.

8. Follow the clearly segregated cycle route through the park. Go past a Millennium Milepost on your right. At the end of the white line segregation continue straight ahead with the river on your right, following signs for Stirchley.

9. The tarmac path swings right to cross the river via a brick and metal bridge (wihout barriers).

10. The track joins a street with terraced houses (Kitchener Road). Turn first left onto Cecil Road then at the T-junction with Dogpool Lane turn left then immediately right onto a continuation of the riverside path.

11. Follow the Rea Valley Route and signs for 'Stirchley, King's Norton'. At the next busy road (Cartland Road) go straight ahead via a toucan crossing onto a continuation of the riverside path.

12. At the T-junction with the trading estate road turn right to cross the bridge then immediately left (with the river now on your left). At the crossroads with the busy Fordhouse Lane, use the toucan crossing to go straight ahead signposted 'King's Norton, Northfield'.

13. At the end of the cycle path by a tall wooden signpost turn left on the quiet estate road (Dacer Close) then shortly first left. Follow Rea Valley Route signs to join the Worcester & Birmingham Canal towpath and turn left.

14. At the next bridge (Lifford Lane Road Bridge) the towpath crosses to the other side of the canal.

15. After 400 yds, at the next bridge (red-brick with a '72' plaque on it) turn right just before a large red-brick house away from the towpath signposted 'Rea Valley Route. King's Norton'. Follow the path across the playing fields. Cross Pershore Road via toucan crossing.

16. The route continues along the valley to Longbridge.

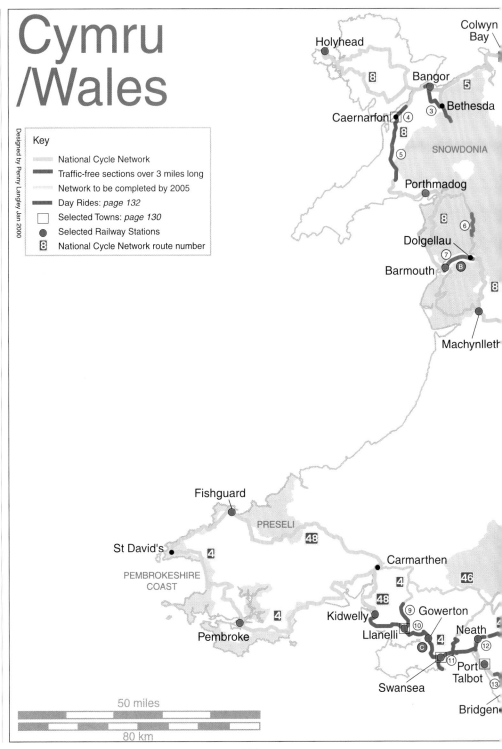

Cymru /Wales

Key

▭	National Cycle Network
▬	Traffic-free sections over 3 miles long
▭	Network to be completed by 2005
▬	Day Rides: *page 132*
☐	Selected Towns: *page 130*
●	Selected Railway Stations
8	National Cycle Network route number

Designed by Penny Langley Jan 2000

Colwyn Bay

Holyhead

8 Bangor

5

● Bethesda

Caernarfon ☐● ④ ③

8

⑤

SNOWDONIA

Porthmadog

8

⑥

Dolgellau

⑦

B

Barmouth

8

Machynlleth

Fishguard

PRESELI

48

St David's ●

4

PEMBROKESHIRE COAST

Carmarthen

4

46

48

4

Kidwelly ●

48

⑨ Gowerton

⑩

Neath

Llanelli ⑪

C 4

⑫

Pembroke

⑪ Port Talbot ⑬

Swansea

Bridgend

50 miles

80 km

Prestatyn
Rhyl

5

Chester

Holyhead
Bangor
Machynlleth

Fishguard
Builth Wells

Swansea
Cardiff

Gloucester Oxford
Chepstow
Reading

Key to long distance routes
— Lôn Las Cymru Gogledd (north)
— Lôn Las Cymru De (south)
— The Celtic Trail (Lôn Geltaidd) East
— The Celtic Trail (Lôn Geltaidd) West
  The Severn & Thames Cycle Route
  Thames Valley Cycle Route

81

Llanidloes

Rhayader

Builth Wells

Glasbury

8
Brecon
RECON
EACONS
42

46 (17) **Abergavenny**
Merthyr
Tydfil
(16) **8** (18) **42**

Cwmbrân **46**
47
(19) (20) **Chepstow**
4 Caldicot
8 **4**
Pontypridd **Newport**
(16) **Cardiff**

Traffic-free paths suitable for families
See page 128
① Connah's Quay - Chester - Mickle Trafford
② North Wales Coast Promenades
③ Bangor - Tregarth
④ Caernarfon to Y Felinheli
⑤ Caernarfon to Bryncir
⑥ Coed y Brenin Forestry
⑦ Mawddach Estuary
⑧ Elan Valley Routes
⑨ Swiss Valley Railway
⑩ Llanelli Coastal Park
⑪ Swansea Bike Paths
⑫ Neath - Briton Ferry
⑬ Afan Argoed Country Park
⑭ Neath to Pontypridd High Level Route
⑮ Ogmore Vale Trail
⑯ Taff Trail
⑰ Llanfoist - Govilon
⑱ Pontypool - Blaenavon
⑲ Sirhowy Country Park
⑳ Newport Canal Paths

© Crown copyright

Day Rides
Ⓐ Colwyn Bay - Prestatyn *16 miles page 148*
Ⓑ Barmouth - Dolgellau *11 miles page 144*
Ⓒ Swansea Bay *9 miles page 132*
Ⓓ Kidwelly to the Wildfowl and Wetlands Centre *15 miles page 136*
Ⓔ Cardiff - Castell Coch *6 miles page 140*

WALES

Wales contains some of Britain's most beautiful countryside and some of its earliest industrial history which has left, particularly in the south, scars but also a plethora of interesting sites. Fortunately many of these scars have disappeared thanks to some of the largest land reclamation schemes in Europe. This juxtaposition of beauty and industry includes the untouched farmland and moors on the ridges between the old coal mining valleys and the dramatic contrast of the heavy industrial complexes at Port Talbot overlooked by sheep-dotted rolling hills.

The Welsh National Cycle Route, also known as Lôn Las Cymru, runs the length of Wales from the Bristol Channel to the island of Anglesey. Highlights along the way include the magnificent development around Cardiff Bay, the fairy-tale

Route 8 from Cardiff to Holyhead follows the remains of the Glamorgan Canal into Merthyr Tydfil under this impressive railway relic.

castle at Castell Coch, the dramatic beauty of the Brecon Beacons, the mountains of Mid Wales, the broad and scenic Mawddach Estuary and the solid splendour of Caernarfon Castle.

Two other Millennium routes cross Wales from east to west. The Bangor to Liverpool route will skirt along the North Coast; in South and West Wales the Celtic Trail/Lôn Geltaidd links the port of Fishguard, via the attractions of Pembrokeshire, to the old coal mining valleys, crossing the Welsh National Route in Pontypridd before running east through Newport and Chepstow to the old Severn Bridge.

NATIONAL CYCLE NETWORK HIGHLIGHTS

Menai Bridge

Telford's suspension bridge across the Menai Straits and a ferry service form Caernarfon provide the links onto Anglesey. The two National Routes in North Wales (5 & 8) combine here to cross over this stretch of water at Menai Bridge.

Caerphilly Castle

Caerphilly Castle is the largest castle in Wales. In 1268 building began on the site of an earlier Roman Fort, by the Anglo-Norman Gilbert de Clare in his struggle with the Welsh ruler Llewellyn ap Griffydd. The Castle's ownership passed to and fro until 1648 during the English Civil War when it was destroyed and the moat drained. The National Cycle Route passes close by the moat and lakes which were reflooded in 1958.

Newport Transporter Bridge

The Newport Transporter Bridge is the largest of a number built by Ferdinand Arnodin. The bridge took four years to build at a cost of £98,000 and was opened by Viscount Tredegar on 12 September 1906. It has a clear span of 592 ft and a height of 177 ft to the underside of the boom. The bridge never paid its way, and once the George Street Bridge was opened in 1964 it fell into dereliction. Eventually Newport Borough had to close the bridge until major funding was found to refurbish this wonderful structure over the years 1992-1995, when it was reopened.

Cefn Coed Viaduct

The magnificent Cefn Coed Viaduct, spans the Afon Taf Fawr in a gentle curve south west of Merthyr Tydfil. The viaduct is a 15-bay structure, 770 ft long, and was completed in 1866 as part of a complex detour insisted on by the owner of Cyfartha Castle, who did not want to see the new Brecon and Merthyr Tydfil Junction Railway from his windows.

Colwyn Bay Promenade

Conwy and Denbighshire's superb promenade route links Colwyn Bay and Rhyl and Prestatyn along a largely traffic-free path overlooking the sea. It runs parallel to the North Coast Railway and has involved heavy engineering to create a continuous route almost entirely separate from traffic.

Llanelli Coastal Park

Sandy Water Park, Llanelli, where the Network divides between routes continuing westwards along the coast to Kidwelly or turning northwards towards the National Botanic Gardens at Middleton Hall.

TRAFFIC-FREE CYCLE PATHS SUITABLE FOR FAMILIES

Listed here is a selection of traffic-free routes, often along disused railways, that are more than three miles long and offer ideal cycling for families. Some are covered by the Day Rides, some are shown on the diagrammatic maps below. (Numbers match the map key on p.124.)

For further information about traffic-free rides, ask for the Traffic-free Information Sheet from Sustrans Information Service, PO Box 21, Bristol BS99 2HA (0117 929 0888) or visit www.sustrans.org.uk

The Family Cycling Trail Guide (£4.95) contains details of 300 traffic-free rides throughout Britain. Also available from Sustrans.

1. Mickle Trafford to Connah's Quay
2. Colwyn Bay to Prestatyn – see page 144
3. Bangor to Tregarth railway path
4. Caernarfon to Y Felinheli railway path
6. Coed y Brenin Forestry Routes
7. Mawddach Estuary path – see page 140
9. Swiss Valley Railway, north of Llanelli
10. Llanelli Coastal Park – see page 132
11. Swansea Bike paths – see page 128
12. Neath to Briton Ferry canal towpath
13. Several routes in Afan Argoed Country Park
15. Ogmore Vale Trail
16. Taff Trail – see page 136
17. Llanfoist to Govilon railway path
18. Pontypool to Blaenavon railway path
19. Routes in Sirhowy Country Park, northwest of Newport, including Crosskeys to Gelligroes along a railway path

5. Caernarfon to Bryncir also known as Lôn Eifion (North Wales)

Two railway paths start in Caernarfon, both are used in the Welsh National Route (Lôn Las Cymru) as it crosses Wales from Cardiff to Anglesey. This, the longer of the two runs south for 12 miles to Bryncir, north of Criccieth. Minor roads lead to Porthmadog.

14. Neath – Llanwonno (Pontypridd) High Level Route

The traffic-free section of this route follows wide gravel roads through the largest forest area in South Wales. From the top of Fairylands Road, north east of Neath, to Llanwonno, north west of Pontypridd, enjoy 20 miles of forest roads climbing to a highpoint of almost 2,000 ft!

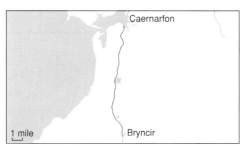

8. Elan Valley Trail

A beautiful six-mile route along the line of the old Birmingham Corporation Railway in the very heart of Mid Wales with panoramic views of four of the Elan Valley Reservoirs, built at the turn of the 20th century to provide a water supply for Birmingham.

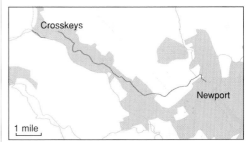

20. Newport – Crosskeys Canal towpath

One of the best canal towpaths in Wales – a wide gravel track runs alongside what was once a major artery carrying coal down to the docks at Newport. There are views of wooded hills rising to over 1,000 ft either side of the canal as you approach Crosskeys.

© Crown copyright

REGIONAL ROUTES AND GOOD CYCLING AREAS

For further information about leaflets covering these routes contact Sustrans Information Service, PO Box 21, Bristol BS99 2HA (0117 929 0888) or visit www.sustrans.org.uk

BRECON BEACONS
RB018

The Brecon Beacons offer some tough but exhilarating cycling, both on-road and off-road. There are also easier trails suitable for families in the forests and along parts of the Monmouthshire & Brecon Canal towpath. Talybont-on-Usk or Hay-on-Wye are good bases to explore the area.

Ordnance Survey Cycle Tours: South, West and Mid Wales includes several routes in the area.
The Mountain Bike Guide to the Brecon Beacons covers the area for mountain biking.

MID WALES
RB018

One of the least densely populated regions in Britain, this area contains some spectacular countryside best appreciated from the saddle. There are plenty of tough challenges on-road and offroad in Mid Wales. The roads and tracks near the Elan Valley Reservoirs west of Rhayader and the road around Lake Vrynwy offer easier family gradients.

Ordnance Survey Cycle Tours: South, West & Mid Wales and *Ordnance Survey Cycle Tours: North Wales & the Marches* both include several routes in the area.

SNOWDONIA NATIONAL PARK
RB013

Snowdonia National Park is crossed by several 'A' roads; unfortunately most of these are busy with traffic, particularly in the summer months. However, there is plenty of easier cycling on quieter lanes in the areas surrounding the Park, notably on the Lleyn Peninsula, the island of Anglesey or in the Vale of Conwy. There are plans to create a traffic-free route south east from Bangor to Betws-y-Coed (Lôn Las Ogwen) which will go right through the heart of the park.

Ordnance Survey Cycle Tours: North Wales & the Marches includes several routes in the area.

The Brecon Beacons.

129

TOWNS AND CITIES ON THE NATIONAL CYCLE NETWORK

Abergavenny

The town has a thriving cycling culture and has long promoted green transport issues. The National Network will eventually run up the spectacular Clydach Gorge whilst the canal already provides a level route to Gilwern.

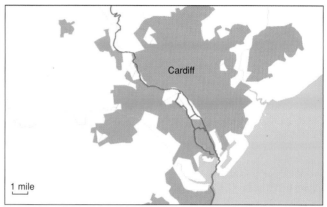

Cardiff

The route from Merthyr Tydfil keeps close to the riverside and its green corridor, threading its way through to the city centre where the route is cantilevered out over the river on the promenade below Wales' spectacular new rugby stadium. From Cardiff Central railway station the route follows the ceremonial Bute Avenue to the National Assembly of Wales and thence around the lake formed by the new tidal barrage.

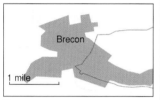

Brecon

The terminus of the Monmouthshire & Brecon Canal from Newport, the towpath of which provides a safe and attractive route into the town.

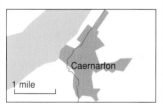

Caernarfon

To the south of the town the railway path of Lôn Eifion brings the cyclist up from Criccieth. Approaching Caernarfon the path runs alongside the newly opened Welsh Highland Railway. The route then passes Caernarfon Castle, built by Edward I and inspired by the walls of Constantinople. A short, signposted urban part leads through the walled part of the medieval town before continuing northwards to Bangor on another railway path.

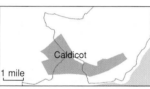

Caldicot

The route passes through the centre of the town and Caldicot Castle then along the edge of the estuary past Sudbrook, which is the site of a spectacular ancient earthworks looking out over the Severn and the M4 bridge.

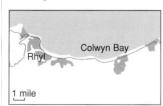

Colwyn Bay/Rhyl

A high proportion of the population in this part of Wales lives along the narrow coastal corridor. The National Cycle Route will follow the coast on an ambitious series of new links to create a route which will serve all the towns along the way. As it is also paralleled by the railway there are numerous opportunities for returning by train.

Llanelli

The National Route here is magnificently provided by the Millennium Coastal Park Project promoted by Carmarthenshire County Council. This links into the town centre via the new Sandy Bridge over the Coastal Link road and the historic Swiss Valley railway route whose new path climbs up to Cynheidre Mine and continues high above the valley floor to Tumble. From here it is a short route to the National Botanic Gardens of Wales at Middleton Hall via the scenic Swiss Valley Railway.

© Crown copyright

Merthyr Tydfil

The highlight of the route through this former industrial powerhouse of South Wales is the magnificent Cefn Coed Viaduct, which was part of Midland Railway's expansion into South Wales. The route heads northwards along this railway corridor. From the viaduct the route drops steeply down the hillside to reach the river corridor running through the town centre.

Pontypridd

The town is very much the hub of the National Cycle Network in South Wales with the Taff Trail meeting the High Level Route to Neath, the equally strenuous route through the South Wales valleys to Port Talbot and the railway path to the Mining and Heritage Park. The routes are expected to be complete by 2002.

Port Talbot

The promenade route along Aberavon Sands is a wide open contrast with the industrial landscape pressing hard behind.

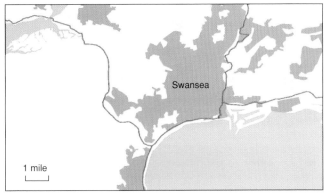

Swansea

Swansea lies at the centre of a network of largely traffic-free routes, the oldest of which runs around Swansea Bay along the line of the former Oystermouth Railway which was variously hauled by steam, horse and even sail!

Ogmore Vale Brick Benches by Dilys Jackson.

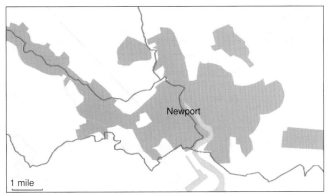

Newport

The routes focus on the refurbished Newport Transporter Bridge. Newport has a good collection of public art including the collapsing town clock which should not be missed.

© Crown copyright

SWANSEA TO GOWERTON & THE MUMBLES

The wide sweep of Swansea Bay provides a dramatic start to both rides, starting from the heart of Swansea, the 'ugly, lovely town' described by Dylan Thomas, who was born here. It is the second largest city in Wales, after Cardiff, with much of it rebuilt after suffering heavy bombing during the Second World War. In the 19th century Swansea was swept along by the rapid industrialisation of South Wales, serving as a port for the local iron and steel industries. In the 20th century the docks fell into decline, but have recently been regenerated with the creation of the new Maritime Quarter, the centrepiece of which is a 600-berth marina at the old South Dock. The Mumbles is a busy sailing and watersports centre which has nevertheless kept its character as a Victorian seaside resort. If you are feeling energetic you may wish to climb up to Mumbles Head for excellent views back over the bay. From Swansea, leading north towards Gowerton, the climb up through the 725 acres of Clyne Valley Country Park is a wooded delight, especially lovely in the changing autumn colours. The gentle three-mile descent on the return trip is a joy for weary legs!

Swansea Waterfront.

Starting point
The seafront by the Marina/County Hall in Swansea.

Distance
Swansea – The Mumbles, 5 miles one way, 10 miles return.
Swansea – Gowerton, 8 miles one way, 16 miles return.

Grade
Easy.

Surface
Swansea – The Mumbles: tarmac.
Swansea – Gowerton: mixture of tarmac and gravel paths.

Roads, traffic, suitability for young children
The two routes are ideal for children. The one busy road crossing (the A4067 at Black Pill) has a toucan crossing.

Hills
Flat ride to The Mumbles. There is a gentle 200ft climb up through Clyne Valley Country Park to the highpoint at Dunvant on the Gowerton ride.

Refreshments
Lots of choice in Swansea and The Mumbles.
Pubs and stores in Gowerton.

Nearest railway stations
Swansea.
There is a restricted service at Gowerton.

The National Cycle Network in the area
The ride described here is part of Route 4, also known as the Celtic

Swansea Harbourside boasts an ambitious series of sculptures including Captain Cat, the blind seafarer in Dylan Thomas' Under Milk Wood.

Trail/Lôn Geltaidd, which runs from Fishguard to the old Severn Bridge at Chepstow.
Route 43 will link Swansea to Builth Wells where it joins the Welsh National Route from Cardiff to Anglesey (Route 8).

Other nearby rides (waymarked or traffic-free)
1. Neath Canal.

Mumbles Pier at the end of the former Oystermouth railway.

2. The High Level Forestry Route from Fairylands Road, east of Neath to Llanwonno, north west of Pontypridd.
3. There are many routes in Afan Argoed Country Park, north east of Port Talbot.

133

SWANSEA TO GOWERTON & THE MUMBLES

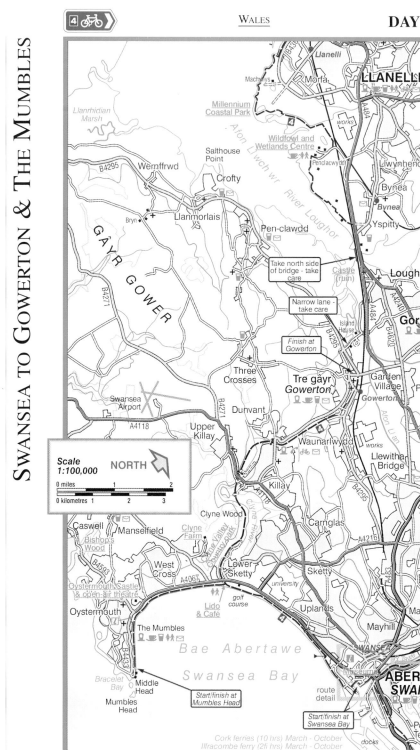

Scale
1:100,000

NORTH

0 miles — 1 — 2
0 kilometres 1 — 2 — 3

Labels within map:

Swiss Valley
Llanelli
Morfa
LLANELLI
works
Machynys
Millennium Coastal Park
Wildfowl and Wetlands Centre
works
Bryn
Llanrhidian Marsh
Salthouse Point
Penclacwydd
Llwynhendy
Bynea
Bynea
Wernffrwd
Crofty
Llanmorlais
Bryn
Pen-clawdd
Yspitty
GÂYR GOWER
Take north side of bridge - take care
Castle (ruin)
Loughor
Narrow lane - take care
Island House
Gorseinon
Finish at Gowerton
Three Crosses
Tre gâyr Gowerton
Garden Village
Penllergaer
Gowerton
Swansea Airport
Dunvant
Upper Killay
Waunarlwydd
works
Llewitha Bridge
Killay
Llewithar Bridge
Clyne Wood
Carnglas
Caswell
Manselfield
Clyne Farm
Lower Sketty
Sketty
Bishop's Wood
West Cross
university
Oystermouth Castle & open-air theatre
Lido & Café
golf course
Uplands
Manselton
Oystermouth
Mayhill
The Mumbles
Bae Abertawe
SWANSEA
Bracelet Bay
Middle Head
Swansea Bay
ABERTAWE
SWANSEA
Mumbles Head
Start/finish at Mumbles Head
route detail
Start/finish at Swansea Bay
Port Tennant
Cork ferries (10 hrs) March - October
Ilfracombe ferry (2¾ hrs) March - October
docks
Visitor Centre

© Crown copyright

Route instructions

A. Swansea to The Mumbles

1. Keeping Swansea Bay to your left, follow the cycle path along the promenade/sea front for five miles, passing the university and golf course. The route stops in The Mumbles where there are plenty of refreshment stops.

B. Swansea to Gowerton

1. Follow the cyclepath along the promenade/sea front for three miles, passing Swansea University.

2. At the end of the golf course on the right, bear right away from the sea front and cross the main A4067 via the traffic lights. Enter Clyne Valley Country Park and start climbing steadily.

3. Climb almost 200 ft to the highpoint at Dunvant. Descend. At the housing estate at the end of the railway path bear left to continue in the same direction, soon rejoining a tarmac track.

4. This becomes a residential road (Woodlands Road). At the crossroads (with the busy B4295) by the shops, go straight ahead through car park to arrive in the centre of Gowerton.

Swansea Bay.

The Clyne Valley Path.

Swansea
route detail

Swansea tourist attractions include: Singleton Park & Botanical Gardens, Dylan Thomas Centre, Maritime & Industrial Museum, Glynn Vivian Art Gallery, The Egypt Centre and Plantasia

Start/finish Swansea Bay

Castle
Plantasia
Leisure Centre
Dylan Thomas Centre
BURNS PL
Swing footbridge - opens periodically
Unfenced paths around harbour - take care!
Tawe Barrage

KIDWELLY TO THE WILDFOWL AND WETLANDS CENTRE, LLANELLI

Starting from Kidwelly with its dramatic castle, you soon join a traffic-free path that continues more or less unbroken to the Wildfowl & Wetlands Centre south of Llanelli. Throughout the ride there are many views of estuaries that flood in exceptionally high tides. The first, Gwendraeth, has a backdrop of rounded green hills rising up over 600 ft from the shoreline. You soon enter the sandy woodlands of Pembrey Forest, where there are many tracks which you could explore, based around the Country Park Visitor Centre. Beyond Pembrey Forest there are long sections of newly-built cycle paths with wonderful views out over the estuary which separates the Gower Peninsula from the mainland. Between Burry Port and Llanelli the railway line is crossed twice via huge bridges covered with earth and grass, a wonderful piece of landscaping. Indeed along the whole length of the route millions of tons of earth have been moved to regenerate what was once a derelict wasteland. At the Wildfowl & Wetlands Centre you have the option of pressing on to Swansea and catching the train back, or cycling all or part of the way back as far as the stations at Llanelli or Burry Port.

New path around the dunes between Burry Port and Pembrey Forest.

Starting points
1. The centre of Kidwelly.
2. The Wildfowl & Wetlands Centre, southeast of Llanelli.

Distance
18 miles one way, 36 miles return. For a shorter ride you might go as far as Pembrey Country Park (14-mile round trip).

Grade
Easy.

Surface
Mixture of tarmac and gravel paths.

Roads, traffic, suitability for young children
There is a short road section at the start in Kidwelly where care should be taken. Very minor roads are used through Burry Port. Otherwise this is an excellent route for young children (as long as you take account of the wind!).

Hills
None.

Refreshments
Lots of choice in Kidwelly.
Cafe at Pembrey Country Park (just off the route).
Cafe at the Wildfowl & Wetlands Centre at the end of the ride.

Nearest railway stations
Kidwelly, Burry Port, Llanelli.

The National Cycle Network in the area
The ride described here is part of Route 4 also known as the Celtic Trail (Lôn Geltaidd) which runs from Fishguard to the old Severn Bridge near Chepstow.
Route 43 will link Swansea to Builth Wells where it joins the Welsh National Route from Cardiff to Anglesey (Route 8).

Construction work on the Llanelli Coastal Park Project.

Other nearby rides (waymarked or traffic-free)
1. There are many more tracks to explore in Pembrey Forest, around the Country Park.
2. Two railway paths run west from Swansea, to Gowerton and The Mumbles – see page 128.

KIDWELLY TO THE WILDFOWL AND WETLAND CENTRE, LLANELLI

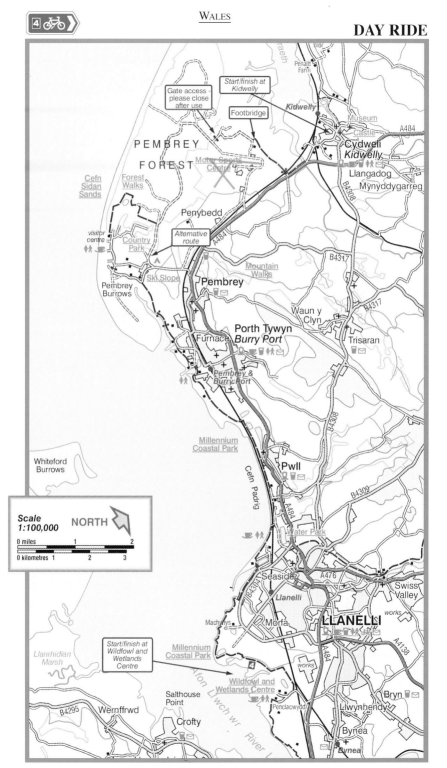

© Crown copyright

138

Route instructions from Kidwelly to the Wildfowl & Wetlands Centre

1. From the church in the centre of Kidwelly follow the B4308 south towards the main road (A484) and Burry Port.

2. Climb then descend. Immediately before the roundabout cross the B4308 onto the pavement/cycle path and follow this round to the right, parallel with the main Llanelli road (A484) for ½-mile.

3. Where the pavement ends, opposite a road turning on the left to Pinged, turn right to pass under a low railway bridge and join a path along the raised embankment with the estuary to your right.

4. At the end of the track turn left down steps, cross the small bridge over the drainage ditch, turn right onto the concrete track and then bear right towards the forest, following 'Route 4' signs.

5. Ignore two left turns, following the main track round a left-hand then right-hand bend to arrive at a T-junction. Turn left through the gate. At the next T-junction (with a tarmac lane) turn right, signposted 'Route 4'.

6. After ¾-mile take the first broad gravel track to the left ('Route 4') and follow this in the same direction, ignoring turnings to left and right for four miles.

7. Exit the forest at the T-junction with tarmac, turn right then left (or keep bearing right to visit Pembrey Country Park for refreshments).

8. Bear to the left of the red-brick buildings. At the end of the fence to the right, on a sharp right-hand bend, turn left between tall stone pillars onto a wide gravel path.

9. At the crossroads at the end of the cycle path go straight ahead and follow the road to the left past the caravan park. At the T-junction at the end of Heol Vaughan turn right.

10. Continue in the same direction to cross a small bridge over the creek, then turn left towards the ornate metal bridge over the railway. At the road turn right and follow alongside a grassy area to the left.

11. Do not cross the level crossing but bear right to join the cycle track through the Millennium Park.

12. Follow this track for four miles roughly parallel to the railway line which you have to cross twice. At the cafe/Visitor Centre turn left and follow round three sides of the dock. Cross the bridge over the creek then just before the roundabout turn right onto the pavement then right towards the creek to join a cycle path.

This bench is made from recycled greenheart timber on the link to Pembrey Forest.

13. Immediately after Copper House roundabout and a wooden plank bridge over the creek turn right by tall wooden posts to continue alongside the water's edge.

14. The tarmac surface turns to good gravel track. Follow this for three miles towards the steel works (Trostre Tin Plate).

15. At the T-junction turn right then shortly fork right for the Wildfowl & Wetlands Site. At this point you have a choice:
(a) go on to Swansea (another 14 miles) and catch the train back to Kidwelly;
(b) cycle all the way back to Kidwelly;
(c) cycle back only as far as Llanelli or Burry Port and catch the train back to Kidwelly.

CARDIFF TO CASTELL COCH

Opened in 1993 and running from Cardiff Bay through Merthyr Tydfil to Brecon, the 55-mile Taff Trail forms part of Lôn Las Cymru, the Welsh National Route (Route 8) which continues beyond Brecon right the way up though Wales to Anglesey. The six-mile section described below (Cardiff to Castell Coch) offers a magnificent exit from the very heart of Cardiff and links together some fine traffic-free trails alongside the River Taff, passing right beneath the splendid new Millennium Stadium. Between Llandaff and Tongwynlais you will pass the Mellingriffith Water Pump, considered to be one of the most important industrial monuments in Europe: a water-powered beam engine erected in 1807 to lift water 11 feet up from the river to the Glamorganshire Canal. The pump worked for 140 years until 1948 when the canal was closed and filled in. Castell Coch, reached after a short road section through Tongwynlais and a very steep climb up the drive, is a Grade 1 listed building described as 'one of the most fascinating surviving relics of Victorian Medievalism'. With its conical turrets rising above the surrounding beech woodland, it is an outstanding landmark.

Cardiff Castle from Bute Park.

Starting points

Cardiff railway station or Cardiff Castle.

Distance

Six miles one way, 12 miles return.

Grade

Easy, with one steep climb up to Castell Coch itself.

Surface

Mixture of tarmac and good quality gravel paths.

Roads, traffic, suitability for young children

The route is almost entirely traffic-free from Cardiff to Tongwynlais. There is a short section on road through Tongwynlais and up the steep drive leading to Castell Coch.

Hills

The route is flat as far as Tongwynlais then there is a short steep climb up to Castell Coch.

Refreshments

Lots of choice in Cardiff centre. Lewis Arms PH in Tongwynlais. Cafe in Castell Coch (you will need to pay to enter the castle).

Leaflets

A pack of leaflets describing the Taff Trail between Cardiff and Brecon is available from Sustrans.

Nearest railway station

Cardiff.

The National Cycle Network in the area

The Taff Trail forms part of Route 8 which links with a number of city centre cycle routes and extends to Holyhead in North Wales. Just north of Castell Coch the Taff Trail joins the Celtic Trail/Lôn Geltaidd (Route 4) which runs from Fishguard to the old Severn Bridge near Chepstow.

Taff Trail Cardiff.

Other nearby rides (waymarked or traffic-free)

1. The Taff Trail continues north from Castell Coch (starting with an exceedingly steep climb!) along dismantled railways through Nantgarw and Rhydyfelin to Pontypridd. South from Cardiff centre the trail runs to Cardiff Bay and the Barrage.

2. There are good quality towpaths along the canals leading from Newport north west to Crosskeys and north to Cwmbran and Pontypool.

The University link, Cardiff.

CARDIFF TO CASTELL COCH

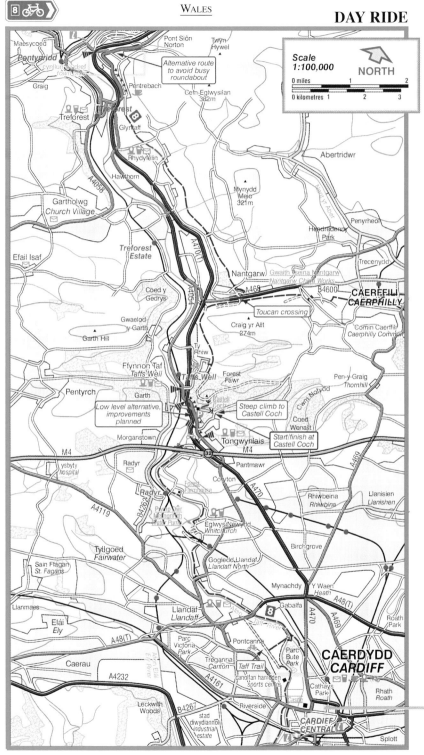

© Crown copyright

Route instructions from Cardiff to Castell Coch

1. Exit Cardiff railway station* and turn left. At the traffic lights by the Empire Pool turn left then immediately after crossing the bridge over the river turn right (use the toucan crossing) and follow the pavement northwards alongside the river. During the course of the ride you will be following 'Taff Trail' and 'Route 8' signs.

*Alternative start from near Cardiff Castle. From the College of Music and Drama on North Road (just north of Cardiff Castle on the A470 towards Merthyr Tydfil) follow signs for Route 8 parallel to and to the east of North Road. You will soon find yourself alongside the River Taff. At a fork of tracks after ¼-mile, pass to the left of a black and white timbered lodge house and follow the riverside path. Rejoin at Instruction no.3.

2. At a round stone pillar and Taff Trail sign turn left away from the river then shortly right along a wide tarmac avenue. Turn right at the next sign to rejoin the river bank at Blackweir Bridge (interim route) –

in future the the Trail will stay on the west bank of the river. Cross Blackweir Bridge and turn left to head north on the riverside track.

3. Go past a weir and alongside playing fields, bear right away from the river at the Taff Trail signs then briefly use the shared-use pavement alongside the road. After ¾-mile, as the road starts climbing on a right hand bend, immediately after passing the old metal and wooden Mellingriffith water pump, turn left onto a tarmac track between newly-built houses to return to the track alongside the river.

4. Briefly use a minor road, continuing in the same direction alongside the river. At a T-junction of tracks by a pylon turn left and pass beneath the M4. Join a minor lane and follow this beneath a second viaduct (the A470). At the T-junction at the end of Iron Bridge Road in Tongwynlais turn left then after 400 yds turn right by the Lewis Arms pub onto Mill Road.

5. Follow for ¾-mile then turn left at the sign for Castell Coch. Steep climb on tarmac.

Taff Trail marker by Angharad Jones.

(If you wish to extend your ride northwards, opposite the castle itself turn right onto track signposted 'Taff Trail' that soon becomes very steep and will involve a push. At the T-junction at the top turn left to continue climbing gently before a fast descent through woodland. Keep following 'Taff Trail'/'Route 8' signs.)

Castle Coch lies at the top of an exceedingly steep hill.

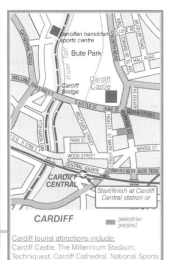

CARDIFF

pedestrian precinct

Cardiff tourist attractions include:
Cardiff Castle, The Millennium Stadium, Techniquest, Cardiff Cathedral, National Sports

BARMOUTH TO DOLGELLAU

The Mawddach Estuary is surely one of the most beautiful in the country, and exploring it by bike is by far the best way to see it. The wooded hills to the north of the estuary rise to over 1000 ft providing a stunning backdrop to the lovely waters of Afon Mawddach. The ride runs south from the seaside resort of Barmouth crossing the estuary on the wonderful wooden railway bridge carrying trains down the coast from Criccieth to Aberystwyth. This links to the seven-mile railway path along the estuary which follows the course of the old line from Barmouth to Ruabon. The railway was opened in 1869 and became popular with Victorian holiday makers, particularly those from North West England visiting the fashionable resort of Barmouth. The line was closed in 1965. Half way along you will pass an excellent refreshment stop at the George III pub at Penmaenpool. Dolgellau is the final destination, solidly built of stone with an attractive square and lots of pubs and tea shops.

Barmouth Bridge.

Starting points

1. Barmouth railway station (on the west coast of Wales, to the north of Aberystwyth).
2. The Tourist Information Centre, Dolgellau.

Distance

11 miles one way, 22 miles return.

Grade

Easy.

Surface

Tarmac and gravel track.

Roads, traffic, suitability for young children

The trail itself (the railway path) is ideal for children. Care should be taken on the road sections linking the trail with the centres of Dolgellau and Barmouth, particularly on the right turn from Barmouth onto the bridge over the estuary.

Hills

One short climb between Barmouth and the bridge over the estuary.

Refreshments

Lots of choice in Barmouth and Dolgellau.
George III pub at Penmaenpool (also does cream teas).

Nearest railway station

Barmouth.

The National Cycle Network in the area

The ride is part of Lôn Las Cymru, the Welsh National Route (Route 8) that runs from Cardiff to Anglesey.
1. North from Barmouth the route uses a four-mile stretch of the busy A496 (interim route) before turning inland on a network of quiet (and hilly!) lanes. To avoid the A496, cycle along the beach at low tide.
2. There is an alternative to the coastal route that runs north from Dolgellau through Coed-y-Brenin

Cyclists on Barmouth Bridge.

Forest and Trawsfynydd. This too uses a section of busy road – three miles along the A470 (interim route).
3. South of Dolgellau the route uses a rough section of coach road to link with a minor road through Aberllefenni and Corris to Machynlleth.
4. There is a tough off-road option south from the Mawddach Estuary to Machynlleth that climbs from Arthog on an old stone track before dropping down Happy Valley.

Other nearby rides (waymarked or traffic-free):

1. Coed-y-Brenin Forestry Commission rides.
2. Traffic-free routes on railway paths run north and south from Caernarfon.

The Barmouth to Ruabon railway path.

145

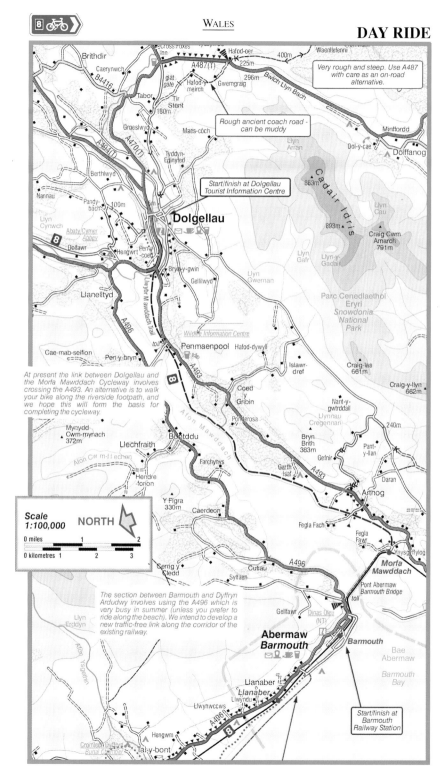

Very rough and steep. Use A487 with care as an on-road alternative.

Rough ancient coach road - can be muddy

Start/finish at Dolgellau Tourist Information Centre

Dolgellau

At present the link between Dolgellau and the Morfa Mawddach Cycleway involves crossing the A493. An alternative is to walk your bike along the riverside footpath, and we hope this will form the basis for completing the cycleway.

Scale
1:100,000

NORTH

0 miles   1   2

0 kilometres 1   2   3

The section between Barmouth and Dyffryn Ardudwy involves using the A496 which is very busy in summer (unless you prefer to ride along the beach). We intend to develop a new traffic-free link along the corridor of the existing railway.

Abermaw
Barmouth

Start/finish at Barmouth Railway Station

© Crown copyright

Route instructions from Barmouth to Dolgellau

1. From Barmouth railway station head for the seafront and turn left along the promenade, passing the Leisure Centre.

2. At the T-junction after passing beneath the railway bridge, turn right. After ¼-mile at the brow of the hill turn right onto a tarmac path towards the bridge signposted 'Route 8'. **TAKE CARE** on this right turn.

3. Cross the bridge, continue along the gravel track parallel with the railway lines and follow the cycle path as it swings round to the left, at first parallel with the minor lane.

4. Follow the old railway path for seven miles, passing the George III pub at Penmaenpool after five miles.

5. At the T-junction with the road at the end of the railway path turn right across the bridge then left,

Aerial view of the Mawddach Estuary and Barmouth Bridge.

signposted 'Dolgellau'. A new path into Dolgellau is planned.

6. Follow this road for two miles to emerge in the square in the heart of Dolgellau (the Tourist Information Centre is on your left).

The wooden bridge at Penmaenpool.

COLWYN BAY TO PRESTATYN

Enjoy this wonderful open breezy ride along the wide sea promenade that stretches almost unbroken for 15 miles from Colwyn Bay to Prestatyn. The ride has a background of wooded hills rising to over 600 ft behind Abergele. In the foreground are myriad caravan sites – there can be few places more popular with caravan owners than the north coast of Wales!

The ride runs along the bustling seafront of Colwyn Bay before passing the curious concrete anchors that have been dumped in great heaps along the coast to prevent erosion from the sea. Two short climbs take you up and over the jetties carrying stone from the quarries out to sea. Up in the wooded hills between Llanddulas and Abergele you will catch a glimpse of the atmospheric Gwrych Castle. The ride continues along the coast past the extensive caravan sites of Towyn to cross the River Clwyd. Rhyl's ice cream stalls will give you the boost you need to complete the last few miles to journey's end at Prestatyn.

NB. This is an open coastal ride where you should be very aware of the wind (normally from the west). If you are going to cycle there and back it is best to cycle into the wind at the start, while you are fresh, and have the wind help you on the return journey. Alternatively, contemplate catching the train then doing a one way trip, blown back to the start!

Colwyn Bay promenade with cycle route.

Starting points

1. Prestatyn railway station (or the Tourist Information Centre on Prestatyn seafront).
2. Colwyn Bay railway station.
3. The Tourist Information Centre at Rhos-on-Sea.

Distance

16 miles one way, 32 miles return.

Grade

Easy but take good note of the wind direction! Catch the train into the wind and cycle with the wind behind you.

Surface

Tarmac or good stone-based track.

Roads, traffic, suitability for young children

The route is almost entirely traffic-free. There are short road sections from Prestatyn railway station to the seafront and at the western end of Rhyl over the Blue Bridge. There are no difficult road crossings along the seafront. The ride is ideal for children.

Hills

None.

Refreshments

Lots of choice in Colwyn Bay.
Lots of choice in Rhyl.
Lots of choice in Prestatyn.

Nearest railway stations

Colwyn Bay, Abergele, Rhyl and Prestatyn.

The National Cycle Network in the area

The ride is part of Route 5, which

Colwyn Bay.

runs east-west from Runcorn to Bangor. At its eastern end Route 5 connects with the Southport to Hull Trans Pennine Trail; at its western end it links with Lôn Las Cymru, the Welsh National Route (Route 8) from Holyhead to Cardiff.

Other nearby rides (waymarked or traffic-free)

1. There are two railway paths starting from Caernarfon, one heads south to Bryncir, the other runs north east towards Bangor.
2. A railway path will run south from Porth Penrhyn (near Bangor) to Bethesda.
3. There are waymarked forestry routes in the woodlands around Betws-y-Coed.

COLWYN BAY TO PRESTATYN

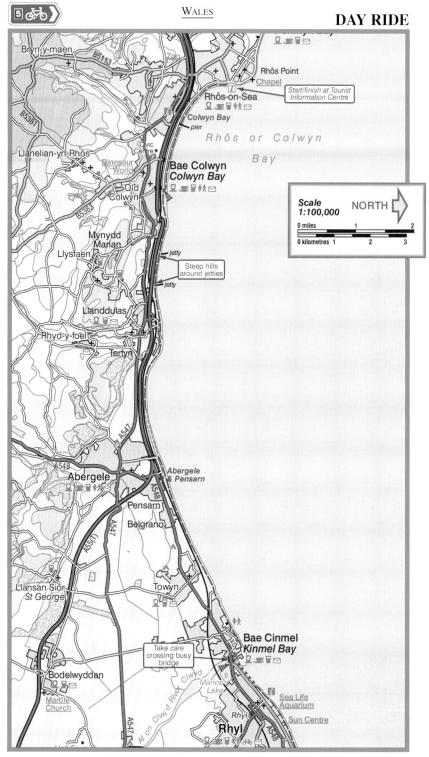

Scale
1:100,000
NORTH ➤

0 miles   1   2
0 kilometres 1   2   3

Bryn-y-maen

B5113

Rhôs Point
Chapel
Rhôs-on-Sea

Start/finish at Tourist
Information Centre

Colwyn Bay
pier

Rhôs or Colwyn
Bay

Llanelian-yn-Rhôs

Civic
Centre

Dinosaur
World

Bae Colwyn
Colwyn Bay

Old
Colwyn

Mynydd
Marian

Llysfaen

jetty

Steep hills
around jetties

jetty

Llanddulas

Rhyd-y-foel

Terfyn

A547

Abergele
& Pensarn

A548

Abergele

Pensarn

A548

Belgrano

A550(T)

A547

Llansan Siôr
St George

Towyn

♂♀

Bae Cinmel
Kinmel Bay

Take care
crossing busy
bridge

Bodelwyddan

Afon Clwyd River Clwyd

Marine
Lake

Marble
Church

Sea Life
Aquarium

Rhyl

Sun Centre

A547

A548

Rhyl

© Crown copyright

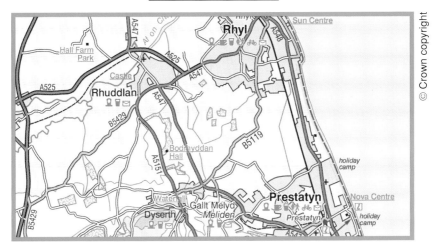

© Crown copyright

Route instructions from Rhos-on-Sea to Prestatyn

1. From the Tourist Information Centre in Rhos-on-Sea (at the western end of Colwyn Bay), with the sea to your left, follow the green cycle path along the sea front.

2. There are two short steep climbs up over the jetties serving the quarries to your right.

3. Towards the end of the road alongside the caravan park the path bears left to join the wide red seafront path.

4. Leave the seafront path at the railway station and follow the path to the right of the wall.

5. Descend to the broad track below the sea wall. Go past the huge sea defence works. Towards the end of Kinmel Bay, turn right away from the seafront at a footpath signpost onto a tarmac path. **Easy to miss.**

6. At the T-junction with wide track turn left then right onto Berwyn Crescent. At the T-junction with Bryn Avenue turn left and follow this round to the main road.

7. Turn left by the Ferry pub and walk your bike along the pavement to cross the metal bridge.

8. Go along the seafront to the end of Rhyl. Continue for a further three miles to end at Prestatyn Tourist Information Centre.

9. For Prestatyn Station, turn right by Prestatyn Tourist Information Centre and follow the road leading directly away from the beach. At the traffic lights go straight ahead to the station.

Colwyn Bay is suitable for young and old.

151

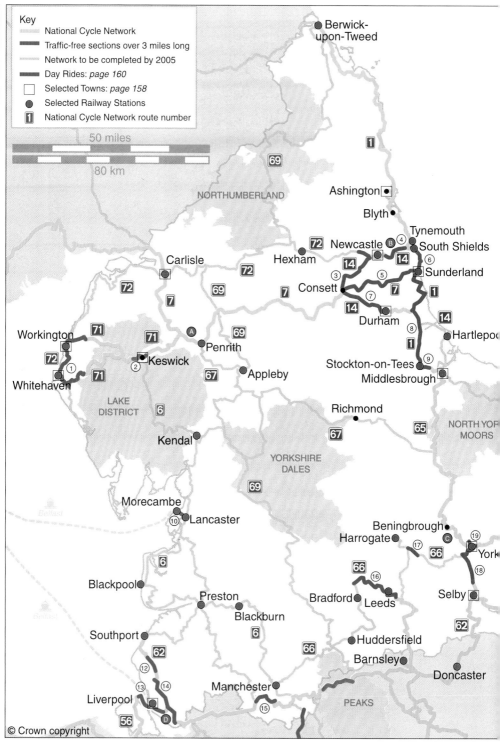

North of England

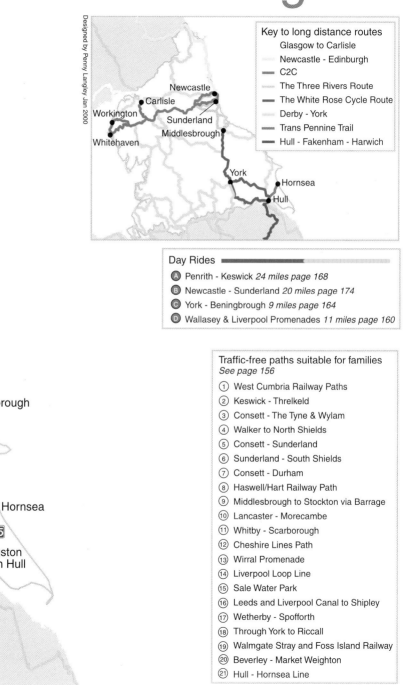

Designed by Penny Langley Jan 2000

Key to long distance routes

Glasgow to Carlisle
Newcastle - Edinburgh
C2C
The Three Rivers Route
The White Rose Cycle Route
Derby - York
Trans Pennine Trail
Hull - Fakenham - Harwich

Day Rides

Ⓐ Penrith - Keswick *24 miles page 168*
Ⓑ Newcastle - Sunderland *20 miles page 174*
Ⓒ York - Beningbrough *9 miles page 164*
Ⓓ Wallasey & Liverpool Promenades *11 miles page 160*

Traffic-free paths suitable for families
See page 156

① West Cumbria Railway Paths
② Keswick - Threlkeld
③ Consett - The Tyne & Wylam
④ Walker to North Shields
⑤ Consett - Sunderland
⑥ Sunderland - South Shields
⑦ Consett - Durham
⑧ Haswell/Hart Railway Path
⑨ Middlesbrough to Stockton via Barrage
⑩ Lancaster - Morecambe
⑪ Whitby - Scarborough
⑫ Cheshire Lines Path
⑬ Wirral Promenade
⑭ Liverpool Loop Line
⑮ Sale Water Park
⑯ Leeds and Liverpool Canal to Shipley
⑰ Wetherby - Spofforth
⑱ Through York to Riccall
⑲ Walmgate Stray and Foss Island Railway
⑳ Beverley - Market Weighton
㉑ Hull - Hornsea Line

THE NORTH

The Tynemouth railway provides an impressive backdrop to Route 72 on its way to the Tyne Tunnel.

The North of England, defined here as the area south from the border with Scotland to a line from Liverpool to Hull, is a region of great contrasts. There are the densely populated areas around Tyneside, Teeside and along the industrial corridor running from Liverpool to Leeds and yet Northumberland is the most lightly populated county in England. The scars of the old heavy industries of coal, steel and shipbuilding and of course the textile mills of Yorkshire and Lancashire lie within a few miles of England's most rugged scenery, its highest mountains and four of its National Parks – The Lake District, The Yorkshire Dales, The North York Moors and Northumberland.

The five open National Cycle Network Routes in the region each present a very different aspect of the Network. The Sea to Sea Route (C2C) from Whitehaven on the Cumbrian Coast to Tynemouth or Sunderland on the North Sea is Sustrans' most popular long-distance route, cycled by thousands of people every year as they cross the country from the Lake District, over the Pennines to the East Coast. The Trans Pennine Trail threads its way through one of the most urbanised areas of Britain between Liverpool and Manchester before crossing the Pennines and reaching the North Sea beyond Hull at Hornsea. The White Rose Cycle Route runs north from Hull along the flat expanse of the Vale of York, then passes through the lush western fringes of the North York Moors before reaching the industrial city of Middlesbrough. The Three Rivers Route (Tees, Wear and Tyne) from Middlesbrough to Newcastle and the Coast and Castles Route (from Newcastle to Edinburgh) complete the picture. With these in place there will be a route all the way up the east coast from Harwich to John o' Groats and the Shetlands, covered by seven long-distance maps.

NATIONAL CYCLE NETWORK HIGHLIGHTS

Liverpool: Pier Head
From the deck of the Mersey Ferry en route from the Wirral at Wallasey, Liverpool presents a memorable frontage. The twin towers of the Liver Building mark the headquarters of the once prestigious Atlantic Passenger trade (1911), whilst on the horizon is the tower of the huge Anglican Cathedral finished in 1924.

Teris Novalis
This stainless steel sculpture by Tony Cragg is a 20 times life-size version of the theodolite and level used in the construction of a mainline railway. It is positioned on the site of the former Consett Steelworks and is both a memorial to this extraordinary industry (which made the Sydney Harbour Bridge) and to the two instruments which set out the lines, levels and directions of our present transport system.

Newcastle Millennium Bridge
The stunning new pedestrian and cycle bridge will be complete by early 2001. Just downstream from the landmark Tyne Bridge this 600 tonne bridge created from a pair of graceful steel arches linked by thin suspension rods will open like a giant lid of a closed eye to form a gateway arch under which ships can sail. The bridge, designed by Chris Wilkinson Architects and Gifford & Partners, will join the two routes on both banks of the Tyne.

Stadium of Light
Sunderland AFC's football ground, the Stadium of Light, towers above the River Wear – a veritable cathedral on the Wear. The new football stadium was opened on 30 July 1997 when 40,000 supporters watched Ajax FC of Amsterdam, and was voted the best in England in 1998. This magnificent building marks the start of a modern riverside route second to none culminating at St. Peter's Quay.

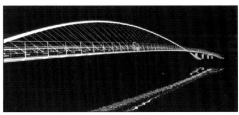

York's Millennium Bridge
This will be one of the most spectacular new links on the whole Network. This design by Whitby Bird is largely built from stainless steel. It not only joins riverside paths on both both sides of the Ouse, but also acts as a focus for a citywide network of purpose-built cycle routes.

Bamburgh Castle
Bamburgh Castle is one of a chain of spectacular castles along the route from Newcastle to Berwick. The basalt outcrop on which it sits has been occupied since the first century. The Castle you see as you cycle past today is the product of centuries of rebuilding with considerable work by the first Lord Armstrong at the end of the 19th Century. Despite its strength the Castle was the first in England to succumb to artillery fire when it was attacked during the War of the Roses.

TRAFFIC-FREE CYCLE PATHS SUITABLE FOR FAMILIES

Listed here is a selection of traffic-free routes, often along disused railways, that are more than three miles long and often ideal cycling for families. Some are covered by the Day Rides, some are shown on the maps below. (Numbers match the map key on p.152.)

2. Keswick to Threlkeld railway path (Lake District) – see pages 168-173
3. Consett via the Derwent Valley Walk to Wylam and the Tyne (near the Metro Centre)
4. Walker to North Shields on the riverside path through Newcastle upon Tyne city centre – see pages 174-177
6. Sunderland to South Shields, shared-use pavement alongside the A183 – see p. 174-177
7. Consett to Durham via Lanchester Valley Path
8. Stockton to Eden Walkway and on to Seaham and Sunderland
9. Middlesbrough to Stockton via the Tees Barrage

11. Whitby to Scarborough railway path
12. Cheshire Lines Path, a railway path from Maghull to Ainsdale
13. Liverpool and Wallasey Promenades from Otterspool to the Liver Buildings on the east side of the river and from Seacombe Ferry Terminal to New Brighton on the west side – see pages 116-119
14. Liverpool Loop Lines, a railway path from Halewood to Aintree, Liverpool
15. Sale Water Park, a riverside path along the River Mersey through South Manchester
17. Wetherby to Spofforth railway path
18. Through York to Riccall on a riverside path and railway path – see pages 164-167
19. Walmgate Stray and Foss Island path, York
20. Beverley to Market Weighton railway path
21. Hull to Hornsea railway path

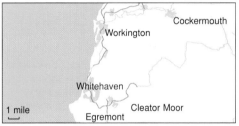

1. West Cumbria Railway Paths
Many of the old mineral tramways have been converted to good cycle routes in this old industrial area of West Cumbria. Workington and Whitehaven are the two starting points for the famous Sea to Sea (C2C) cycle route. The Groundwork Trust built projects make extensive use of wayside sculpture.

5. Consett to Sunderland
This is one of the two options for finishing the Sea to Sea (C2C) Route. The railway path drops 1,000 ft over 24 miles on its way from the crossroads of four railway paths at Consett down to the North Sea in Sunderland. This early Sustrans route, built throughout with a Manpower Services Community Programme team, includes a number of major sculptures including earthworks by Andy Goldsworthy.

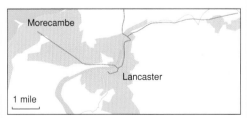

10. Lancaster to Morecambe via the new Millennium Bridge
The new Millennium Bridge over the River Lune makes the key connection between a number of excellent railway paths and links Lancaster to Morecambe seafront with its memorable new promenade filled with mosaics and sculpture.

16. Leeds to Shipley along the Leeds & Liverpool Canal
The canal follows the valley formed by the River Aire (Airedale) offering a safe and attractive route through this highly built-up area to the north west of Leeds with views of the 12th-century Cistercian Abbey at Kirkstall.

© Crown copyright

REGIONAL ROUTES AND GOOD CYCLING AREAS

For further information about the leaflets and guidebooks covering these routes/areas contact Sustrans Information Service, PO Box 21, Bristol BS99 2HA (0117 929 0888) or visit www.sustrans.org.uk

YORKSHIRE DALES CYCLE WAY RPR04
130 miles

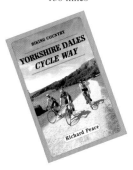

Links with National Route 67. 80-page pocket-size book describing the 130-mile cycle route on lanes through the Yorkshire Dales. Hand-drawn black and white mapping, illustrations and gradient profiles. Historic background detail plus accommodation and refreshment stops.

REIVERS CYCLE ROUTE RPR07
187 miles

Links with National Route 1, 7, 71. Full colour fold-out map showing the 187-mile route running north west from Newcastle through unspoilt Northumberland and the

Kielder Forest before turning southwest to Carlisle and the Lake District to the coast at Whitehaven. An alternative return route for C2C.

THE YORKSHIRE WOLDS RB014

Lying to the north of Hull and to the east of York, the Yorkshire Wolds offer superb quiet cycling on a network of gently graded lanes through rolling countryside and attractive small villages, one of the best of which is Thixendale, lying at the very heart of the Wolds. *Ordnance Survey Cycle Tours: North York Moors and Teeside* contains several routes through the Yorkshire Wolds.

THE EDEN VALLEY

Running between the Cumbrian Fells to the west and the Pennines to the east, the valley formed by the River Eden enjoys the views of both these mountain ranges without making great physical demands on the leisure cyclist exploring the area. There are quiet, gently graded lanes almost all the way down both sides of the valley from Carlisle as far south as Kirkby Stephen. *Ordnance Survey Cycle Tours: Cumbria & the Lakes* contains several routes through the Eden Valley.

NORTH CUMBRIA AND THE SOLWAY FIRTH RB007

To the north of the Lake District National Park and to the west of the M6 corridor lies a little explored network of quiet, flat lanes with fine views of the Cumbrian Fells to the south and across the Solway Firth to the north, views of the hills of Dumfries & Galloway. *Ordnance Survey Cycle Tours: Cumbria & the Lakes* contains a route in this area.

NORTHUMBERLAND RB015

Between Tyneside and the Scottish Borders lies a wide coastal corridor of quiet lanes crossing rolling, sparsely populated Northumberland with many castles dotted throughout the region. *Ordnance Survey Cycle Tours: Northumberland & County Durham* contains several routes in the area.

TOWNS AND CITIES ON THE CYCLE NETWORK

Ashington
High quality cycle routes serve Ashington, which was once the centre of the coal industry. The dragline buckets at the entrance to the Queen Elizabeth Park are a small reminder of the mining industries of the area.

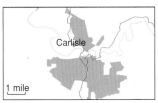

Carlisle
A new Millennium Bridge high over the River Eden marks the entry to this border stronghold. The castle is the focus of two converging National Routes – one heading for the Scottish border at Gretna, the other following the course of Hadrian's Wall from Whitehaven to Newcastle.

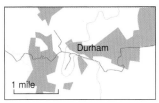

Durham City
Not an easy place to cycle! The River Wear winds around the citadel of the castle and cathedral and all access routes are barred by steep hills. But persevere – just to the west lies Britain's most extensive network of railway paths, whilst to the east the route winds along the riverside.

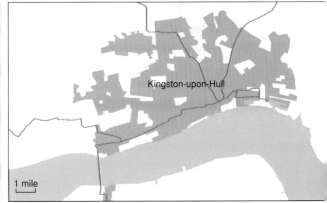

Hull
The city boasts one of the highest levels of cycling in Britain, and the National Routes make use of some of the extensive network of green-painted cycle routes. This is the home city of John Prescott, who as Secretary of State launched the Transport White Paper of 1998 which placed walking, cycling and the Safe Routes to Schools Project squarely on the agenda. The National Cycle Network is a key part of the strategy to quadruple cycling by 2012. A particular feature for those travelling to and from the continent is the route to the King George Dock.

Keswick
The capital of the northern Lakes. Take a rest here and go boating on Derwent Water or walking in the hills. There is an excellent short bike trip to Castlerigg Stone Circle returning by the railway path which crosses back and forth over the River Greta (see page 164).

Liverpool
Here the National Cycle Network connects together two early traffic-free paths – the Liverpool Loop Line and Otterspool Promenade and at the same time provides a route serving university and colleges.

Middlesbrough
The town has early 1970s examples of cycle routes designed to foster cycling in this flat area. A new tidal barrage has provided the focus for a riverside route linking Middlesbrough with Stockton-on-Tees. Middlesbrough has extensive public sculpture including the 'Bottle of Notes' by Claes Oldenburg to commemorate Captain Cook's voyages. North from here the route follows two routes – one via the Castle Eden County Park, the other via Hartlepool.

© Crown copyright

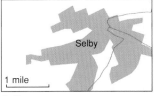

Selby

The town's abbey is contemporary with Westminster Abbey and should not be missed. Selby District Council played a pivotal role in the development of the National Cycle Network when it supported Sustrans acquiring its first railway route (to York) in 1984. This became the foundation of a programme which led to the successful promotion of the National Cycle Network as a Millennium project.

Sunderland

The riverside route makes a spacious entry into the city, running below the Stadium of Light and under Wearmouth Bridge to reach St Peter's Wharf, rebuilt alongside the University and the National Glass Centre. To the south the route follows the old coal waggonways to reach the Tunstall Hills and the coastal town of Seaham.

Whitehaven

The town lies at the western end of the Sea to Sea (C2C) cycle route to Tynemouth/Sunderland. It was built as a model town in the 18th century to serve the iron industry which was springing up in this remote area

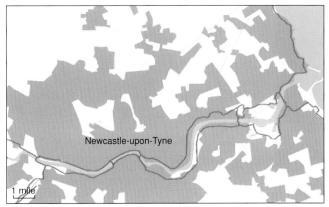

Tyneside

Newcastle, Gateshead, Wallsend, North Shields, Tynemouth and South Shields make up this bustling community which is based around the River Tyne. The National Routes run both north and south of the river mostly within sight of it but not always directly on its banks. The five crossings include three which are only for walkers and cyclists, the latest of which is the magnificent Millennium bridge. There is also a tunnel beneath the river for use exclusively by cyclists and pedestrians.

beyond the Lakes. At Moor Row the route picks up the Way of the Ironmasters railway to Egremont, also used further north at Workington.

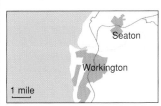

Workington

The route through the town largely follows the disused railway – the Way of the Ironmasters – built when West Cumbria was a major steel-producing area and the world's largest supplier of rails. Limestone needed for smelting was plentiful in the area and the path has been designed with features based on stone and iron. Northwards the routes divide, one going eastwards through Seaton towards Cockermouth, the other following the coast to eventually complete Hadrian's Trail to Newcastle.

York

The extensive network of largely traffic-free routes shown here has been built up year by year since Sustrans first acquired the old main line railway running south towards Selby in 1984. The Millennium opening of a spectacular new bridge over the River Ouse completes the programme and provides a direct route to the University across Walmgate Stray – one of the ancient city pastures belonging to the Freemen of York. This links to the Foss Islands Railway Path which continues east on fragments of the Derwent Light Railway and wayside tracks to reach Stamford Bridge. Northwards the route follows the banks of the Ouse towards Skelton and Beningbrough Hall.

© Crown copyright

ALONG THE MERSEY IN LIVERPOOL

Here is a ride taking in the best of Liverpool's tourist attractions: the famous Liver Buildings loom over the wide open square at Pier Head, a little way down the Mersey is Albert Dock with the Beatles Museum. Linking the two parts of the ride is the quintessential experience for the visitor to the city, the ferry across the Mersey. Liverpool has made giant steps in improving the riverside area, and the promenade from Otterspool to Pier Head is a wide attractive path with big open breezy views across to the Wirral. At every stage there are signs of regeneration: Albert Dock had fallen into disuse but is now the largest group of Grade 1 listed buildings in Great Britain – a quayside complex with many museums, galleries and restaurants. The views are just as good from the Birkenhead side as you make your way north to New Brighton.

Pier Head from the Wallasey Ferry.

The Royal Albert Docks now house the Tate Gallery.

Starting point
Pier Head Ferry Terminal (by the Liver Buildings), Liverpool.

Distance
(a) Seacombe Ferry Terminal to New Brighton – four miles one way, eight miles return.
(b) Pier Head to Otterspool Promenade – five miles one way, 10 miles return.

Grade
Easy.

Surface
All tarmac.

Roads, traffic, suitability for young children
Both sections of the ride are ideal for children and they will love the crossing on the ferry!

Hills
No hills.

Refreshments
Lots of choice around Pier Head and Albert Dock.
Plenty of choice in New Brighton.

Nearest railway stations
James Street Station, Cressington Station, New Brighton.

The National Cycle Network in the area
The Trans Pennine Trail starts in Southport and runs south east along the traffic-free Cheshire Lines Path and the Liverpool Loop Line through Ainsdale, Maghull, Aintree and Halewood to Widnes (and thence eastwards towards South Manchester and the Pennines). Route 56 runs down through the Wirral to Chester and joins the North Wales Route at Queensferry/ Connah's Quay.

Other nearby rides (waymarked or traffic-free)
1. The Cheshire Lines Path, the Liverpool Loop Line, and St Helen's Canal through Sankey Valley Park are all traffic-free sections of the Trans Pennine Trail.
2. The North Wirral Coastal Park continues west from New Brighton along the edge of the Wirral.
3. It is hoped that in the future there will be a good quality path all the way around the outside of the Wirral, connecting up with the Wirral Way through West Kirby, Heswall and Neston to Hooton. (At present only short sections are appropriate for cyclists.)

The Mersey Ferry.

DAY RIDE

62

ALONG THE MERSEY IN LIVERPOOL

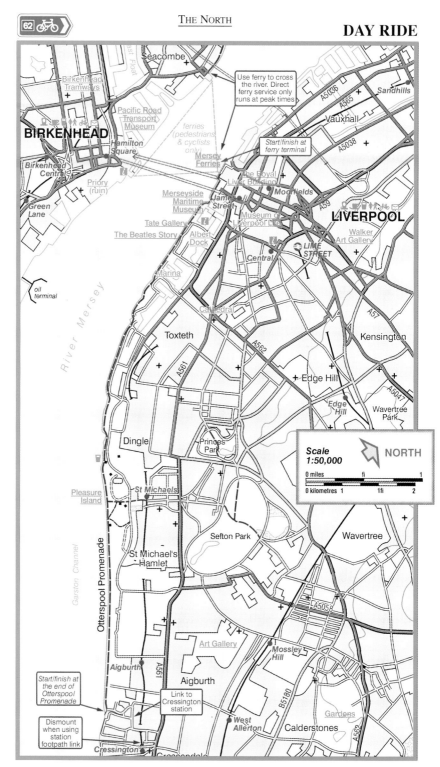

Use ferry to cross the river. Direct ferry service only runs at peak times

Start/finish at ferry terminal

Start/finish at the end of Otterspool Promenade

Dismount when using station footpath link

Link to Cressington station

BIRKENHEAD

LIVERPOOL

Seacombe

Birkenhead Tramways

Pacific Road Transport Museum

Hamilton Square

Birkenhead Central

Priory (ruin)

Green Lane

ferries (pedestrians & cyclists only)

Mersey Ferries

The Royal Liver Building

Moorfields

Merseyside Maritime Museum

James Street

Museum of Liverpool Life

Tate Gallery

The Beatles Story

Albert Dock

Walker Art Gallery

Marina

LIME STREET

Central

oil terminal

River Mersey

Cathedral

Toxteth

Kensington

A562

A561

Edge Hill

Edge Hill

Wavertree Park

A5047

A57

Dingle

Princes Park

Sandhills

Vauxhall

A5036

A565

A5038

A59

Scale 1:50,000

NORTH

0 miles · · fi · · 1

0 kilometres 1 · 1fi · 2

Pleasure Island

St Michaels

Sefton Park

Wavertree

Garston Channel

Otterspool Promenade

St Michael's Hamlet

A5058

Art Gallery

Mossley Hill

Aigburth

A561

Aigburth

West Allerton

Calderstones

Gardens

B5180

A562

Cressington

Grassendale

© Crown copyright

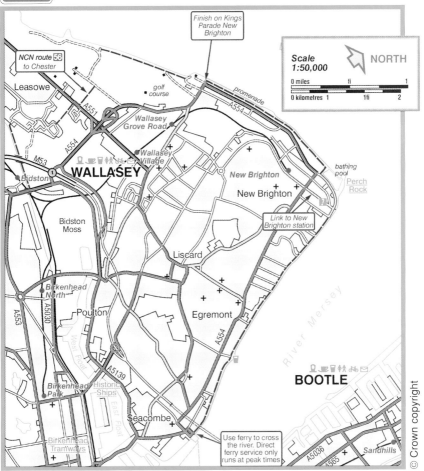

Finish on Kings Parade New Brighton

NCN route 56 to Chester

Leasowe

golf course

promenade

Scale 1:50,000
NORTH

0 miles   fi   1
0 kilometres   1   1fi   2

Wallasey Grove Road

Wallasey Village

WALLASEY

Bidston

New Brighton

New Brighton

bathing pool

Perch Rock

Bidston Moss

Liscard

Link to New Brighton station

Birkenhead North

Poulton

Egremont

River Mersey

BOOTLE

Birkenhead Park

Historic Ships

Seacombe

West Float

East Float

Birkenhead Tramways

Use ferry to cross the river. Direct ferry service only runs at peak times

Sandhills

© Crown copyright

Route Instructions

From Pier Head you have two choices:

1. New Brighton. Catch the Mersey Ferry to Seacombe Terminal, Birkenhead and turn right along the promenade for four miles to New Brighton. You may wish to continue west along the promenade on the North Wirral Coastal Park. Alternatively, Route 56 turns inland after passing the outdoor bathing pool and before the golf course. It runs down through the west side of Birkenhead to Neston and Chester.

2. Otterspool. Stay on the Liverpool side of the Mersey and turn south (keep the Mersey to your right) along the promenade for five miles to Otterspool, passing Albert Dock and the marina.

The Mersey Ferry
Monday to Friday there is a half-hourly service until 10.00AM and after 4.00PM.
In the middle of the day (10.00AM to 4.00PM) there is an hourly service.
At the weekends there is an hourly service.

There is plenty to do around Albert Dock, including the Beatles Museum, allowing you to fill the time while waiting for the ferry. For further information about ferries call 0151 630 1030 or 0151 236 7676.

New Brighton Promenade.

YORK TO BENINGBROUGH

York has done more than most cities in Britain to cater for the needs of the cyclist and although its achievements may still be some way behind Holland and Denmark, a start has been made in the acceptance of the role the bike can play in helping to solve traffic congestion. The ride starts near the heart of the beautiful walled city and runs parallel with the broad, slow-moving River Ouse. Be warned that after heavy winter rains the riverside path can completely disappear under water! The ride crosses the grazed Rawcliffe Meadows – a managed 25 acres of wildflowers and birdlife. You will pass several curious sculptures – seats looking like horse-drawn carriages and farm implements, a weather vane with a bicycle and dog, and a metalwork globe with depictions of York Cathedral and the walled city. The ride joins the network of quiet lanes and crosses the flat and fertile land of the Vale of York. This is the route of the East Coast Main Line and a sign alongside the railway indicates that you are 200 miles south of Edinburgh and 200 miles north of London. The National Trust property of Beningbrough Hall offers a view of life in an English country house from Georgian to Victorian times. It is open from Easter to October. If you wish to push on to a pub, you have a choice of two in Newton-on-Ouse, a small village just beyond Beningbrough.

York Minster is a focus for National routes. It is visible for miles and a cycle route passes right outside its walls.

Starting point

The riverside path at the end of Marygate in the centre of York.

Distance

Nine miles one way, 18 miles return. For a longer linear ride you could follow Route 65 to Thirsk (36 miles one way) or to Northallerton (46 miles one way) and catch the train back to York.

Grade

Easy.

Surface

Sealed riverside paths and quiet lanes.

Roads, traffic, suitability for young children

The four miles at the start of the ride are traffic-free and flat, thus offering an ideal ride for young children. Five miles of the route (from Overton to Beningbrough) are along quiet lanes.

Hills

None.

Refreshments

Lots of choice in York.
The Sidings Hotel & Restaurant, Shipton (open for coffee, lunch, tea).
The cafe at Beningbrough Hall is open from Easter to October.
Downay Arms pub, Blacksmith Arms pub, Newton-on-Ouse (just beyond Beningbrough).

Leaflets

A superb map of cycle facilities in York is produced by York City Council. It is available from: The Cycling Officer, York City Council, Directorate of Development Services, 9 St Leonard's Place, York YO1 2ET (01904 613161).

Nearest railway station

York.

The National Cycle Network in the area

York is at a crossroads of the Network. The north-south section from Middlesbrough to Selby is already signed and mapped (Route 65) as is the route from Beverley and Pocklington to the east (Route 66). The western section to Harrogate and Leeds (a continuation of Route 66) will be completed in the future.

Other nearby rides (waymarked or traffic-free)

York has two other waymarked, traffic-free routes, both used in the National Cycle Network. To the south, a route runs alongside the River Ouse, past the new Millennium cycle/foot bridge, the racecourse then down the course of the former Selby railway to Riccall. Crossing the Millennium Bridge a route over Walmgate Stray past the University to the Foss Island Railway Path and on to Stamford Bridge.

Beside the River Ouse just upstream from Scarborough Bridge.

Bridge across Hurn's Gutter modelled on the Forth Bridge!

YORK TO BENINGBROUGH

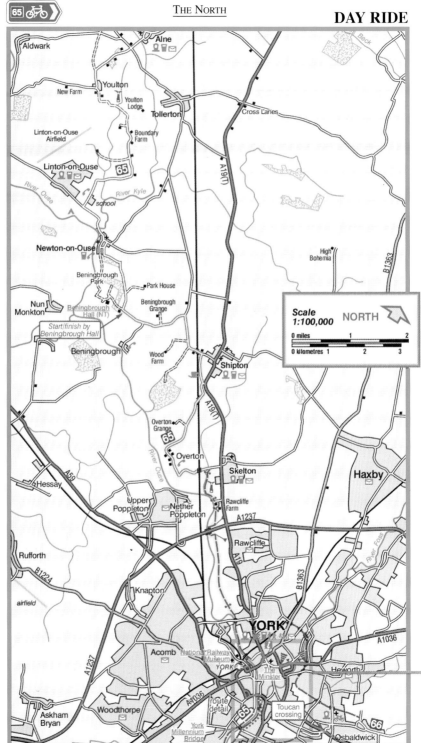

© Crown copyright

The Clifton Ings on the way to Skelton are grazed in the summer!

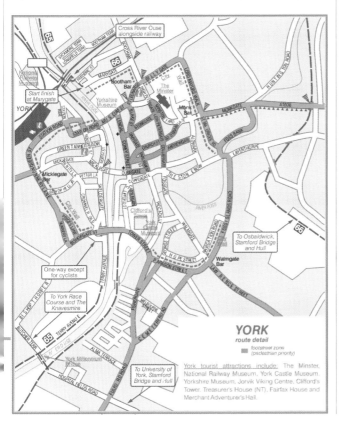

York
route detail

■ footstreet zone
(pedestrian priority)

York tourist attractions include: The Minster,
National Railway Museum, York Castle Museum,
Yorkshire Museum, Jorvik Viking Centre, Clifford's
Tower, Treasurer's House (NT), Fairfax House and
Merchant Adventurer's Hall.

Route instructions from York to Beningbrough

1. From the end of Marygate follow the riverside path alongside the River Ouse away from the centre of York (ie keep the river to your left).

2. Pass through Rawcliffe Meadows.

3. After four miles, having passed beneath the bridge carrying the Ring Road over the River Ouse, at the T-junction by a row of terraced houses, turn left to rejoin the riverside path.

4. At the end of the cycle path by the National Cycle Network sign turn left. At the T-junction near to main road turn left signposted 'Beningbrough, Newton-on-Ouse'.

5. At the next T-junction turn left to cross the railway bridge (same sign).

6. After one mile turn left by 'Coaches only' signpost (Route 65) then after 1½ miles go into Beningbrough Park to visit the Hall. If you wish to go on to the pubs in Newton-on-Ouse, go past the hall to the further entrance.

Waymarking by Andy Hazell at Skelton Lane on the turning to Overton.

PENRITH TO KESWICK

Forming part of the popular Sea to Sea (C2C) Cycle Route which crosses the country from coast to coast, this section from Penrith to Keswick takes you right into the heart of the Lake District, with much of the ride dominated by the majestic outline of Blencathtra, rising to almost 3000ft. Once out of the busy town of Penrith the ride links together a series of small hamlets and villages built of stone, almost all of which have a pub, so that if you wish to shorten the ride there are several good turnaround points. This is a land of drystone walls and sheep grazing, with solid farmhouses and the occasional fortified hall (the ride runs across the southern end of what was once a vast lawless area between England and Scotland, frequently raided by the Reivers in the 15th and 16th centuries). If you make it as far as Keswick there are scores of possibilities for refreshments from cafes to fine restaurants. With luck the prevailing westerly winds should help blow you back to Penrith! There is a tough alternative heading east from Keswick which passes the magnificently located Castlerigg Stone Circle then climbs steeply on a challenging off-road section using the course of an old coach road that ascends to almost 1,500 ft.

N.B. The old coach road should only be undertaken by fit cyclists on mountain bikes in good weather.

It's worth the climb to Castlerigg Stone Circle, east of Keswick.

Starting points

1. Stricklandgate (the A6 Scotland Road) in the centre of Penrith.
2. Keswick Tourist Information Centre in the centre of Keswick.

Distance

24 miles one way, 48 miles return. For shorter rides, starting from Penrith, there are pubs at Newton Reigny (7 miles round trip), Blencow (11 miles round trip), Greystoke (15 miles round trip) or Troutbeck (24 miles round trip).

Grade

Moderate (with challenging off-road options).

Surface

Almost all on road except a short section of farm track on the outskirts of Penrith and a three mile stretch of gravel-based railway path at the Keswick end. The challenging and adventurous off-road option along the old coach road is rough and should only be undertaken by fit cyclists on mountain bikes in good weather.

Roads, traffic, suitability for young children

The ride is almost all on minor roads. There is a short section on busy streets from Penrith to the start of the minor road network. A good option for young children would be to follow the course of the dismantled railway from Keswick to Threlkeld alongside the River Greta. This route crosses and recrosses the river as it runs through its wooded gorge.

Hills

There is a steady climb of over 500 ft from Penrith to the highpoint of the ride just north of Troutbeck. If you return to Penrith via the coach road you will be faced with a climb of almost 1,000 ft from crossing St John's Beck to the highpoint of the old road.

Refreshments

Lots of choice in Penrith.
Sun Inn, Newton Reigny.
Crown Inn, Great Blencow.
Boot & Shoe PH, Greystoke.
Sportsmans Inn, Troutbeck Inn, Troutbeck.
Salutation Inn, Horse & Farrier PH, Threlkeld.
Lots of choice in Keswick.

Nearest railway station

Penrith.

The National Cycle Network in the area

The ride forms part of the C2C Cycle Route (Routes 7, 71, 72) from Whitehaven/Workington to Tynemouth/Sunderland. Route 1 branches off through Skelton and Dalston to Carlisle to link with the Scottish National Route (Carlisle – Glasgow – Inverness, Route 7). In the future Route 67 will link

The Coach Road to Matterdale End provides a wonderfully remote route on fine days.

Penrith across the Pennines to Richmond, Northallerton and York. South from Keswick, Route 6 will pass through Kendal, Lancaster and Preston to Manchester.

Other nearby rides (waymarked or traffic-free)

In Cumbria, the Reivers Cycle Route runs from Carlisle south west towards the Cumbrian Coast, passing around the north side of Caldbeck Fells to Cockermouth, Workington and Whitehaven. This offers the possibility of a signposted, circular ride of 150 miles linking Whitehaven, Penrith and Carlisle.

The Munsgrisdale Road from Scales.

169

PENRITH TO KESWICK

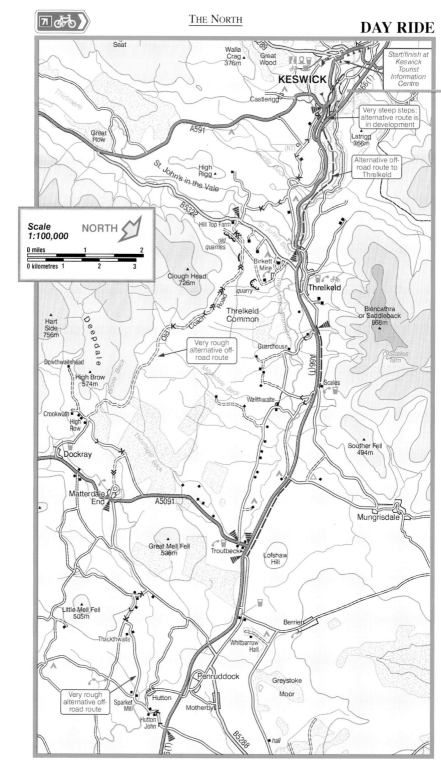

© Crown copyright

170

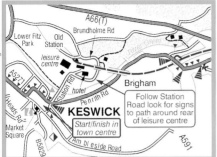

Route instructions from Penrith to Keswick

1. Take care on the busy roads through Penrith and follow signs for 'A6 (north)'. Shortly after passing petrol stations to the right then left, bear left by the Grey Bull pub signposted 'Caravan Park'.

2. The tarmac turns to track by the farm. Go past barns and alongside the M6 then turn left through the subway beneath the motorway. Ignore the turning to the right. Climb the hill.

3. At the fork of tracks by the group of college buildings bear left onto the concrete track to pass through the college itself. Shortly at a crossroads go straight ahead signposted 'Residents only. No exit'. At the road turn right.

4. Follow signs for Skelton and Laithes through Newton Reigny. Go through the hamlet of Laithes. At a crossroads by a Give Way sign turn left signposted 'Blencow, Greystoke'.

5. Follow signs for Greystoke. At the crossroads in the village turn right signposted 'Berrier'. Steady climb.

6. Long fabulous descent. At T-junction turn left signposted 'Troutbeck, Keswick'. At the next T-junction by the Sportsmans Inn turn right signposted 'Keswick' then on a sharp left-hand bend bear right onto a minor lane running parallel with the main road.

7. At the T-junction with the A66, turn right onto the cycle path alongside the main road. After 150 yds take the first road to the right by Hillcrest B&B. Fine descent. At the T-junction with the main road turn right on the cycle lane.

8. Second fine descent. Take the next road to the right 'Mungrisdale, Caldbeck C2C'. Turn left on the second drive/track signposted 'Southerfell'

9. At the T-junction with a minor road turn left. At the end of this gated road turn right past the White Horse Inn. At the T-junction with the A66 turn right. Follow the cycle lane up to the right away from the A66 to go through a bridlegate onto the old road.

10. At the T-junction at the end of the old road (Fellside) turn right. Go past the pubs in Threlkeld. Just before rejoining the A66 turn right onto the cyclepath. Tarmac turns to gravel track.

11. Follow the Cockermouth, Keswick & Penrith (1869) railway path for three miles. This crosses the River Greta on a number of impressive bridges, and towards the end creeps around the hillside below the A66 viaduct on a newly built boardwalk.

12. At the end of the railway path continue straight ahead then bear to the left of the Leisure Centre and descend to the road. Turn right then at the crossroads at the end of Station Road go straight ahead for Keswick town centre.

Keswick to Greystoke (challenging offroad option via the old coach road)

13. With your back to Keswick Tourist Information Centre go straight ahead towards Keswick Lodge Hotel. At the crossroads go straight ahead onto Station Road.

14. On a sharp right-hand bend bear left up towards the Leisure Centre. Pass to the right of the building then bear right onto the railway path and past the old station.

Coach road near its junction with St. John's in the Vale.

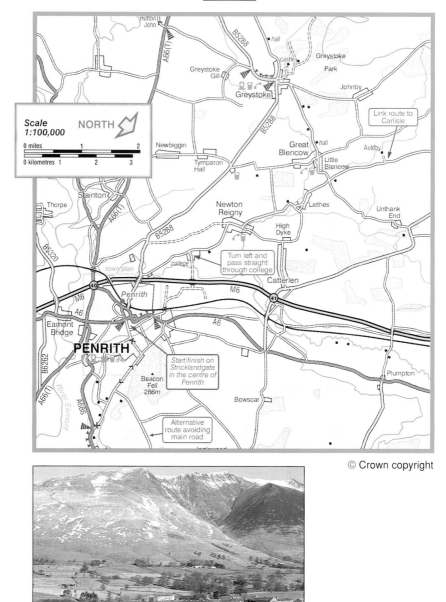

© Crown copyright

Blencathra towers over the route between Threlkeld and Scales.

15. Immediately after passing beneath the first bridge, leave the railway path, turn left up the steps then left on the road. Take the first road left then the first road to the right signposted 'Castlerigg, C2C'.

16. Climb steeply and go past the Castlerigg Stone Circle. Fast descent. At the T-junction at the bottom of the hill turn right signposted 'C2C, Grasmere Bike Route'. At the next T-junction turn right again (same sign).

17. Take the first road to the right signposted 'Shundraw, St John's in the Vale'. At the T-junction with the B5322 turn right signposted 'Thirlmere' then left 'Matterdale. C2C'. Climb steeply.

18. At a fork of tracks by a farm bear left. At a diagonally offset crossroads (with a level tarmac path) go straight ahead. Follow the old coach road for five miles, climbing to almost 1,500 ft.

19. At the crossroads at the end of the old coach road, turn left signposted 'Troutbeck'. Climb then descend past a wood on the left. Shortly after the start of a second wood, close to a stone barn, turn sharp right onto a broad stone track signposted 'Bridleway to Matterdale End'.

20. At the road (A5091) turn left then right 'Penruddock, Penrith'. Ignore a right to 'Dockray, Ullswater'. Take the next right after 1¼ miles 'Thackthwaite C2C'.

21. Steep climb. Follow the road round a sharp left-hand bend. Descend. **Easy to miss**. Take the first road left 'Thackthwaite'.

22. At T-junction by Sparket Mill turn left 'Penrith, Greystoke'. At the crossroads with the A66 go straight ahead 'Greystoke'. At the T-junction with the B5288 turn right 'Greystoke, Penrith'.

23. At the crossroads by the stone cross in the centre of Greystoke take the road signposted 'Johnby, Blencow, C2C'. Rejoin the outward route.

Spanning the River Greta, Brundholme Bridge is one of the bowstring bridges designed by Sir Thomas Bouch and built in 1862-64.

NEWCASTLE TO SUNDERLAND

Tyne & Wear has seen the creation of a highly developed network of cycle routes in the past few years, much of it tied in closely with the overall regeneration of the industrialised area alongside the River Tyne. Many loops are possible using the cycle routes on either side of the river and crossing via the bridges in the centre of the city, including the magnificent new Millennium Bridge at Gateshead, at Blaydon in the west or via the foot and cycle tunnel near Jarrow to the east. Using a mixture of quiet streets, riverside paths and railway paths the route described here runs along the north side of the Tyne to the ferry terminal at North Shields, crosses the water via the ferry then soon joins the shared-use path alongside the A183 with fine views out to the North Sea. Along this section you pass Souter Lighthouse, built in 1871 and the first lighthouse specifically constructed to use electric light. As with the Tyne, so too the River Wear has seen attractive regeneration and development along the waterfront, including many fine sculptures and the National Glass Centre.

Tyneside Ferry.

Starting point

The Quayside in the centre of Newcastle upon Tyne.

Distance

19 miles one way, 38 miles return. For shorter rides, starting from Newcastle, there are good turnaround points at the Segedunum Heritage Centre at Wallsend (10 miles round trip), North Shields Ferry Terminal (18 miles round trip), Souter Lighthouse (28 miles round trip).
Alternatively you may wish to push on beyond North Shields to Tynemouth and then return to Newcastle (23 miles round trip).

Grade

Easy.

Surface

Mixture of tarmac and stone cycle path.

Roads, traffic, suitability for young children

Traffic-free paths are mixed with sections along quiet streets all the way from Newcastle to Sunderland. There is a long stretch of shared-use pavement alongside the A183 between South Shields and Sunderland but care should be taken crossing the many side roads.

Hills

No major hills.

Refreshments

Plenty of choice in the centres of Newcastle, South Shields, North Shields and Sunderland. There is a tea room at Souter Lighthouse, to the south of South Shields.

Leaflets

1. *CycleCity's Tyneside Cycling Map* is an excellent publication showing the traffic-free paths, signposted cycle routes, advisory routes plus a wealth of other information. It costs £4.95 and is available from Sustrans Information Service, PO Box 21, Bristol BS99 2HA (0117 929 0888) or visit www.sustrans.org.uk

2. *Pedalling Paths – a map and guide to cycle routes in North Tyneside* – The Environment Strategy Team, Environment Function, Graham House, Whitley Road, Benton, Newcastle upon Tyne NE12 9TQ (0191 201 0033).

3. *Leisure Cycling in South Tyneside* – South Tyneside MBC, Development Services Dept, Town Hall and Civic Offices, Westhoe Road, South Shields, Tyne & Wear NE33 2RL (0191 427 1717).

Nearest railway stations

Newcastle upon Tyne, Sunderland. Two bikes are allowed on each train. From Monday to Friday you are not allowed to travel with your bike before 0900 or between 1600 and 1800. No bikes are allowed on the train on Saturdays. There are no restrictions on Sundays.

The National Cycle Network in the area

1. The C2C has two possible endings: Consett to Tynemouth and Consett to Sunderland. The latter uses 24 miles of railway path between the two points, passing through Stanley, Washington and Pallion on its way to the North Sea Coast.

2. Route 1 links South Shields with Sunderland and Seaham and runs further south to Teeside and the White Rose Cycle Route (Routes 65 & 66).

3. Hadrian's Way (the North Tyne Cycleway) continues west from Blaydon to Wylam.

4. The Reivers Cycle Route runs from Tynemouth to North Shields then turns north through Seaton Burn and Ponteland towards Bellingham and Kielder.

5. The Three Rivers Route (Routes 1, 14, 7) links Middlesbrough, Stockton, Hartlepool, Durham, Consett, Newcastle, Gateshead and North and South Tyneside.

6. The Coast & Castles Route (Route 1) runs north along the coast of Northumberland from Tynemouth to Berwick-on-Tweed then through the Scottish Borders to Edinburgh.

Other nearby rides (waymarked or traffic-free)

You are spoilt for choice for traffic-free routes in the North East: there are all the Durham Railway paths such as the Lanchester Valley and the Waskerley Way plus the routes on either side of the Tyne such as Keelman's Way and Hadrian's Way. See the Regional Map on page 152 and the 'Traffic-free paths' section on page 156.

Along the railway path at Walker.

175

DAY RIDE

NEWCASTLE TO SUNDERLAND

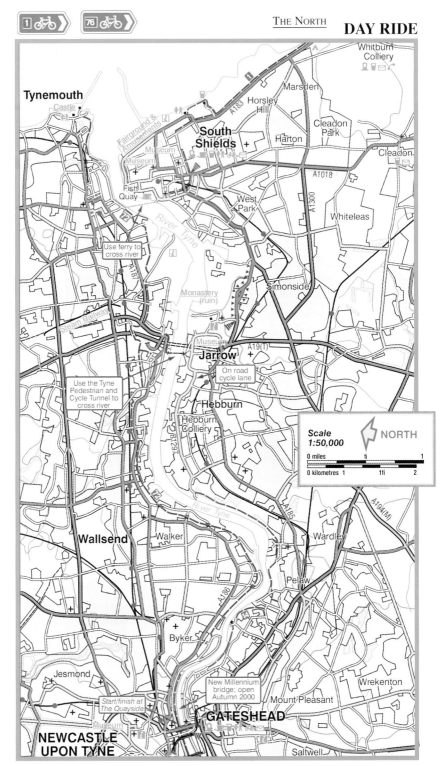

© Crown copyright

© Crown copyright

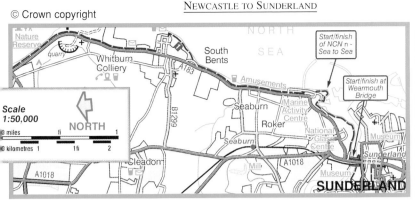

obvious cycle lane through several barriers.

10. Cross the busy Westoe Road, climb past a big, tree-filled cemetery. Sea views open up at the top of the rise. Continue in the same direction downhill. At the T-junction at the end of Sea Way, turn right then left onto cyclepath.

Route instructions from Newcastle upon Tyne city centre to North Shields (Tynemouth) and Sunderland

1. From the Swing Bridge in Newcastle city centre follow the riverside path east (ie river to right).

2. At the Spillers building bear left uphill away from the river. At the mini-roundabout continue straight ahead, after the car park on the left, turn left opposite Foundry Court, pass between stone barriers onto the railway path. Follow for four miles.

3. At the T-junction with Hadrian Road (A187) in Wallsend, at the end of the railway path, cross to the cycle path on the other side of the road. Shortly, bear left downhill away from the main road, cross the bridge over the small river then at the T-junction turn right.

4. Before rejoining the main road (Hadrian Road/A187) turn left onto Bewicke Road immediately before the PH, then left onto cycle path.

5. Cross the open ground then the bridge over the A19, bearing right. Follow the cycle signs (and the C2C signs) then turn right down towards the shops at the Royal Quays.

6. Just before the second roundabout turn left onto Redburn Dene signposted 'C2C, Route 72'.

Follow this downhill through a landscape of boulders and timbers and bear left at the bottom. At the roundabout go straight ahead.

7. Follow the waymarking closely as there are few street names. At a second roundabout go straight ahead then shortly turn left then first right between warehouses. At a T-junction turn right then left. Follow 'Route 10' signs down the wheeling ramp parallel with a flight of steps and either push your bike or cycle down the ramp to the ferry terminal*.

*Side trip to Tynemouth
(a) At the bottom of the ramp follow New Quay, Clive Street, Liddell Street and Bell Street (all the same road!) to Union Quay.

(b) Go through the car park and along the promenade above Tynemouth harbour and pier.

Main Route to Sunderland
8. Cross the Tyne on the ferry. From the South Shields Ferry Terminal go up ramp, then right at T-junction with Ferry St signposted 'Sunderland, Souter Lighthouse, Sea Front Cycle Route'.

9. At the first roundabout, go straight ahead. At the second roundabout, turn left onto the cycle lane then first right onto Old Coronation Street. Follow the

11. At the roundabout, go straight ahead signposted 'Two Rivers Cycleway, Route 1, Sunderland, Souter Lighthouse'.

12. Go past Souter Lighthouse and through an area where there are houses on both sides of the road. **Easy to miss**. Opposite small chapel by Whitburn Cemetery on the right, turn left signposted 'Route 1', follow signs to the sea.

13. Lovely section along the cliffs. Rejoin the road. After two miles, as the main road swings sharp right away from the coast turn left sharply back on yourself down towards the beach signposted 'City Centre, C2C, Route 1'.

14. At the bottom of the hill follow the cyclepath close to the water and alongside the marina, the route is now signposted 'Route 7'. Go past the National Glass Centre and along the riverfront.

15. It is suggested you go as far as the end of the riverside path just beyond the metal tree sculpture. For Sunderland station bear right, away from the river soon after the metal tree, signposted 'C2C, Route 7'. At the T-junction turn left on the green cycle lane to cross bridge. Follow one-way system to station.

177

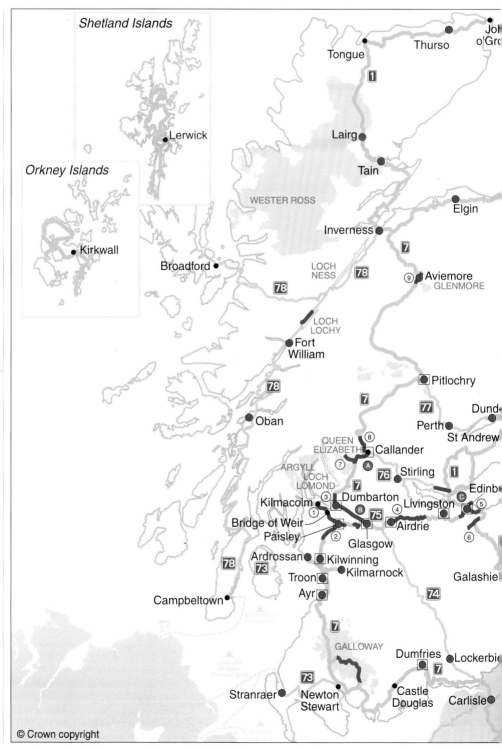

Scotland

Traffic-free paths suitable for families
See Page 182

1. Johnstone - Greenock
2. Johnstone - Kilbirnie
3. Glasgow - Loch Lomond
4. Airdrie - Bathgate Railway Path
5. Edinburgh Urban Railway Paths
6. Dalkeith - Penicuik Railway Path
7. Loch Katrine
8. Aberfoyle - Callander - Strathyre
9. Aviemore to Boat of Garten
10. Formartine and Buchan Way

Key

▬▬▬	National Cycle Network
▬▬▬	Traffic-free sections over 3 miles long
▬▬▬	Network to be completed by 2005
▬▬▬	Day Rides: *page 186*
☐	Selected Towns: *page 184*
●	Selected Railway Stations
1	National Cycle Network route number

50 miles

80 km

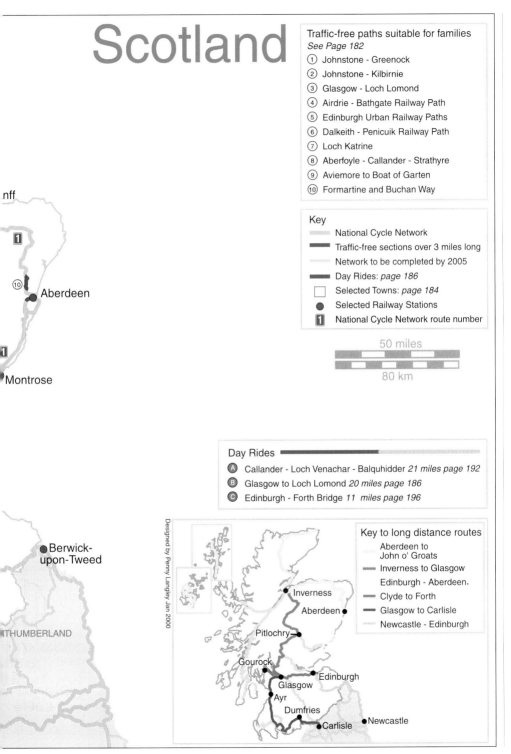

nff

1

10

● Aberdeen

1

● Montrose

Day Rides ▬▬▬

- Ⓐ Callander - Loch Venachar - Balquhidder *21 miles page 192*
- Ⓑ Glasgow to Loch Lomond *20 miles page 186*
- Ⓒ Edinburgh - Forth Bridge *11 miles page 196*

Designed by Penny Langley Jan 2000

● Berwick-upon-Tweed

THUMBERLAND

Inverness

Aberdeen ●

Pitlochry

Gourock

Edinburgh

Glasgow

Ayr

Dumfries

Carlisle ● Newcastle

Key to long distance routes

▬▬▬	Aberdeen to John o' Groats
▬▬▬	Inverness to Glasgow
▬▬▬	Edinburgh - Aberdeen.
▬▬▬	Clyde to Forth
▬▬▬	Glasgow to Carlisle
▬▬▬	Newcastle - Edinburgh

SCOTLAND

Loch Achray in the Trossachs.

Scotland is the most mountainous and spectacular region in the United Kingdom, and the National Cycle Network enables you to explore the area on a mixture of forestry tracks, paths alongside rivers and lochs, dismantled railways and quiet roads. The population of Scotland is concentrated in the Glasgow-Edinburgh corridor: outside this narrow strip lies one of the least densely populated areas of Europe, ideal for exploration by bike. Fewer people means fewer cars, and for anyone arriving here from the more densely populated parts of Britain there is a very pleasant surprise in store - many roads carry such little traffic that you can plan quiet, safe rides on B roads and in some cases even on A roads.

Sustrans work started many years ago in Scotland and there are several traffic-free routes around Glasgow that date back to the 1980s, including the Glasgow to Loch Lomond route which is featured as a Day Ride (see page 182). The Scottish National Route (from Carlisle to Inverness) was opened in 1995 and makes good use of many of these railway paths. The Clyde to Forth Route crosses the country from the architectural masterpieces of Edinburgh to the vibrant atmosphere of Glasgow.

NATIONAL CYCLE NETWORK HIGHLIGHTS

Arran Ferry

A highlight of many journeys will be the ferry trips, often run by Caledonian MacBrayne. The Ardrossan ferry, shown here, can readily be reached from the Glasgow and Ayr cycle route, and the crossing leads to Brodick, Arran and the Lochranza ferry to Kintyre.

Arran to Oban

A view over Loch Sween and the Sound of Jura near Kilmory. Once away from the cities, Scotland abounds with spectacular open views which are a memorable part of every cyclist's journey through the Highlands.

Bell's Bridge, Glasgow

This key link across the Clyde was built for the Glasgow Garden Festival. It now leads to the Scottish Convention Centre and will eventually become the centrepiece of future redevelopment of the Festival site.

Queen Elizabeth Forest Park

The Trossachs are close to Glasgow and provide wonderful wild countryside. The National Cycle Route follows forest roads from Aberfoyle, lochside paths past Achray and Venachar and the former main line railway to Oban from Callander to the Falls of Leny and eventually Glen Ogle – all marvellous!

Sluggan Bridge

It is well worth following the gravel forest roads to find Sluggan Bridge standing in splendid isolation across the River Dulnain. The bridge was built between 1729 and 1730 on General Wade's military road to Inverness. The road was realigned to bypass the bridge in 1813.

John o'Groats

The culmination of many a challenge cycle ride from Land's End and elsewhere. The launch of the National Cycle Netwok was preceded by a Trailblazing Ride from John o'Groats to Dover during which support was pledged by each local authority along the course of the route.

TRAFFIC-FREE CYCLE PATHS SUITABLE FOR FAMILIES

Listed here is a selection of traffic-free routes, often along disused railways, that are more than three miles long and offer ideal cycling for families. Some are covered by the Day Rides, some are shown on the maps below. (Numbers match the map key on page 178)

For further information about traffic-free rides, ask for the Traffic-free Information Sheet from Sustrans Information Service, PO Box 21, Bristol. BS99 2HA (0117 929 0888) or visit www.sustrans.org.uk

The Family Cycling Trail Guide (RB01) (£4.95) contains details of 300 traffic-free rides throughout Britain. Also available from Sustrans.

1. Johnstone to Greenock
2. Johnstone to Kilbirnie railway path (south west of Glasgow)
3. Glasgow to Loch Lomond – see page 186
4. Airdrie to Bathgate railway path
5. Edinburgh Railway Path Network
6. Dalkeith to Penicuik railway path
7. Along the shores of Loch Katrine (Trossachs, north of Glasgow)
8. Aberfoyle-Callander-Strathyre (Trossachs, north of Glasgow) – see page 192
9. Aviemore to Boat of Garten (Highlands)
10. Formartine and Buchan Way

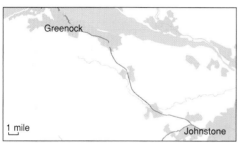

1. Johnstone to Greenock

This eastern section of the Clyde to Forth Cycle Route follows 13 miles of railway paths from Johnstone through Bridge of Weir and Kilmacolm to Greenock. The views from above Port Glasgow northwards across the Firth of Clyde to the hills beyond Helensburgh are stunning.

4. Airdrie & Bathgate railway path

This 14-mile trail across Scotland's central plateau follows the course of the old Airdrie and Bathgate Junction Railway which used to carry coal, ironstone and limestone. Many interesting sculptures have been erected along its course.

6. Dalkeith to Penicuik railway path

The longest of the dismantled railways close to Edinburgh is also the most scenic, passing through many beautiful wooded cuttings and alongside the tumbling waters of the River North Esk. The trail runs south west from Eskbank (Dalkeith) to Penicuik.

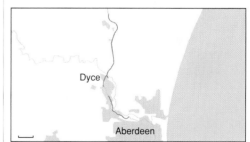

10. Formartine and Buchan Way

The trail follows the course of the old Great North of Scotland Railway from Aberdeen (Dyce) to Peterhead and Fraserburgh, which ran for 100 years from 1865 to 1965. There are fine views of the mountains of Donside and Deeside including such famous ones as Bennachie and Lochnagar.

© Crown copyright

REGIONAL ROUTES AND GOOD CYCLING AREAS

For further information about leaflets/guidebooks covering these routes contact Sustrans Information Service, PO Box 21, Bristol BS99 2HA (0117 929 0888) or visit www.sustrans.org.uk

FOUR ABBEYS ROUTE (SCOTTISH BORDERS) RPR06

55 miles

Links with National Route 1. A 16-page booklet with full colour photos and mapping describes the 55-mile route around the glorious countryside of the Scottish Borders, visiting the abbeys at Melrose, Dryburgh, Kelso and Jedburgh.

THE SCOTTISH BORDERS FPL17

Big spaces, rolling hills and empty roads create a wonderful cycling environment with many attractive towns such as Peebles, Melrose and Kelso offering a variety of refreshment stops and accommodation. The weather also tends to be a lot drier than in the west!

Ordnance Survey Cycle Tours: Southern Scotland contains several road rides in the Scottish Borders.

Cycling in the Scottish Borders is a free booklet with 20 road and forestry rides in the region. It is available from Scottish Borders Tourist Board, Tourist Information Centre, Murray's Green, Jedburgh, Roxburghshire TD8 6BE (01835 863435). Also available from Sustrans.

GALLOWAY FOREST PARK

Two strands of the Scottish National Route cross Dumfries and Galloway. One follows minor roads via Dumfries, Castle Douglas, Kirkudbright, Gatehouse of Fleet and Newton Stewart. The other uses forestry tracks and paths, through the Galloway Forest Park between Gatehouse and Glen Trool, between Loch Ken and Clatteringshaws Loch, then down Glen Trool past Loch Trool to Glen Trool Village. There are over 20 waymarked forestry routes of all grades in this vast expanse of woodland, including four starting from Clatteringshaws Loch and five from Glen Trool Visitor Centre.
Ordnance Survey Cycle Tours: Southern Scotland contains several road rides in Dumfries & Galloway.

QUEEN ELIZABETH PARK, THE TROSSACHS RB005

After leaving the banks of Loch Lomond, the Scottish National Route goes right through the heart of the Trossachs, using a mixture of railway paths, forestry tracks and loch side paths. There are several other waymarked routes in Queen Elizabeth Park and a superb ride from Loch Achray around the northern shores of Loch Katrine to Stronachlachar and on to Inversnaid on the eastern bank of Loch Lomond.

Ordnance Survey Cycle Tours: Central Scotland contains several rides between Glasgow and the Highlands.

HIGHLANDS AND ISLANDS

A vast spectacular area to be explored by fit cyclists, with many of the A roads carrying surprisingly little traffic outside the main season. The terrain is easier on the east coast. Be prepared for wet weather in the Western Highlands.

101 Bike Routes in Scotland devotes half of its space to routes in the Highlands and Islands.

TOWNS AND CITIES ON THE NATIONAL CYCLE NETWORK

Airdrie

The Monklands area was the cradle of the Industrial Revolution in Scotland – the first canals and railways were built here and these form the basis for National Route 75 (Clyde to Forth) through the heavily urbanised areas of Coatbridge and Airdrie. Even the in-filled Monkland Canal has been used for the route. Features include an imposing railway viaduct, a new bridge over a dual carriageway and a new subway under a railway line. This area is a model for the imaginative creation of a largely traffic-free cycle route through a busy and congested area.

Ayr

Scottish National Route 7 through Ayr exhibits all the characteristics of a typical National Cycle Network route – promenade, disused railways, traffic-calming and a Millennium Bridge. Once complete, an impressive and attractive route will be available, onto which further sustainable transport routes can be grafted.

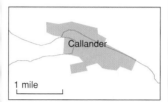

Callander

When Dr Beeching closed the Callander to Oban Railway in 1965 he left a legacy of a scenic disused line through the Central Highlands. With the support of the local authority, Sustrans has created one of the most popular routes in Scotland now forming part of the Scottish National Route 7. Skirting rivers, lochs and mountains, this is being extended north into the Highlands and south towards Stirling. The route continues west through the Queen Elizabeth Forest Park. Callander is a thriving tourist destination for cyclists and a number of new cycle businesses have sprung up on the back of the excellent traffic-free network.

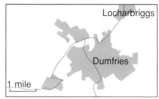

Dumfries

Serving a large rural hinterland and hence busy with traffic, the town is bisected by the River Nith which offers the opportunity to use riverside paths, parks and a new bridge for the National Route. The railway, which until recently served the chemical works at Cargenbridge, may be the basis of traffic-free route to the west of the town linking into the minor road network. Locharbriggs and Heathhall will also be linked to the town centre via the Caledonian Cycleway, which will include new crossings of the A75 and A702 trunk roads.

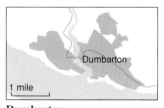

Dumbarton

The town lies on Scotland's first long distance cycle route – from

Edinburgh

In the mid 1980s Sustrans produced a comprehensive report on cycling in the city as well as a detailed Safe Routes to School study. Many of the proposals contained in the report have been implemented thanks to the forward-thinking transport policy of the Council and the excellent campaigning by SPOKES, the Lothian Cycle Campaign Group. National Routes 1 and 75 converge on the city and use much of the extensive disused railway network and the Union Canal.

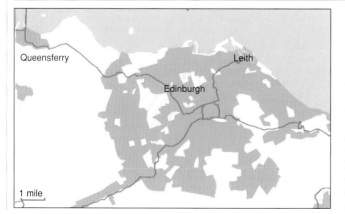

© Crown copyright

Glasgow to Loch Lomond. This is now a very popular facility linking the city to what is soon to be Scotland's first National Park. Through Dumbarton the route changes from largely disused railways towards Glasgow, to a riverside path towards Loch Lomond.

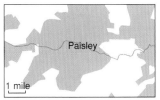

Paisley

National Routes 7 (the Scottish National Route) and 75 (the Clyde to Forth Route) coincide through Paisley where Sustrans routes in Scotland were born. The proposals to create cycle routes out of disused railways came at the right time for the area when three lines became redundant (the Lochwinnoch Loop Line, the Johnstone to Kilmacolm Line and the Paisley Canal Line). Sustrans was quick to acquire these and develop an excellent network of routes linking the city to the countryside and coast. Subsequent developments have enabled Paisley to be linked to the centre of Glasgow.

Livingston

Well-known as a New Town and capital of Scotland's Silicon Glen. What is not so well-known is the wealth of open spaces, woodlands and waterways which make up Livingston's unique countryside. The network of greenways and footpaths, provide a safe and attractive environment whether for recreation or as part of an everyday journey. National Route 75 (Clyde to Forth) passes right through the heart of Livingston's green space. There is extensive public art along the route.

Kilwinning

The town lies at the junction of the Scottish National Route and the link to Arran and Northern Ireland (via the Campbeltown-Ballycastle ferry). One of Sustrans' earliest routes enters the town over a disused viaduct, partly owned by Sustrans.

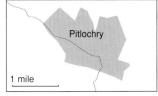

Pitlochry

The Scottish National Route 7 passes through the centre of this popular tourist destination and gateway to the Highlands, thus adding to a sustainable local economy. The area is popular with cyclists and the local Tourist Board have produced a pack of leaflets describing a network of six signed local routes in the area.

Troon

Due to its situation and topography the seaside town of Troon has one of the highest levels of cycling in Scotland. However, links to and from the town are very much constrained by the many golf courses which surround it. National Route 7 gets over this problem by using existing estate roads and paths as well as a new link southwards beside the railway line to Ayr.

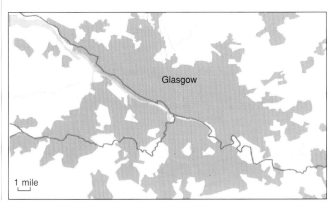

Glasgow

Glasgow is served by an excellent network of National Routes. To the south and west, quiet roads and paths through parks lead to the disused railway system all the way to the Clyde Coast at Ardrossan and Gourock. To the north, the Glasgow to Loch Lomond Cycle Route uses disused railways, canal and riverside paths to reach Scotland's first National Park. To the east the Clyde Walkway forms the start of an traffic-free route to Edinburgh.

© Crown copyright

GLASGOW TO LOCH LOMOND

This ride out of Scotland's largest city starts from the Scottish Exhibition & Conference Centre, an important National Cycle Network junction of the Clyde to Forth Route (Route 75) and the Carlisle to Inverness Route (Route 7). Standing here one has the sense of Glasgow re-inventing itself: all around are new buildings with just the occasional one dating back to previous generations. After a short spell on a cycle path alongside the busy A814 you join a railway path, a green corridor through first an industrial then a residential setting with many older buildings of red or yellow sandstone. You pass John Brown's shipyard in the centre of Clydebank, where the great ships the *Queen Mary*, *Queen Elizabeth* and *Queen Elizabeth II* were built. Beyond Clydebank, the route joins the Forth & Clyde Canal on a broad, well-maintained towpath. The canal, built in 1790, and soon to be reopened to boats, was the main route across

Scotland linking the Clyde at Bowling, west of Glasgow with the Forth near to Falkirk and Grangemouth. The ride becomes more open with green views of the Kilpatrick Hills behind Erskine Bridge. A second railway path starting at the end of the canal takes you through woodland and rocky outcrops to the outkirts of Dumbarton, the ancient fortress-capital of the Kingdom of Strathclyde. The route through Dumbarton is on quiet roads and soon you join the waterside path alongside the River Leven which leads to Balloch and the banks of Loch Lomond. It is worth stopping to read the information boards along the river with interesting background detail about the history and wildlife of the riverside.

The River Leven approaching Balloch.

Starting points

The Scottish Exhibition &
Conference Centre near Bell's
Bridge in the centre of Glasgow.

Distance

20 miles one way, 40 miles return.
For shorter rides there are good
turnaround points at the cafe at
Bowling Basin (20 miles round trip)
or Dumbarton (28 miles round trip).
There are railway stations along the
route if you wish to catch the train
back.

Grade

Easy.

Surface

A mixture of tarmac and gravel
paths.

Roads, traffic, suitability for young children

The route is traffic-free apart from
the section through Dumbarton
where quiet streets are used. There
are several road crossings, mostly
via toucan crossings or traffic
islands. The best sections for
children are the Forth & Clyde
Canal towpath between Clydebank
and Bowling and the stretch
alongside the River Leven north
from Dumbarton to Balloch.

Hills

None.

Refreshments

There is a cafe by the bike shop in
Bowling at the end of the canal
towpath.
Plenty of choice in Dumbarton.
Plenty of choice in Balloch.

Leaflets:

*CycleCity's Glasgow Cycling Map –
City Centre and Suburbs* is an
excellent publication showing the
traffic-free paths, signposted cycle
routes, advisory routes plus a
wealth of other information. It costs
£4.95 and is available from Sustrans

Information Service, PO Box 21,
Bristol BS99 2HA (0117 929 0888)
or visit www.sustrans.org.uk

Nearest railway stations

There are stations along the route
from the Exhibition Centre in
Glasgow at the start to Balloch at
the end of the ride.

The National Cycle Network in the area

Glasgow is at a crossroads of the ·
National Cycle Network: Route 7
runs north-south from Inverness to
Carlisle; Route 75 (the Clyde to
Forth Cycle Route) runs west-east
from Gourock to Leith.

*Forth & Clyde Canal approaching
Erskine Bridge.*

Other nearby rides (waymarked or traffic-free)

1. Johnstone to Kilbirnie railway
path.
2. Johnstone to Greenock railway
path.
3. Airdrie to Bathgate railway path.
4. River Clyde Walkway to the east
of Crown Street/Saltmarket.
5. Forth & Clyde Canal.

Railway path near Clyde tunnel.

GLASGOW TO LOCH LOMOND

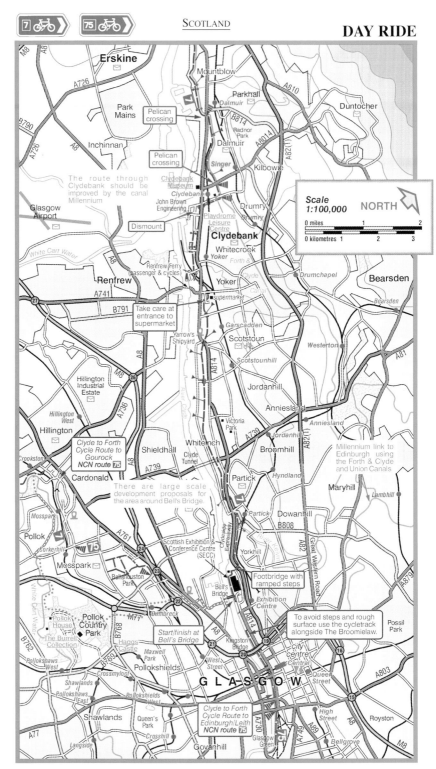

© Crown copyright

Route instructions from Glasgow to Loch Lomond

The railway path through Whiteinch provides elevated parkland through Glasgow.

1. From the Scottish Exhibition & Conference Centre in the centre of Glasgow, follow the cobbled promenade, with the river to your left. Go around the perimeter fence of the heliport, turn left onto Stobcross Road, cross the main road via the footbridge then turn sharp left alongside the main road 'Loch Lomond Cycleway'.

2. Follow the cycle path parallel with the main road. Shortly after passing the old red-brick building of Partick Fire Brigade, turn left into the subway then right through the subway to join the railway path.

3. After three miles, at the end of the railway path turn right by a discount store and continue in the same direction towards Brown Engineering.

4. At Brown Engineering turn right to go through subway, cross Stanford Street (take care) then turn left at the toucan crossing to join the towpath of the Clyde & Forth Canal.

Approaching Bowling on the Forth & Clyde Canal towpath with the Kilpatrick Hills in the background.

GLASGOW TO LOCH LOMOND

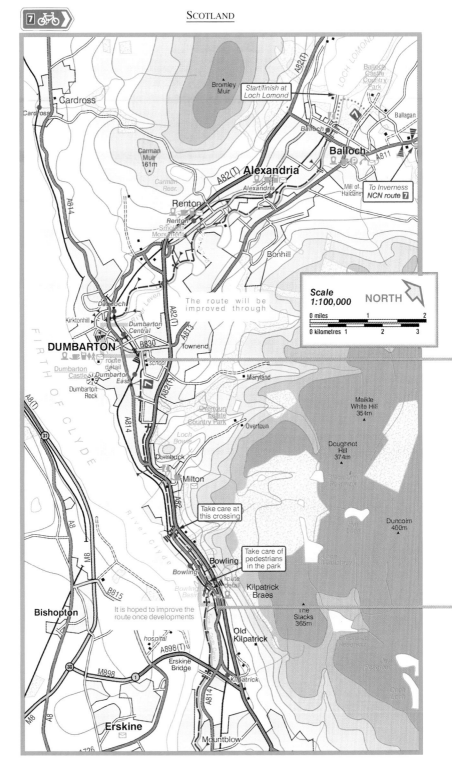

Start/finish at Loch Lomond

To Inverness NCN route 7

The route will be improved through

Scale
1:100,000

NORTH

| 0 miles | | 1 | | 2 |
| 0 kilometres | 1 | | 2 | 3 |

Take care at this crossing

Take care of pedestrians in the park

It is hoped to improve the route once developments

© Crown copyright

Bowling Tunnel.

5. Dismount to cross the main thoroughfare through the Shopping Centre at Clydebank. (This will change once the canal is reopened in 2001).

6. After four miles, at a large metal bridge over the canal by a bike hire outlet and small marina, turn right uphill, cross the road then turn left through the park.

7. Follow the railway path section for 2½ miles through woodland and exposed rocks. At the T-junction with Third Avenue on the outskirts of Dumbarton turn left and follow the excellent signposting for two miles through Dumbarton to the banks of the River Leven. (Follow the inset mapping.)

8. Join the cycle path along the banks of River Leven and follow this for five miles to Balloch.

9. Cross the bridge and turn left into Balloch Castle Country Park to reach the shores of Loch Lomond.

The start of the River Leven route from Dumbarton to Loch Lomond.

CALLANDER TO BALQUIDDER AND LOCH VENACHAR

A most spectacular setting of lochs and mountains forms the backdrop to these two rides north and south from the holiday centre of Callander. The ride north to Balquidder runs along the course of the old Caledonian railway line which until 1965 used to run from Stirling to Oban. Passing through broadleaf woodland alongside the swift waters and spectacular falls of the River Leny, the ride runs a parallel course to the A84 through the Pass of Leny, known as the entrance to the Highlands. There are fine views of Ben Ledi where it is said that 2,000 years ago the Druids lit fires at the top to celebrate the changing of the seasons. A quiet road is followed from the end of Loch Lubnaig to Balquidder, where you may wish to visit Rob Roy's grave.

The southern ride follows the shores of Loch Venachar past splendid isolated houses set above the water's edge, with views across to the mighty shape of Ben Ledi. You may well see colourful dinghies and windsurfers on the water. The loch ends at Blackwater Marshes, a raised bog classed as a Site of Special Scientific Interest. There are reeds, willow, birch trees and patches of bog myrtle. This special combination of plants and water provides home and food for Greylag Geese, Goosanders, Teal and Wigeons. The open territory is also excellent for birds of prey. A short section on forest roads takes you to the refreshment stop/turnaround point at Brig o'Turk.

Falls of Leny on an ancient packhorse road.

Starting point

The centre of Callander.

Distance:

(a) 13 miles from Callander to Balquidder, 26 miles return. The trip could be shortened by going only as far as Strathyre (18 miles round trip).
(b) Eight miles from Callander via Invertrossachs to Brig o'Turk, 16 miles return.

Grade

Moderate.

Surface

Mixture of tarmac and stone-based tracks. There is a rougher section at the north end of Loch Lubnaig.

Roads, traffic, suitability for young children

(a) Callander-Balquidder. A traffic-free path starts from the central car park in Callander. There may be a little traffic along the road serving the holiday chalets at the southern end of Loch Lubnaig. A very quiet road is used between Strathyre and Balquidder.
(b) Callander-Loch Venachar. There is a short section (½ mile) on the A81 south from the centre of Callander where care should be taken. You then join the minor road to Invertrossachs, which carries very little traffic. There is a three mile cycle path/forestry track between Invertrossachs and Brig o'Turk.

Hills

(a) Callander-Strathyre. There is a steady 200 ft climb from Callander past the Falls of Leny up to Loch Lubnaig. There are several other short climbs, including a steep one up a series of zig zags at the north end of Loch Lubnaig (fantastic views!).
(b) Callander-Brig o'Turk. Generally rolling with the occasional short steep climb.

Flooded car park, Callander.

Refreshments

Lots of choice in Callander.
(a) Cafe and pubs in Strathyre. Teashop at the museum in Stronvar (just south of Balquidder).
(b) The Byre Inn at Brig o'Turk.

Nearest railway station

The nearest is at Dunblane (12 miles to the east).

The National Cycle Network in the area:

1. To the north of Balquidder, Route 7 passes through Lochearnhead and Glen Ogle on its way to Killin, Pitlochry, Aviemore and Inverness.
2. To the south of Loch Venachar, Route 7 crosses the Dukes Pass via forestry tracks then passes through Aberfoyle and Drymen on its way to Loch Lomond and Glasgow (see page 186).

Other nearby rides (waymarked or traffic-free)

1. There are plenty of forest routes in Queen Elizabeth Forest Park (maps from Tourist Information Centres or the Visitor Centre north of Aberfoyle).
2. There is also a delightful ride along the northern side of Loch Katrine which can be followed on a minor road as far as Loch Lomond.

Southside Loch Venachar avoiding the main Dukes Road.

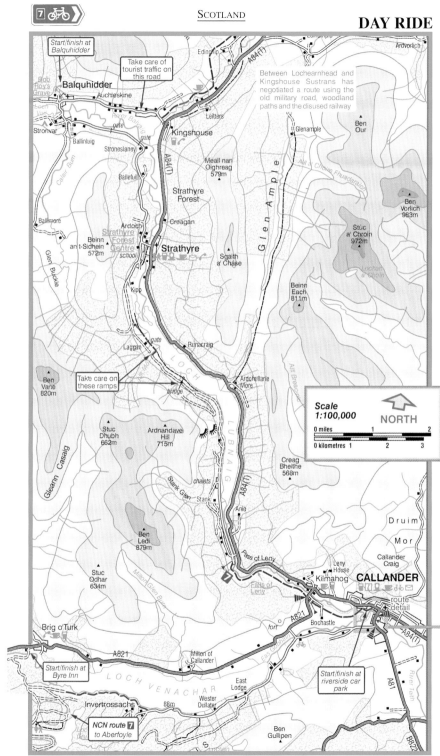

CALLANDER TO BALQUIDDER

Start/finish at Balquhidder

Take care of tourist traffic on this road

Bob Roy's Grave

Balquhidder

Auchleskine

Between Lochearnhead and Kingshouse Sustrans has negotiated a route using the old military road, woodland paths and the disused railway

Ardvorlich

Edinchip

Leitters

Stronvar

Ballinluig

gate

Stroneslaney

gate

Kingshouse

Glenample

Ben Our

Ballefull

Meall nan Oighreag 579m

Ballimore

Ardoch

Strathyre Forest Centre

school

Creagan

Strathyre Forest

Beinn an t-Sidhein 572m

Strathyre

Sgaith a' Chase

Glen Ample

Ben Vorlich 983m

Stùc a' Chroin 972m

Beinn Each 811m

Glen Buckie

Kipp

Glen Buckie

Laggan

gate

Take care on these ramps

bridge

Runacraig

Ardchullarie More

Ben Vane 820m

Gleann Casaig

Stuc Dhubh 662m

Ardnandave Hill 715m

chalets

Stank Glen

Stank

Creag Bheithe 568m

Anie

Druim

Mor

Ben Ledi 879m

Stuc Odhar 634m

Pass of Leny

Leny House

Callander Craig

Kilmahog

CALLANDER

route detail

Brig o'Turk

A821

Milton of Callander

Falls of Leny

fort

Bochastle

A821

Start/finish at Byre Inn

LOCH VENACHAR

East Lodge

Start/finish at riverside car park

Invertrossachs

Wester Dullater

88m

Ben Gullipen

NCN route 7 to Aberfoyle

Scale 1:100,000

NORTH

0 miles   1   2
0 kilometres 1   2   3

© Crown copyright

Route instructions:
A. From Callander to Balquidder

1. From the western end of the central car park in Callander, follow the cyclepath across the parkland signposted 'Balquidder, Strathyre' to join the railway path.

2. Cross the river then after one mile cross the road (A821). **CARE!** Climb steadily beside the beautiful river.

3. The track turns to tarmac. Where the road forks take the right-hand of the two lanes, staying close to the water. The tarmac turns back to track at the end of the wooden holiday cabins.

4. After two miles bear left uphill then right following blue arrows and signs for 'Strathyre'.

5. The path descends to rejoin the lakeside then shortly climbs again on a steep section of zig zags. At the T-junction with the forest road turn right (remember this point for the return trip, it is **easy to miss**).

6. The track turns to tarmac. Follow this beautiful, narrow road for five miles through woodland to the T-junction in Balquidder. Here, after visiting Rob Roy's grave, you can:

(a) turn around and return, perhaps stopping at the Museum of Bygones tearoom at Stronvar or at the variety

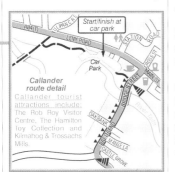

Callander route detail
Callander tourist attractions include: The Rob Roy Visitor Centre, The Hamilton Toy Collection and Kilmahog & Trossachs Mills.

of refreshment stops in Strathyre;

(b) turn left for four miles along the lochside on the no through road for refreshments at the Monachyle Mhor hotel and restaurant; or

(c) turn right and follow Route 7 over Glen Ogle towards Killin.

If you decide to extend your trip you should return to Callander the same way, following blue arrows and 'Callander' cycle signs and avoid spending time on the busy A84.

B. Callander along the banks of Loch Venachar to Brig o'Turk

1. From the centre of Callander follow the A81 towards Glasgow for ½-mile. Cross the bridge over the river. Towards the end of Callander, on a sharp left-hand bend, turn right signposted 'Invertrossachs'.

Loch Lubnaig - Route 7 follows the disused railway around the promontory.

2. Keep following signs for Invertrossachs, Aberfoyle and Route 7 for five miles along this tarmac road.

3. When you come to a 'Private Road. No cycling' sign ahead, bear right off the tarmac road onto a gravel path signposted 'Aberfoyle. Route 7'.

4. Follow this lovely lochside path for two miles. At a T-junction with a wider forestry path turn right (or turn left for Route 7 to Aberfoyle). **Remember** this point for your return.

5. Keep bearing right, ignoring two turns to the left. At the major T-junction with 'Forest Drive' signposted to the left, turn right and go past Achray Farm to the Byre Inn at Brig o'Turk.

EDINBURGH TO THE FORTH BRIDGE

Riding across the Forth Road Bridge must be one of the most extraordinary cycling experiences in Scotland. There you are, hundreds of feet above the waters of the Firth of Forth, with views to the east of the magnificent Forth Rail Bridge (the one where, as the saying goes, they start painting at one end the moment they have stopped at the other!) cyclists can cross from South Queensferry to North Queensferry in complete traffic-free safety along the cycle lanes that run either side of the bridge. The ride out from central Edinburgh uses a mixture of bus lanes, shared-use pavements, railway paths and quiet roads through Barnton, Braepark and over the lovely old Cramond Brig to cross the River Almond. You pass under the Forth Rail Bridge on the course of an old dismantled railway before climbing through Queensferry, named after Queen Margaret who used the ferry to cross the Forth in the 11th century. After crossing the bridge you have the choice of returning on the other side or dropping down into North Queensferry for refreshments, a visit to Deep Sea World and a train trip back to Edinburgh across the Forth Rail Bridge.

The Forth Road Bridge cycle track carries Route 1 into Fife.

Starting point
Haymarket Station, Edinburgh.

Distance
11 miles one way, 22 miles return.

Grade
Easy.

Surface
Mixture of stone-based paths and tarmac.

Roads, traffic, suitability for young children
The bus lane along Haymarket/West Coates is used from Haymarket Station until the start of the railway path. Care should be taken at the road crossings in Davidson's Mains, Braepark, Dalmeny and Queensferry. If you decide to visit North Queensferry there is a road section from the cycle path across the bridge down to the village. The most exciting section for children is the crossing of the Forth Road Bridge itself which has traffic-free cycle lanes on both sides.

Hills
Rolling. There is a climb up to the cycle lane on the bridge.

Refreshments
Albert Hotel, Ferrybridge Hotel, Post Office Cafe, North Queensferry.
The tearoom in Dalmeny House is open on Sunday, Monday and Tuesday afternoons in July and August.

Leaflets
An excellent large map showing all the cycle facilities in Edinburgh is produced by SPOKES, the Edinburgh cycle campaign group and is available from Sustrans Information Service, PO Box 21, Bristol BS99 2HA (0117 929 0888) or visit www.sustrans.org.uk

Nearest railway stations
Edinburgh Haymarket, Dalmeny and North Queensferry.

The National Cycle Network in the area
1. Route 75, the Clyde to Forth Cycle Route runs across Scotland from Gourock to Leith.
2. Route 1 northbound connects Edinburgh with St Andrew's and Dundee and will continue along the coast to Aberdeen and Inverness.
3. Route 1 southbound runs east to Dalkeith then south through the Scottish Borders to Berwick-upon-

Princes Street, Edinburgh.

Tweed to join the Coast and Castles Route which follows the coast down to Newcastle upon Tyne.

Other nearby rides (waymarked or traffic-free)
There are many traffic-free trails in or near Edinburgh such as the Innocent Railway Path, the Water of Leith, the Union Canal, plus several sections of railway path in North Edinburgh.

EDINBURGH TO THE FORTH BRIDGE

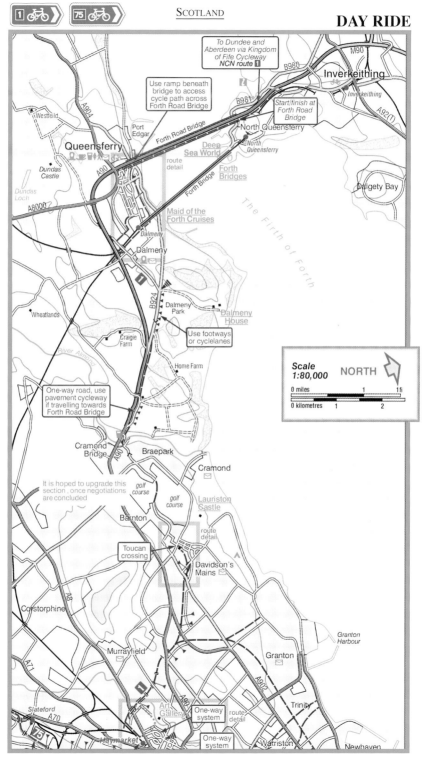

Scale 1:80,000   NORTH

0 miles   1   1fi

0 kilometres   1   2

© Crown copyright

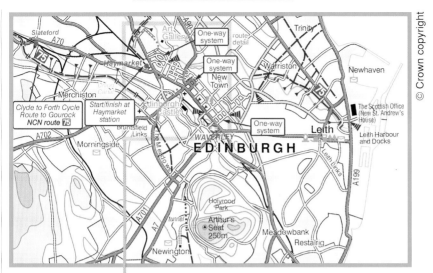

© Crown copyright

3. At the second fork of tracks bear right and follow Silverknowes Drive and Terrace and at right hand bend, a short path on the left leads to Cramond Road South. Cross into Barnton Avenue.

4. At the end of the path bear left through the supermarket car park. At the road (Cramond Road South) turn right (**TAKE CARE**) then take the first left onto Barnton Avenue.

Route instructions from Edinburgh to Forth Road Bridge

1. From Haymarket Station in the centre of Edinburgh turn left along the cycle lane on Haymarket/West Coates. After ½-mile and just before a painted metal bridge, turn left onto Balbirnie Place then bear right uphill onto the tarmac path and sharp right on the railway path to cross the bridge over the road.

2. Shortly, at the obvious fork of tracks (with Sainsbury's petrol station to the right) bear left.

5. Continue in the same direction, ignoring turnings as tarmac turns to a rough path then back to tarmac. At the crossroads go straight ahead onto Brae Park Road signposted 'Cramond Brig, Queensferry'.

6. Cross the bridge, climb, then immediately before the main road, turn right onto the pavement/cyclepath alongside the road (A90).

7. Follow the same direction for two miles on the pavement along the one way road, the A90 and the B924. Opposite the gates to Dalmeny House turn left to 'Dalmeny'.

8. At the end of Dalmeny village, on a sharp left-hand bend, bear right onto a no through road called The Glebe. Shortly, turn left by a cycle sign 'Dalmeny Station, Forth Road Bridge', descend to the railway path and turn sharp right. (**Remember** this point if you decide to cycle back from the Forth Road Bridge).

9. At the end of the railway path, exit the left-hand corner of the supermarket car park. Turn right into Morrison Gardens.

10. At the T-junction at the end of Morrison Gardens turn left then left again onto the ramp road signposted 'Cyclists only'. Shortly, at the T-junction turn right, up the slope then at the bridge turn left on the cycle lane.

11. Cross the Firth of Forth. At the end of the bridge turn left down the steps, then either go back up the steps on the other side and return to Edinburgh (or to Dalmeny railway station) OR continue downhill for the pubs and cafes in North Queensferry (and the railway station).

Northern Ireland

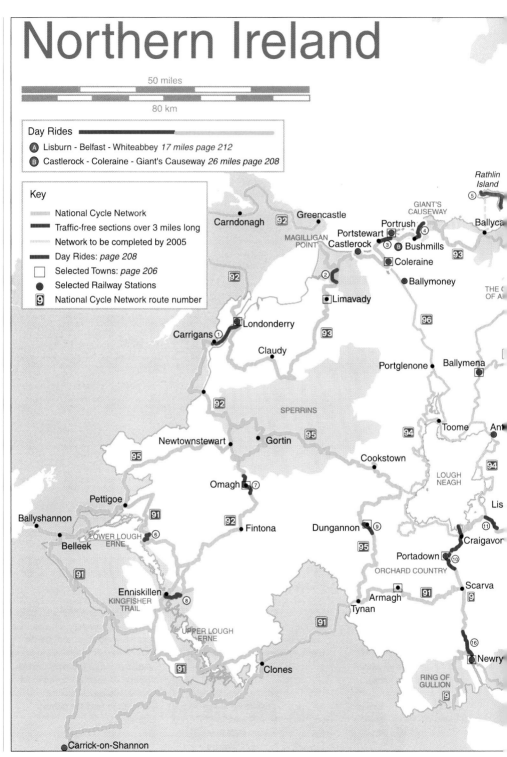

50 miles

80 km

Day Rides

Ⓐ Lisburn - Belfast - Whiteabbey *17 miles page 212*
Ⓑ Castlerock - Coleraine - Giant's Causeway *26 miles page 208*

Key

- National Cycle Network
- Traffic-free sections over 3 miles long
- Network to be completed by 2005
- Day Rides: *page 208*
- ☐ Selected Towns: *page 206*
- ⬤ Selected Railway Stations
- 9 National Cycle Network route number

Rathlin Island ⑤

Carndonagh · | 92 | Greencastle

GIANT'S CAUSEWAY
Portrush Ballyca
Portstewart
MAGILLIGAN POINT
Castlerock ③ Ⓑ Bushmills ④
Coleraine | 93 |

| 92 | Ballymoney

THE C OF A

Limavady | 93 |

| 96 |

Londonderry
Carrigans ①
Claudy

Portglenone · Ballymena

| 92 |

SPERRINS

| 95 | | 94 | Toome An

Newtownstewart · Gortin
Cookstown | 94 |

| 95 |

LOUGH NEAGH

Omagh ⑦

Pettigoe
Ballyshannon | 91 |
Belleek LOWER LOUGH ERNE ⑥ | 92 | Fintona Dungannon ⑨ Lis

| 95 | | 11 | Craigavor

Portadown ⑩
ORCHARD COUNTRY Scarva
| 91 | Armagh | 91 | 9
Enniskillen
KINGFISHER TRAIL ⑧
Tynan
UPPER LOUGH ERNE | 91 |

| 91 | Clones | 16 | Newry

RING OF GULLION 9

Carrick-on-Shannon

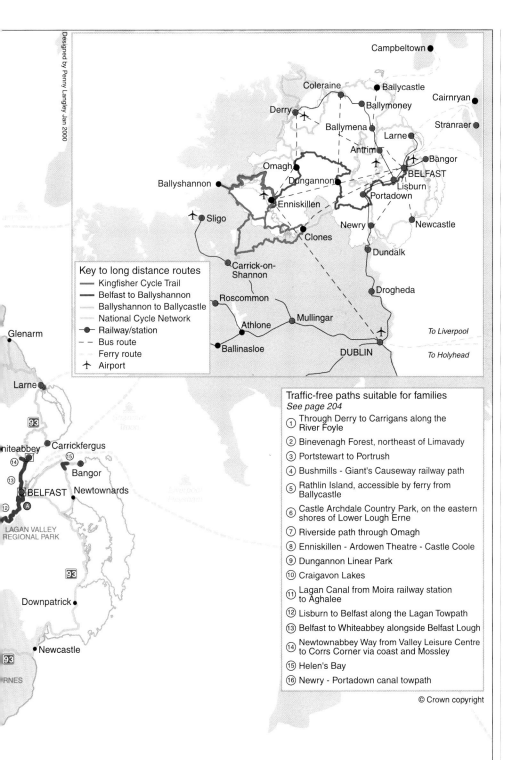

Campbeltown ●

Coleraine ● Ballycastle ●
Cairnryan ●
Derry ● Ballymoney ●
Ballymena ● Stranraer ●
Larne ●
Antrim ●
Bangor ●
Omagh ● BELFAST
Dungannon ● Lisburn
Ballyshannon ● Portadown
Enniskillen ●
Sligo ● Newry ● Newcastle ●
Clones ● Dundalk ●
Carrick-on-Shannon
Drogheda ●
Roscommon ●
Mullingar ●
Athlone ●
Ballinasloe ● DUBLIN

To Liverpool
To Holyhead

Glenarm ●
Larne ●
93
niteabbey ● Carrickfergus
14 15
13 Bangor ●
BELFAST Newtownards
12 A
LAGAN VALLEY REGIONAL PARK
93
Downpatrick ●
93
● Newcastle
RNES

Key to long distance routes
— Kingfisher Cycle Trail
— Belfast to Ballyshannon
— Ballyshannon to Ballycastle
— National Cycle Network
●— Railway/station
– – Bus route
— Ferry route
✈ Airport

Traffic-free paths suitable for families
See page 204

① Through Derry to Carrigans along the River Foyle

② Binevenagh Forest, northeast of Limavady

③ Portstewart to Portrush

④ Bushmills - Giant's Causeway railway path

⑤ Rathlin Island, accessible by ferry from Ballycastle

⑥ Castle Archdale Country Park, on the eastern shores of Lower Lough Erne

⑦ Riverside path through Omagh

⑧ Enniskillen - Ardowen Theatre - Castle Coole

⑨ Dungannon Linear Park

⑩ Craigavon Lakes

⑪ Lagan Canal from Moira railway station to Aghalee

⑫ Lisburn to Belfast along the Lagan Towpath

⑬ Belfast to Whiteabbey alongside Belfast Lough

⑭ Newtownabbey Way from Valley Leisure Centre to Corrs Corner via coast and Mossley

⑮ Helen's Bay

⑯ Newry - Portadown canal towpath

© Crown copyright

NORTHERN IRELAND

The rural road network of Northern Ireland provides a range of cycling opportunities suitable for everyone from the occasional cyclist to the semi-professional. There are rich farmlands and a dramatic coastline. The area abounds in castles, iron age forts, prehistoric burial sites, cathedrals and churches, fine country houses and parks. The countryside is full of pleasant, relaxed towns and villages, and most important, there are Ireland's welcoming people, always glad of a chat, especially in the pub in the evening. The pub is also the best place to hear traditional Irish music.

Water is perhaps the dominant theme in defining the National Cycle Network in Northern Ireland. The route through Belfast runs alongside the River Lagan and Belfast Lough; likewise the

Gad Tower, Upper Lough Erne. Ferry ride to the National Trust's estate at Crom on the Kingfisher Trail.

River Foyle in Derry provides the best routes through the city; on the spectacular north coast the Network runs close to the sea from Magilligan Point to Giant's Causeway; the first mapped long distance route in Ireland, the Kingfisher Trail, explores Upper and Lower Lough Erne; the Portadown to Newry Canal is used extensively in both towns whilst the Camowen River in Omagh and the Callan River in Armagh offer traffic-free routes through the towns. Lastly, there are plans for a route around Lough Neagh, the largest inland lake in the United Kingdom.

NATIONAL CYCLE NETWORK HIGHLIGHTS

Oxford Island

The Lough Neagh Discovery Centre is situated within Oxford Island National Nature Reserve. In the Centre, learn about the history and wildlife of the Lough, then go for gentle cycles and walks along the trails of this reserve, which is particularly famous for bird life.

Causeway Coast

This beautiful and dramatic coastal route is one of the most visited attractions in Northern Ireland and as such has a wide range of tourist facilities. The route leads to the Giant's Causeway which is even more stunning. The towns have playgrounds for children.

Lagan Valley Regional Park

The delightful riverside towpath route meanders through this well managed Park from Lisburn to Belfast. The route is peaceful and flat and is home to birds such as swans, moorhens, ducks and kingfishers. Cyclists need to take care as this popular path is shared with many walkers.

Kingfisher Trail

The Kingfisher Trail at approximately 230 miles is the first long distance cycle trail in Ireland. It is a fully signed route and runs through the counties of Fermanagh, Leitrim, Cavan, Donegal and Monaghan. This is a beautiful rural area of quiet country roads well suited to cycling.

Beaghmore Stone Circles, Sperrins

The Sperrin Mountains are a marvellously quiet area to cycle through. Half way between Gortin and Cookstown on Route 95 are the Beaghmore Stone Circles. These ancient stone structures hold many secrets and the site offers panoramic views of Tyrone.

Foyle Valley Linear Park, Derry

Riverside paths run through Derry along both sides of the Foyle. The path along the railway line is part of a six-mile traffic-free route through this historic city.

TRAFFIC-FREE CYCLE PATHS SUITABLE FOR FAMILIES

Listed here is a selection of traffic-free routes, often along disused railways, that are more than three miles long and offer ideal cycling for families. Some are covered by the Day Rides, some are shown on the maps below. (Numbers match the map key on page 200)

For further information about traffic-free rides, ask for the Traffic-free Information Sheet FF06 from Sustrans Information Service, PO Box 21, Bristol BS99 2HA (0117 929 0888) or visit www.sustrans.org.uk

1. Derry to Carrigans
2. Binevenagh Forest, northeast of Limavady
3. Portstewart to Portrush (see page 208)
4. Bushmills to Giant's Causeway railway path (see page 208)
5. Rathlin Island, via the ferry from Ballycastle

6. Castle Archdale Country Park, on the eastern shores of Lower Lough Erne
7. Riverside path through Omagh
8. Enniskillen to Castle Coole via Ardowen
9. Dungannon Linear Park
10. Oxford Island to Portadown
11. Lisburn to Belfast along the Lagan Towpath (see page 212)
12. Belfast to Whiteabbey alongside Belfast Lough (see page 212)
13. Newtownabbey Way from Valley Leisure Centre to Corrs Corner via the coast and Mossley
14. Woodburn Forest, west of Carrickfergus
15. Helen's Bay near Bangor
16. Newry to Portadown Canal towpath

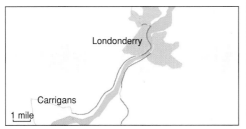

1. Derry to Carrigans

This delightful path runs from the new Sainsbury's store alongside the River Foyle to Carrigans in Donegal. The route is a combination of high grade urban paths and a trail alongside the tourist railway line that runs south from Craigavon Bridge. When the path stops, the route links to the quiet Balloughry Road.

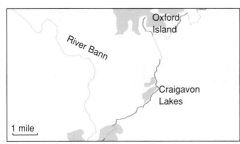

10. Oxford Island to Portadown

This six-mile route runs from the Lough Neagh Discovery Centre to the hospital in Portadown along a series of wide traffic-free paths which were built as part of the town development in the 1960s. This scenic and flat route runs alongside Craigavon Lakes.

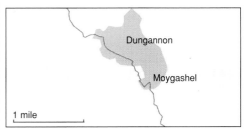

9. Dungannon Linear Park

Starting at the Linengreen Centre in Moygashel, the route runs alongside the Mill Race through Dungannon Park with its attractive lakeside setting. A new link has been formed to the regenerated railway park. The two-mile railway path provides an enjoyable flat ride through this attractive market town.

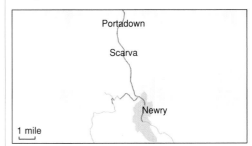

16. Newry-Portadown Canal towpath

South from Portadown the three-mile stretch runs along the River Bann over the Point of Whitecoat Bridge and onto Moneypenny's Lock. North from Newry, the towpath starts at the Canal Street entrance. Of interest are the stone-arched Steenson's Bridge and the old canal locks.

© Crown copyright

REGIONAL ROUTES AND GOOD CYCLING AREAS

For further information about leaflets/guidebooks covering these routes contact Sustrans Information Service, PO Box 21, Bristol BS99 2HA (0117 929 0888) or visit www.sustrans.org.uk

THE KINGFISHER TRAIL
(covered by a National Cycle Network Map)
NN9A (NATIONAL) ROUTE 91

A 230-mile figure-of-eight route through Northern Ireland and the Republic visiting the border counties of Fermanagh, Leitrim, Cavan, Donegal and Monaghan. Mostly rural, the trail includes the appealing towns of Enniskillen and Carrick-on-Shannon. The terrain is mixed (and not green for nothing - take waterproofs!) and the route is mainly on very lightly trafficked roads, passing through many villages with accommodation and pubs. The communities are welcoming and hospitable, as you would expect.

Ferries go from Stranraer, Troon, and Larne. Heysham or Liverpool to Belfast and from Holyhead to Dublin. The Kingfisher Company (028 6632 0121) will put together total or part packages in hotel, hostel or B&B, suggest itineraries and provide general advice.

THE CARLETON TRAIL

The Clogher Valley is often called 'Carleton Country' as it was the home of the acclaimed 19th-century poet and novelist, William Carleton, who immortalised the area in his best-loved works. The Carleton Trail takes in many landmarks which have Carleton associations. There are three waymarked routes, all starting from the Clogher Valley Rural Centre. There are information panels at various points along the way. **The Red Route** is 30 miles long and contains some steep sections. **The Green Route** is also 30 miles long and passes through

Fardross Forest. **The Black Route** is just 10 miles long, a much shortened version of the Red Route. The routes are signed and covered by a leaflet available from Dungannon Council – 028 8772 0330.

THE SPERRINS

The Sperrin Mountains, straddling the Derry-Tyrone border and stretching 35 miles from north west to south east, represent a truly unspoilt world of gentle ridges and winding valleys. A network of quiet country lanes (some have grass growing up the middle!) enable the cyclist to explore this beautiful area. The stone circles at Beaghmore are well worth visiting, as is the Sperrins Visitor Centre. The latest edition of Ordnance Survey map (N.I.) No. 13 shows the course of the National Cycle Network in the area and is vital for planning your trip whether you intend to cycle for a day or a week. Attractions in the area include the Ulster History Park and Ulster American Folk Park to the north of Omagh, the Sperrin Heritage Centre at Cranagh and the Wellbrook Beetling Mill near Cookstown. Contact Sperrins Tourism – 028 7963 4570.

ORCHARD COUNTRY

The compact cathedral city of Armagh is the perfect starting point for a trip around the orchards for which the county is renowned. The countryside is transformed into a sea of white and pink during the apple blossom season. Other highlights along the route include Navan Fort, an important Celtic site and Gosford Forest Park. The area is criss-crossed by quiet, flat lanes along the line of the disused Ulster

Canal, the remains of which can be seen in the form of old arch bridges and disused locks e.g. at Benburb.

THE MOURNES

Distinctive and self-contained, the Mourne Mountains are tucked away in the south east corner of Northern Ireland with twelve summits rising above 2,000 ft. The coast from Newcastle to Greencastle was notorious for smuggling in the 18th century. Ten signposted and mapped cycle routes have been developed in this hilly and beautiful area. Contact the Mournes Heritage Trust – 028 4372 4059.

LOUGH NEAGH WAY (NATIONAL) ROUTE 41

Lough Neagh is the largest inland lake in the United Kingdom and this 150 km route goes all the way around the lake, including a crossing of a newly-built bridge at Bannfoot. Where possible, the route chooses lanes that carry little traffic but stay close to the lake, passing tourist attractions such as Oxford Island Nature Reserve, Ardboe Celtic Cross, Ballyronan Marina, the Randalstown Viaduct and Antrim's Castle Gardens. Route opening 2001.

INISHOWEN PENINSULA

Highlights of the 130-mile circuit of this beautiful peninsula include spectacular views of the Atlantic Ocean and Binevenagh Mountain, the Gap of Mamore, Malin Head (the most northerly point of the island of Ireland), Five Finger Strand and a succession of incredible white sandy beaches. Contact Inishowen Tourism – 00353 77 74933. Route will be signed in 2001.

TOWNS AND CITIES ON THE NATIONAL CYCLE NETWORK

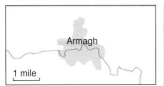

Armagh

An ecclesiastic centre with two cathedrals and the oldest library in the country. The old cobbled city of Armagh is served by Route 91 with a new traffic-free riverside path alongside the River Callan linking to the Visitor Centre for Navan Fort, the famous old burial chamber. In the east, a new urban riverside path connects the minor roads of Route 91 from the Portadown to Newry Canal to the Mall in the city centre.

Ballymena

The Ecos centre, a Millennium project, is situated off the A42 in Ballymena, and Route 93 runs through it. To the east, a cycle lane runs three miles to Broughshane, a village on the road towards remote moorland country, famous for its peat cutting, stone walls and quiet roads.

Belfast

The weir and the regeneration of the River Lagan have acted as a spur to create a highly attractive riverside route right through the heart of Belfast, passing the impressive

Waterfront Hall, the Central Railway Station and the ferry terminals. Road space has been reallocated to cyclists to create continuous routes linking city with country along Belfast Lough to the north and through the splendid Lagan Valley Regional Park to the south. Leaflet available from Sustrans.

Coleraine

This university town in the north of the region was the first in Northern Ireland to install cycle lanes. A new Millennium Bridge offers a safe crossing of the River Bann for pedestrians and cyclists. The Network links the main shopping area, the newly-built Council Offices and the University on the outskirts of town. It forms part of the scenic North Coast route from Castlerock to Portstewart, Portrush, the Giant's Causeway and on to Ballycastle.

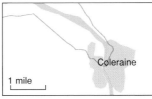

Dungannon

A hilly market town served by a recently improved traffic-free route along the course of an old railway, offering a good connection to the west of town. Dungannon Lake Park is a very popular walking and cycling area. There is a network of flat, minor roads between Dungannon and Armagh, following the line of the disused Ulster Canal.

Limavady

Backburn Park uses the course of an old railway line to link Limavady's main street to residential areas. This traffic-free spine also serves the town's main supermarket, council offices, schools and leisure centres. Route 93 connects with the Roe Valley Country Park to the south of Limavady and into North Sperrins. The National Cycle Network has helped develop what was already a healthy cycling culture in this flat town. To the north east there is a route planned through Binevenagh Forest with magnifcent views over Lough Foyle to Innishowen.

Lisburn

Two new bridges, one across the River Lagan and the other across a restored section of the Lagan Canal, put Lisburn's Civic and Arts Centres at the heart of Route 9. This runs from Belfast through the Lagan Valley Regional Park to Union Locks. From here, via the Horseback Bridge, the National Cycle Network will cross the river and follow minor roads and the line of the old canal towards Lough Neagh. Links to the town centre and the Irish Linen Centre are being examined, possibly through Wallace Park or Castle Gardens.

© Crown copyright

Derry

The River Foyle is the focus of the National Cycle Network in Derry. A traffic-free riverside route runs for six miles right through the centre then alongside the Foyle Valley Railway towards Carrigans in Donegal. Several new retail, housing and office regeneration schemes along the river have incorporated cycle paths, giving easy access to rail and bus stations and the famous city walls. Signalled crossings will create a safe crossing of Craigavon Bridge, the city's famous double decker bridge. On the east side of the river, the path runs south to the residential areas of Prehen and New Buildings.

Newry

The river and canal (Portadown to Newry) run parallel down the valley through the centre of the town. The canal towpath provides Route 9 with an entrance into the town centre, whilst the route of the former Bessbrook tram line, under the spectacular Craigmore Viaduct, the highest in Ireland, will form the basis of a route towards Dundalk and Dublin. To the southwest of Newry is the Ring of Gullion, an Area of Outstanding Natural Beauty with signed local routes. There are plans for an improvement to the coastal route to the Mournes. Contact South Armagh Tourism Initiative 028 3086 8900.

Omagh

A market town and the county town of Tyrone. The traffic-free riverside route along the Camowen River links, via a bridge, to housing estates and schools, and goes past the leisure centre and health centre. A new path leads north past the council offices to Omagh's main tourist attractions: the Ulster American Folk Park and the Ulster History Park. Further north still is the attractive village of Gortin, a good base for exploring the Sperrins.

Portadown

A cycle lane network connects Portadown to Oxford Island on the shores of Lough Neagh passing the Craigavon Lakes. In Portadown itself, a traffic-free path runs past schools and the F.E. College. Many new developments near the Craigavon Lakes are utilising the cycle lane network. The canal towpath comes right into the centre of town and there are plans for it to be improved all the way south to Newry. A new bridge at Bannfoot on the shores of Lough Neagh will avoid a 10-mile detour as part of Lough Neagh Way, Route 94. There is a leaflet available covering Craigavon Lakes. Contact Craigavon Borough Council 028 3832 2205.

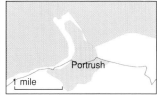

Portrush

The busiest holiday resort in Northern Ireland is well served with a traffic-free path running alongside the coast road offering stunning views of the Atlantic. The caravan and camping parks to the east of the town are linked to the town centre by cycle lanes. To the west the magnificent Port to Port path offers a grand coastal experience as you travel to Portstewart. This area is well served by all sorts of accomodation.

Whiteabbey

The new coastal path coming north from Belfast links Hazelbank Park to Whiteabbey, serving the Rathcoole housing estate. A spur leads off the University of Ulster at Jordanstown campus. The National Cycle Network turns inland from Belfast Lough where the Three Mile Water route continues under some very impressive old viaducts to the new Council Offices at Mossley. An additional route runs from the coast via Glas-na-Bradan Glen linking Rathcoole to the Valley Leisure Centre.

© Crown copyright

CASTLEROCK TO GIANT'S CAUSEWAY

The Giant's Causeway is a World Heritage Site and a splendid destination for this scenic ride along the beautiful north coast of Ireland. You may well choose to break this ride up into several shorter sections, with Coleraine or Portrush as good starting points, both served by railway stations. North from Coleraine the ride links cycle lanes and segregated cycle tracks past the University of Ulster and onto two of the most popular resorts on the north coast – Portstewart and Portrush, linked by another length of cycle track with fine sea views across to the Mull of Kintyre. From Portrush to Bushmills, home of the famous Irish whiskey, the route follows quiet lanes parallel to the busy coast road. As the lanes climb to almost 300 ft you have all of the views with very little of the traffic – just the right combination! From Bushmills, a delightful section of railway path takes you almost to the door of the Giant's Causeway Visitor Centre. To the west of Coleraine, the route climbs steeply to almost 300 ft affording wonderful views out to sea over the sand dunes at The Barmouth. Once you have reached Castlerock railway station it is well worth the effort to explore the ruins of Downhill Castle and the dramatically located Mussenden Temple just to the west of the village.

NB For safety reasons (a steep hill with a blind bend and lots of pedestrians) you are NOT allowed to cycle the ½-mile down to the Giant's Causeway from the Visitor Centre. Please do not abuse this sensible safety precaution.

Views of the seven-mile Magilligan Strand from Mussenden Temple, Route 93.

Starting points

1. Castlerock Station.
2. The new Millennium Bridge over the River Bann in Coleraine.
3. West Strand, Portrush.

Distances

Castlerock to Coleraine: seven miles one way, (14 miles return). Coleraine to Portrush seven miles one way, (14 miles return). Portrush to Giant's Causeway: nine miles one way, 18 miles return.

Grade

Moderate.

Surface

All tarmac, with the exception of the railway path into Giant's Causeway which is a high-grade stone path.

Roads, traffic, suitability for young children

Most of the ride is on quiet roads, cycle lanes and segregated cycleways where the route runs (safely) alongside busier roads. The section between Portstewart and Portrush has fine views out to the sea. The final traffic-free section from Bushmills to Giant's Causeway is along the course of a disused railway.

Hills

There are several short hills and two longer climbs of almost 300 ft: one to the north west of Coleraine on the way towards Castlerock, the other between Portrush and Bushmills, both on very quiet stretches of road.

Refreshments

Pubs, cafe in Castlerock.
Lots of choice in Coleraine.
Lots of choice in Portstewart.
Lots of choice in Portrush.
Cafe at the Giant's Causeway.

Nearest railway stations

Castlerock, Coleraine, Portrush.

The National Cycle Network in the area

1. West of Castlerock, Route 93 climbs steeply on Bishop's Road to over 1,000 ft with magnificent views to the Inishowen Peninsula and, on a fine day, to the Scottish Isles of Islay and Jura. It then drops down to Limavady via Binevenagh Forest.
2. East of Giant's Causeway Route 93 continues inland towards Ballycastle and the ferries to Scotland and Rathlin.

Dramatic rock formations at the Giant's Causeway, World Heritage Site.

Other nearby rides (waymarked or traffic-free)

1. There are plans to create a ferry link from Magilligan Point to Greencastle on the Innishowen Peninsula, linking the round-the-peninsula ride.
2. Rathlin Island, a ferry ride from Ballycastle, offers challenging cycling and walking to famous birdnesting sites and dramatic cliffs.

Railway path from Bushmills to the Giant's Causeway.

CASTLEROCK TO GIANT'S CAUSEWAY

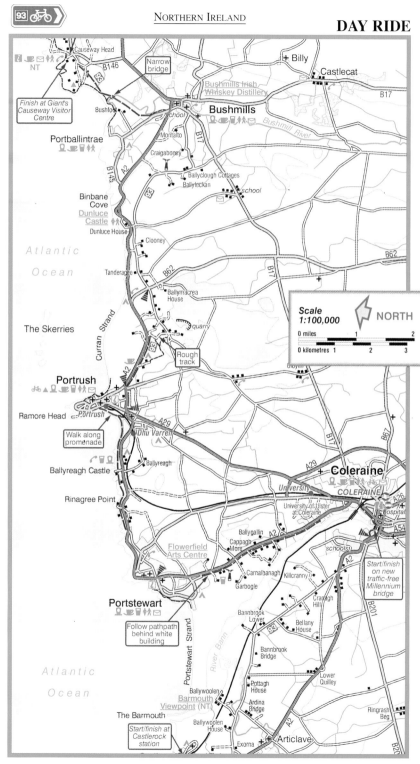

Causeway Head
NT
Finish at Giant's
Causeway Visitor
Centre

Narrow
bridge

Billy
Castlecat

B146

B17

Bushmills Irish
Whiskey Distillery

Bushmills

Bushfoot
school

Portballintrae

Montalto

Bushmill River

B17

Craigaboney

B145

A2

Ballyclough Cottages
Ballyfeckan
school

Binbane
Cove
Dunluce
Castle

Clooney

Dunluce House

Atlantic
Ocean

Tanderagee

B62

B17

B62

Ballymacrea
House

The Skerries

Curran Strand

quarry

Rough
track

Portrush

Ramore Head
Portrush

A2

Scale
1:100,000

NORTH

0 miles   1   2
0 kilometres 1   2   3

Cloyin

Walk along
promenade

A29

Dhu Varren

B17

B67

Ballyreagh Castle

Ballyreagh

Coleraine

A29

COLERAINE

University

A26

Rinagree Point

University of Ulster
at Coleraine

Hospital
A54

Ballygallin

Flowerfield
Arts Centre

Cappagh
More

A2

schools

A2

Carnalbanagh

Killcranny

Start/finish
on new
traffic-free
Millennium
bridge

Garbogle

Portstewart

Cranagh
Hill

B201

Follow pathpath
behind white
building

Portstewart Strand

River Bann

Bannbrook
Lower

Bellany
House

93

Bannbrook
Bridge

Lower
Quilley

Atlantic
Ocean

Ballywoolen
Barmouth
Viewpoint (NT)

Pottagh
House

The Barmouth

Ardina
Bridge

Ballywoolen
House

Ringrash
Beg

Start/finish at
Castlerock
station

A2

Exorna

Articlave

B20

© Crown copyright

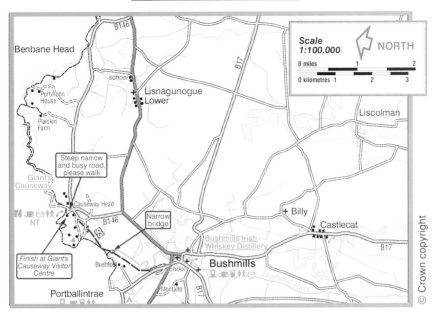

© Crown copyright

Route instructions from Castlerock to Giant's Causeway

1. From Castlerock Station, climb gently up the hill away from the sea and turn left along the segregated cycleway. Shortly, turn left down Ballywoolen Road at the school.

2. Follow this road for five miles, climbing 270 ft. At the T-junction with the A2 at the end of Cranagh Road, turn left downhill on the cycle lane. **Easy to miss**. Halfway down the hill (after the roundabout) turn left onto a no through road, signposted 'Route 93'.

3. Follow National Cycle Network 93 signs through Coleraine, crossing the new bridge over the River Bann and following the cycle lane round to the left. Continue alongside the A2 towards Portstewart on segregated track.

4. **Easy to miss**. On the outskirts of Portstewart follow signs carefully, turning left and immediately right behind a new white apartment.

Follow the waymarked route through the quiet residential streets of the town. (You may prefer to go along the main street of Portstewart with views out to sea – this is a more scenic route but obviously a lot busier with traffic.)

5. A segregated cycleway takes you from 'Port to Port' (Portstewart to Portrush) with fine views out to sea. On the outskirts of Portrush, the cycle track descends to the promenade. **Easy to miss**. At the bottom of the descent follow the promenade and after 100 m turn right away from the sea and pass under the railway bridge.

6. Follow the signposted route through Portrush on a combination of quiet streets, cycle lanes and segregated cycleways. On the outskirts of Portrush, following the coast road to Bushmills, go past the the Golf Links Hotel (Kelly's) on your right then (**easy to miss**) after 1 mile turn right uphill by a small wood onto a track to join a minor road. Turn left along the minor road.

7. Follow the waymarked route for six miles along quiet lanes parallel with the main coast road. You may wish to visit Dunluce Castle, a castle with a turbulent and fascinating history. There is one easily missed left turn on a fast descent just after a set of holiday cottages, about one mile before Bushmills. Look out for signs!

8. Soon after crossing the A2 onto the road towards Portballintrae, turn right at the Route 93 signpost onto the railway path and follow this for almost three miles to Giant's Causeway. This path is under construction in 2000 with the main road as an alternative. You will need to retrace your steps as far as Portrush for a train station.

NB For safety reasons (steep hill, blind bend, lots of walkers, the shuttle bus) you are not allowed to cycle from the Visitor Centre to the Giant's Causeway itself. It is best to leave yourself enough time to do the full two-mile walk along the cliff top, down to the Giant's Causeway then back along the road.

LISBURN TO WHITEABBEY

Water is the linking theme of this ride as it makes its way along the River Lagan from Lisburn into the regenerated heart of Belfast, then out along the shores of Belfast Lough towards Whiteabbey and the Newtownabbey Way. Starting in Lisburn, on an island formed by the River Lagan and the canal, a long wooded, riverside section leads past old linen mills and right into the centre of Belfast via a safe crossing on the Ormeau Bridge. Many fine old stone buildings punctuate the riverside route through the city centre, and Clarendon Docks have been completely rebuilt, now boasting an attractive mixture of residential and commercial buildings. The Belfast Hills, particularly the dramatic outline of Cave Hill, form a fine backdrop to the second half of the ride. After passing the ferry terminals, a short section takes you on the narrow corridor between the docks and the motorway through Duncrue Industrial Estate where your nose will be assailed by a variety of powerful smells! This unavoidable section is soon over and you cross onto the north foreshore path that takes you all the way to Whiteabbey with the vast shimmering expanse of Belfast Lough away to your right. The fence alongside the first section has been erected to protect the wading birds from being disturbed by dogs and walkers.

Cyclists pass a Millennium Milepost on the Newtonabbey Way.

Starting points

1. The Waterfront Hall in the heart of Belfast.
2. Lisburn Borough Council Offices on Island Mill, Lisburn.
3. Whiteabbey village, at the edge of Belfast Lough.

Distance

13 miles one way from Lisburn to the Waterfront Hall, Belfast (26 miles return).

Six miles one way from the Waterfront Hall, Belfast to Whiteabbey village (12 miles return).

Grade

Easy.

Surface

Tarmac surface throughout.

Roads, traffic, suitability for young children

There are two, traffic-free sections ideal for young children:
1. Island Mill in Lisburn to Central Station in Belfast.
2. Dargan Road in North Belfast to Whiteabbey alongside Belfast Lough.

Hills

None.

Refreshments

Plenty of choice in Lisburn.
Cafe at Lisburn Civic Centre, Island Mill.
Cutters Wharf PH, Stranmillis.
The Stables Tearoom in Sir Thomas and Lady Dixon Park (just off the route, near Drumbeg).
Malone House Restaurant in Barnett Demesne (just off the route near Shaw's Bridge).
Lots of choice in the centre of Belfast.
Glenavna Hotel, Whiteabbey.
Ice cream and tea shops in Whiteabbey village.

Nearest railway stations

1. The route goes right past Belfast Central Station.
2. The best connection to Lisburn station takes you through Castle Gardens.
3. Whiteabbey Station, across the busy A2, about ¼-mile to the west of the village.

The National Cycle Network in the area

1. West from Lisburn Route 9 continues over the newly-built Horseback Bridge at Union Locks and on towards Lough Neagh and the Portadown to Newry Canal towpath.
2. North from Whiteabbey, Route 93 follows Three Mile Water

Route 93 in Belfast passes the ferry terminals to England and Scotland.

Conservation Park under the spectacular Bleach Green Viaducts to the council offices at Mossley Mill before continuing towards the coast at Carrickfergus and Larne.
3. Route 93 will also run east, crossing the River Lagan via Queen Elizabeth Bridge and then fork with one route running north east to Bangor and the other south east to Comber, passing the Odyssey, Millennium Cafe.

Traffic-free path along the River Lagan in central Belfast.

LISBURN TO WHITEABBEY

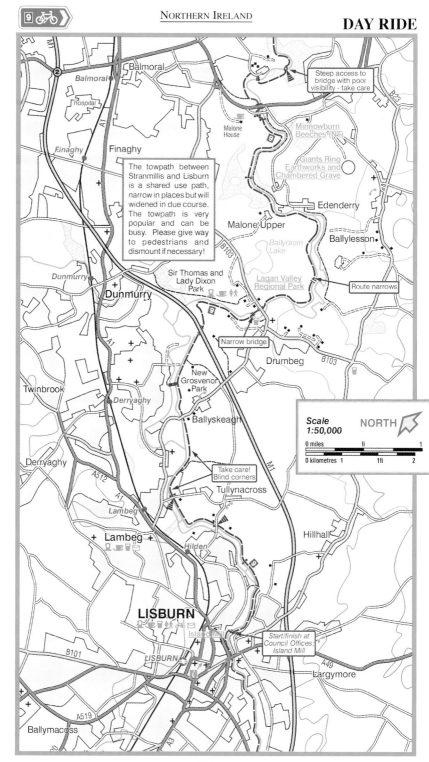

Balmoral

Balmoral

hospital

Finaghy · Finaghy

Steep access to bridge with poor visibility - take care

Malone House

Minnowburn Beeches (Ni)

Giants Ring Earthworks and Chambered Grave

Edenderry

Malone Upper

Ballylesson

The towpath between Stranmillis and Lisburn is a shared use path, narrow in places but will widened in due course. The towpath is very popular and can be busy. Please give way to pedestrians and dismount if necessary!

Dunmurry

Dunmurry

Sir Thomas and Lady Dixon Park

Ballydrain Lake

Lagan Valley Regional Park

Route narrows

Narrow bridge

Drumbeg

Twinbrook

New Grosvenor Park

Derryaghy

Ballyskeagh

Derryaghy

Scale 1:50,000   NORTH

| 0 miles | | fi | | 1 |
| 0 kilometres | 1 | | 1fi | 2 |

Take care! Blind corners

Tullynacross

Lambeg

Hillhall

Lambeg

Hilden

LISBURN

Island Mill

LISBURN

Start/finish at Council Offices, Island Mill

Largymore

B101

B519

Ballymacoss

A3

© Crown copyright

Route instructions

The route is well-signposted and once alongside either the River Lagan or Belfast Lough it is very difficult to get lost.

1. From the new Lisburn Civic Centre at Island Mill, follow the wooded riverside path on the east bank of the River Lagan north east towards Belfast for 10 miles, passing old linen mills and the relics of the old Lagan Canal.

2. Cross under Governor's Bridge (Stranmillis) to continue in the same direction along the newly-built segregated cycle lane along Stranmillis Embankment.

3. Cross the Ormeau Road (via controlled crossing) onto a continuation of the riverside route on a wide path. Go past Central Station, the Waterfront Hall, the Lagan Weir and the terminals for the ferries to England and Scotland.

4. Follow the waymarked route through Clarendon Dock and Duncrue Industrial Estate, across Dargan Road and onto the newly-built path alongside Belfast Lough.

5. Follow this for a further three miles, passing a tall fence on the right, the motorway to the left, then alongside Hazelbank Park as far as Whiteabbey village, following the coast the whole way.

Haulers Way Riverside Path, Belfast.

6. The Newtownabbey Way continues to Mossley Mill under the Bleach Green Viaducts.

The red bridge between Belfast and Lisburn in the Lagan Valley Regional Park.

LISBURN TO WHITEABBEY

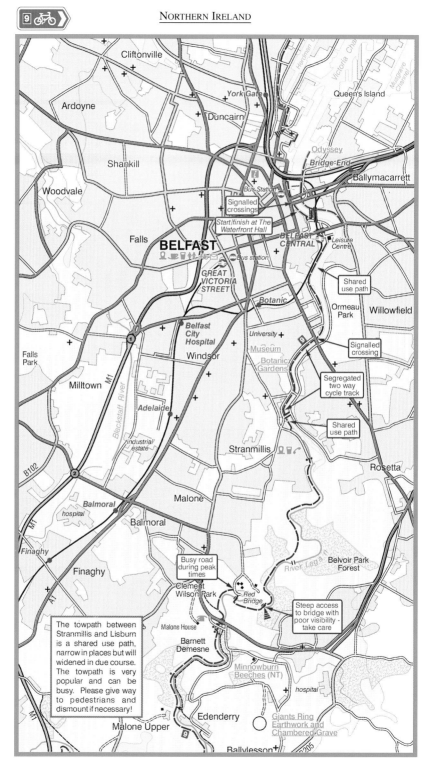

The towpath between Stranmillis and Lisburn is a shared use path, narrow in places but will widened in due course. The towpath is very popular and can be busy. Please give way to pedestrians and dismount if necessary!

© Crown copyright

216

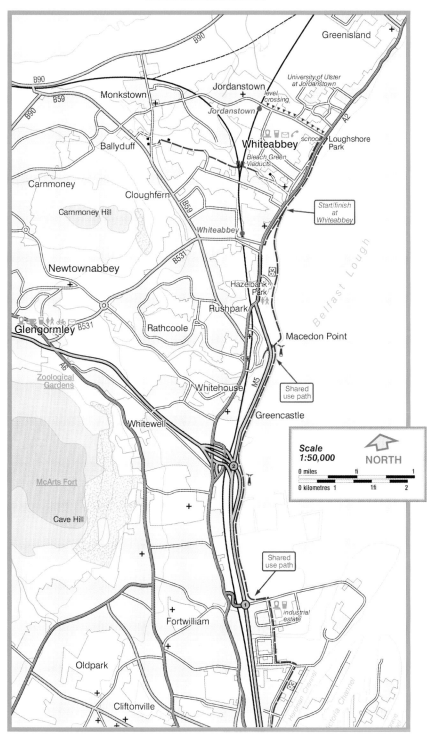

LONG DISTANCE AND HOLIDAY ROUTES

This section of the book gives a brief description of each of the long distance routes which are available as maps from Sustrans and are shown on the map below. Several sections of the National Cycle Network make ideal challenges for a holiday lasting from a few days to a few weeks. The award-winning National Route Maps published by Sustrans show the routes in easy-to-use strip form with daily route profiles, mileages and details of Tourist Information Centres, for help in finding accommodation along the way. The routes are a mixture of quiet lanes and traffic-free paths including dismantled railways, canal towpaths and forestry tracks.

To order any of the maps or books listed below please contact Sustrans Information Service, PO Box 21, Bristol BS99 2HA (0117 929 0888) visit the Sustrans website at www. sustrans.org.uk or see page 253.

What sort of bike should I use?
You can use any type of bike to ride most parts of the Network. However, not all the surfaces are sealed, so the best sort of bike to use would be a hybrid bike, a mountain bike fitted with road tyres or a robust touring bike with strong wheels and a wide range of gears. Fit mudguards and carry your luggage in panniers on a rack – far more comfortable than cycling with a rucksack!

The Network keeps on getting better!
The partners in the National Cycle Network are determined to continue developing and improving the routes. For example over time road junctions may be made safer; more traffic-calming measures may be introduced to slow down traffic on the road sections; better quality surfacing, drainage and regular maintenance of encroaching vegetation may be required on the traffic-free sections; in some cases entirely new traffic-free routes will be built to replace existing sections along roads. As the creation of the Network is an ongoing project, old maps will become out of date, so if in doubt, follow the signs on the ground.

Schematic arrangement of route numbering

KEY

Route number marker

DOVER TO LONDON AND HASTINGS
£5.99/NN1X (180 miles)

LONDON TO EASTBOURNE AND HASTINGS
£5.99/NN2A (150 miles)

These two routes in the South East link London to Dover. The first route is arranged to suit those arriving in Britain at the gateway port of Dover. The main route follows the coast and its extraordinary chain of defences – Dover, Walmer, Deal and Richborough Castles – the last being the Romans' gateway to the country. Then inland to Canterbury before following as close as possible the whole length of the North Kent coast to Dartford, and then the River back to Erith, Thamesmead, Woolwich, the Barrier, the Dome and Greenwich.

South from Greenwich, the second map follows a route to Gatwick and Three Bridges, from where a series of railway paths and deep Sussex lanes reach the sea at Eastbourne. The route then follows the coast as closely as possible through to Bexhill and Hastings with a spur west to Newhaven.

Public transport
There are numerous stations on the routes. **Three Bridges**, **East Grinstead**, **Polegate**, **Sandwich**,

The railway path from Norwich to Drayton and Reepham (Hull-Harwich Route).

Canterbury, **Whitstable** and **Sittingbourne** are just a few of those on the route.

HULL-HARWICH CYCLE ROUTE
Easy: 369 miles (+ 44 miles of link routes)

Easy gradients are a welcome feature of the Hull to Harwich route as it crosses the gentle countryside of eastern England from the Lincolnshire Wolds and Fens down into Norfolk and Suffolk. After the Wolds the route rarely rises above 200ft making it ideal for families or adults returning to cycling after a few years absence. Linking the ports of Hull and Harwich, the route explores the cathedral cities of Lincoln and Norwich and visits many attractive East Anglian villages on its way through Constable Country to Harwich.

Hull-Fakenham
MAP: 206 miles/£5.99/NN1A

Fakenham-Harwich
MAP: 163 miles/£5.99/NN1B

Hull-Harwich Holiday Planner
£4.50/RG14
84-page full colour booklet packed with general

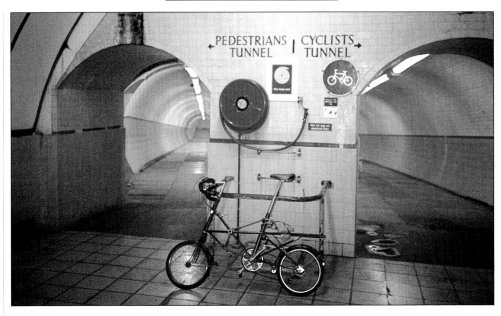

background details about the region plus specific information about villages, towns, accommodation and cycle shops.

Public transport options
Kingston upon Hull: main line services via York, Leeds and Doncaster.
Harwich: main line services from London Liverpool Street. Local rail services from Ipswich, Colchester and Manningtree.

It is also possible to join the route from the following stations: **Market Rasen**, **Lincoln**, **Boston**, **King's Lynn**, **Norwich**, **Beccles**, **Halesworth** and **Ipswich**.

The coastal option in Suffolk uses three somewhat irregular ferries!

 **THE THREE RIVERS CYCLE ROUTE NEWCASTLE, SUNDERLAND AND MIDDLESBROUGH**
MAP: 135 miles/£5.99/NN14
The three rivers are the Tyne, the Wear and the Tees which together define the industrial North East. Following the decline of the shipbuilding, steel and coal industries, much derelict land has been regenerated into attractive parks and many old railway lines have become recreational paths. Put this together with the success of the riverside

The Tyne Tunnel carries Route 1 from Jarrow to North Shields. Further east there is the alternative of the Tyne Crossing - spoilt for choice!

development along the Tyne through Newcastle, the attractions of the marina and National Glass Centre in Wearmouth and the barrage crossing of the Tees between Stockton and Middlesbrough, and you can see that the area offers far more to the cyclist than you might suppose! Circular rides can easily be fashioned by picking up the C2C route from Sunderland to Consett and thence northwards to the Tyne via Rowlands Gill and the magnificent viaducts of the Derwent Railway Path; or turn southwards to pick up the Lanchester Railway Path to the cathedral city of Durham and eventually the coast again at Seaham.

At the southern end of the Three Rivers Routes a further circular trip can be made by using first the route through Hartlepool for the Middlesbrough Transporter, and then the Eden Valley railway path north from Stockton-on-Tees.

Public transport options
As the Metro does not take cycles, the start of the route is probably best reached by cycling along either the South or North Tyne cycle route from **Newcastle Central**. Further south **Sunderland**, **Seaham**, **Hartlepool** and **Middlesbrough** all lie very close to the route.

COAST & CASTLES CYCLE ROUTE
NEWCASTLE TO EDINBURGH
MAP: 169 miles/£5.99/NN1C

This beautiful section of the National Cycle Network runs north from Tynemouth along the lovely coastline of Northumberland, England's least densely populated county. There are castles along the way at Warkworth, Dunstanburgh and Bamburgh, not forgetting Lindisfarne Castle and the Priory on Holy Island. The Scottish border is crossed soon after visiting the elegant Georgian streets of Berwick-upon-Tweed, England's northernmost town. The Scottish Borders are wonderful cycling country with little traffic and many fine, small towns – the route passes through Melrose, one of the most attractive in the region. After crossing the Moorfoot Hills, the River Esk Valley is followed through Dalkeith. The Innocent Railway Path takes you right into the heart of Edinburgh.

Transport
Apart from **Newcastle** and **Edinburgh** stations at either end, the East Coast Main Line Railway also stops at **Berwick** and **Alnmouth**, both squarely on the route.

EDINBURGH-ABERDEEN
CYCLE ROUTE
Moderate: 125 miles

From the beautiful city of Edinburgh the route crosses the famous Forth Road Bridge into the Kingdom of Fife and the historic town of St Andrews before continuing north along the coast via Dundee and smoky ol' Arbroath up to the granite city of Aberdeen.

Edinburgh-Aberdeen
MAP: 125 miles/£5.99/NN1D

Public transport options
Edinburgh Waverley: main line service from all parts of Britain.
Aberdeen: main line services from all parts of Britain including Edinburgh, Glasgow and Inverness.
It is also possible to join the route from the following stations: **Dundee**, **Arbroath**, **Montrose** and **Stonehaven**.

Cullen Viaduct has been restored to take cyclists on the spectacular coastal route between Banff and Buckie (Aberdeen-John o'Groats Route).

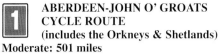

ABERDEEN-JOHN O' GROATS CYCLE ROUTE
(includes the Orkneys & Shetlands)
Moderate: 501 miles

North of Aberdeen, 'the granite city with the warm heart', the route passes through the red-sandstone town of Turriff before reaching the Moray Firth at the fishing port of Banff. West from here you pass through the attractive settlements at Portsoy, Forres and Nairn. Beyond Inverness, 'capital' of the Highlands, the route continues north to Thurso, Wick and John o' Groats. The map also shows routes in the Shetlands and Orkneys.

Aberdeen-John o' Groats
MAP: 501 miles/£5.99/NN1E

Note that the northern half of this route is shown to a deceptively comforting small scale which belies the time distances!

Public transport options
Aberdeen: main line services from all parts of the UK including Edinburgh, Glasgow and Inverness.
John o' Groats: The nearest railway stations are either at **Thurso** (20 miles) or **Wick** (17 miles).

It is also possible to join the route from the following stations: **Elgin**, **Forres**, **Nairn** and **Inverness**, plus six stations between **Dingwall** and **Lairg**.

DEVON COAST TO COAST
(PLYMOUTH-ILFRACOMBE)
Moderate: 90 miles

Cross beautiful Devon from the English Channel to the Bristol Channel, starting with a climb from Plymouth along the popular traffic-free Plym Valley Trail. After visiting the handsome town of Tavistock, skirt the western edge of the vast granite mass of Dartmoor to reach Okehampton. Sunken lanes through rolling green countryside take you to the start of the traffic-free Tarka Trail, descending to the coast at Bideford and following the Taw estuary through Barnstaple. The route finishes at the seaside resort of Ilfracombe.

Plymouth-Ilfracombe
MAP: 102 miles/£5.99/NN27

Public transport options
Plymouth: main line services from all parts of Britain including Bristol Temple Meads, Birmingham New Street and London Paddington. Ilfracombe has no railway station (but can often be reached by pleasure steamer from Penarth). The closest is at **Barnstaple** (accessed via Exeter).

THE CORNISH WAY: LAND'S END-BUDE

MAP: 170 miles/£5.99/NN3B

The Cornish Way runs the length of the county from Land's End to Bude. Significant sections of cycle route include Land's End to Sennen, the promenades around St. Michael's Bay (due for completion 2001), the fascinating Cornish Mineral Railways which pick up the remains of the once great tin industry, and a railway path for an easy route into Truro. From here the route divides into two, each equally hilly. The southern route crosses the Fal at King Harry's Ferry to generally follow the coast to Mevagissey, where it joins extensive new construction to Heligan Gardens and St. Austell. Again the route splits, either to follow a mineral route to the China Clay Museum at Wheal Martyn before joining the second at the Eden Project – Cornwall's monumental Millennium tropical gardens due to open in 2001. North from here follow a maze of minor roads to Llanhydrock House, with its much needed new bridge over the A30 to Bodmin. At Bodmin the second route from Truro via some serious hills at Newquay eventually joins the easy Camel Trail railway path to Wenfordbridge, the wild open spaces of Bodmin Moor and finally the coast again at Bude.

Public transport
The route is well served by trains to **Bodmin Parkway**, **St. Austell**, **Truro**, **Redruth**, **Camborne**, **Hayle** and **Penzance**.

Right: Truro Cathedral welcomes the Trailblazing Riders on their way to Land's End (The Cornish Way).

King Harry's Ferry provides a secure crossing of the River Fal on route from Truro to Mevagissey.
Note: the very small (3 bikes) ferry at Malpas provides a delightful alternative (The Cornish Way).

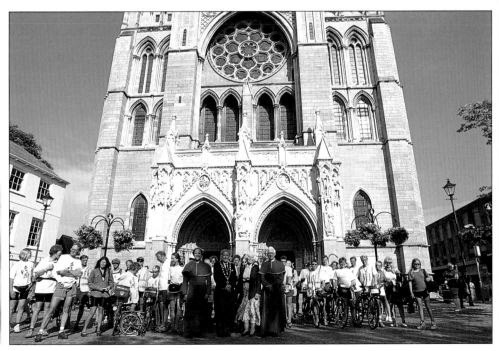

THE WEST COUNTRY WAY PADSTOW-BRISTOL/BATH
Moderate/challenging: 252 miles
(Mileage is for Padstow-Bath)

The West Country Way runs from the north Cornish coast to the historic cities of Bath and Bristol via a mixture of quiet lanes and popular traffic-free sections such as the Camel and Tarka Trails and the Bridgwater & Taunton Canal. On its West Country meanderings it takes in an exhilarating ridge ride over the roof of Exmoor, the atmospheric Somerset Levels, the mystical town of Glastonbury and the glory of Wells Cathedral.

Padstow-Bristol/Bath
MAP: 252 miles/£5.99/NN3A

The West Country Way B&B Guide
RG32 £3.99
Handy, pocket-size book listing B&Bs, Youth Hostels and camping sites along the course of the West Country Way. There are also details of trains, Tourist Information Centres, bike shops, places to visit and suggestions for eating out.

Public transport options
Bodmin Parkway: main line services from Exeter, Bristol and London Paddington.
Bristol: main line services from all parts of Britain to Bristol Temple Meads.

Glastonbury Tor from the route to Wells. Nine incised standing stones are located between the Tor and Wells Cathedral (The West Country Way).

It is also possible to join the route from the following stations:
Barnstaple (via Exeter), **Tiverton Parkway**, **Taunton** and **Bridgwater**.

THAMES VALLEY CYCLE ROUTE (LONDON-OXFORD)
Easy: 97 miles

Starting at Putney Bridge, escape from London through Richmond Park and along the banks of the majestic River Thames passing Hampton Court and Runnymede. After the vast splendour of Windsor Castle the route travels cross-country to rejoin the river at Wargrave, then threads its way through Reading. Glorious Chiltern beechwoods form a canopy over the lanes as you climb north past the Maharajah's Well at Stoke Row to historic Wallingford and Abingdon before reaching journey's end at Oxford.

London-Oxford
MAP: 97 miles/£5.99/NN5A

Public transport options
London: Main line services from all parts of the UK. Then cycle to the start of the route at Putney Bridge.

Oxford: Main line services from London Paddington via Reading and from Birmingham.

It is also possible to join the route from the following stations:
Richmond, **Staines** and **Windsor** from London Waterloo.
Maidenhead, **Twyford**, **Reading** and **Didcot** from London Paddington.

 **SEVERN & THAMES CYCLE ROUTE (GLOUCESTER-NEWBURY)**
Easy: 128 miles (+ 51 miles of link routes)
Cross southern England from the cathedral city of Gloucester to the busy market town of Newbury. After the lush pastures of the Severn Vale, follow the railway path from Bristol into the beautiful city of Bath then onwards along the Kennet & Avon towpath with its spectacular viaducts and locks. The main route leaves the canal at Bradford-on-Avon to pass through Corsham, Chippenham, Calne, Avebury and Marlborough. A parallel route follows the canal to Devizes then diverts onto quiet lanes through Etchilhampton, Woodborough and Wootton Rivers. The north route (via Chippenham) and the south route (via Devizes) link up on the edge of Savernake Forest, to the east of Marlborough. From here, quiet lanes lead through the attractive town of Hungerford and a final canal section takes you into the heart of Newbury. Most of the remainder of the journey to Reading follows the course of the canalised river.

Gloucester-Newbury
MAP: 128 miles/£5.99/NN4A

Public transport options
Gloucester: main line services from all parts of Britain including Bristol Temple Meads, Birmingham New Street and London Paddington.
Newbury: main line services from all parts of Britain including Bristol Temple Meads and London Paddington.

It is also possible to join the route from the following stations: **Bristol Temple Meads**, **Bath**, **Bradford-on-Avon**, **Trowbridge**, **Swindon** and **Hungerford**, as well as local stations to Reading.

Route 4 from London to Fishguard passes right through the centre of Avebury Stone Circle (Severn & Thames Route).

 **CELTIC TRAIL (LÔN GELTAIDD)**

The new coastal path from Burry Port to Pembrey Forest doubles as coastal defence works (Celtic Trail).

WEST (FISHGUARD-SWANSEA)
Moderate (with challenging options): 128 miles
EAST (SWANSEA-SEVERN BRIDGE)
Moderate (with challenging options): 217 miles

The route explores the beautiful Pembrokeshire coastline as far as St David's before turning south east towards Pembroke Castle and Laugharne, home of Dylan Thomas. Beyond Carmarthen the route enters the Llanelli Millennium Coastal Park and finishes along the wide sweep of Swansea Bay.

South Wales was once the world's greatest coal-producing area and although the pits have gone, there are still many signs of the area's rich industrial heritage in the form of old railways, viaducts and canals, many of which are used on this route through the Welsh Valleys to the old Severn Bridge at Chepstow.

Fishguard-Swansea
MAP: 128 miles/£5.99/NN4C

Public transport options
Fishguard: occasional services from Swansea.
Swansea: main line services from London Paddington.

It is also possible to join the route from the following stations: **Haverfordwest**, **Pembroke**, **Carmarthen**, **Kidwelly**, **Burry Port** and **Llanelli**.

Swansea-Severn Bridge
MAP: 217 miles/£5.99/NN4B

Public transport options
Swansea: main line services from London Paddington.
Chepstow: on the Cardiff to Gloucester line.

It is also possible to join the route from the following stations: **Neath**, **Port Talbot**, **Pontypridd**, **Cardiff** and **Newport**.

The National Cycle Network officially opened on June 21st 2000, when the whole 10,000 mile Network was ridden on this single long day. 260 separate rides celebrated this event.

On the following few days the Network hosted the World's largest Cyclethon, when local authorities, groups and interests of every kind staged events on the Network throughout the country. Details available on the Sustrans website - www.sustrans.org.uk

WEST MIDLANDS CYCLE ROUTE (OXFORD-DERBY VIA BIRMINGHAM)

MAP: 162 miles/£5.99/NN5B

This route uses railway paths from Derby to Etwall and then it picks up canal side routes through Burton on Trent. At Alrewas the route uses a delightful section of the Trent Valley. Major new construction takes the route past Lichfield Cathedral and into the centre of Walsall. Sandwell Valley Country Park is the next open space before the traveller links into the extensive network of canal paths which thread through Birmingham and lead to Centenary Square. South from the City centre the route follows the Rea Valley and splits with the direct route following the Roman road straight to Redditch whilst the western route takes in the Waseley Hills and Bromsgrove. The approach to Stratford upon Avon follows the towpath and leaves via the railway greenway to Milcote. From here the route mostly follows minor roads around the edge of the Cotswolds to reach Banbury, Blenheim and Oxford.

EAST MIDLANDS CYCLE ROUTE (OXFORD TO DERBY VIA LEICESTER)

Moderate: 178 miles

Highlights along this route through the geographical centre of England include the old town of Winslow and the amazing cycle network in Milton Keynes. Traffic-free sections include the Brampton Valley Way between Northampton and Market Harborough, a riverside path through Leicester and the finish along the River Derwent into Derby.

Oxford-Derby, via Leicester
MAP: 178 miles/£5.99/NN6A

Public transport options
Oxford and **Derby:** Main line services from London

It is also possible to join the route from the following stations: **Milton Keynes, Northampton, Market Harborough, Leicester** and **Loughborough.**

The route of the East Midlands Cycle Route goes over the Grand Union Canal to Frog Island, Leicester.

TRANS PENNINE TRAIL WEST (SOUTHPORT-BARNSLEY)

£5.99/NN62A (available Winter 2000)

TRANS PENNINE TRAIL EAST (BARNSLEY-HORNSEA)

£5.99/NN62B (available Winter 2000)

This crucial route is currently mapped by a free guide available from the Sustrans Information Service. The consortium of local authorities who are building this route as a separate Millennium Project will be covering this route in two separately produced maps. This route starts at the Ferryport at Hull, and so makes for a most important route from coast to coast for visitors from Europe.

The route from Hull takes in the Earth Centre Millennium Project at Conisborough, and as far as Barnsley is mapped on NN6B. West of there it crosses the Pennines at Dunford Bridge and follows the magnificent Longdendale Valley (reservoir and railway paths) to the whole built-up area of Greater Manchester. The route navigates via the Mersey Valley to the Mersey ferry at Liverpool's Pier Head.

DERBY-YORK CYCLE ROUTE

Moderate: 154 miles

Travel down the Vale of York from Britain's most cycle-friendly city on a mixture of railway paths and quiet lanes to the busy industrial town of Doncaster. Follow the Trans Pennine Trail to visit the Earth Centre at Conisbrough, ride through the steel city of Sheffield before reaching Rother Valley Park and crossing the great estates of the Dukeries. The route runs across Sherwood Forest and D.H. Lawrence country into the heart of Nottingham.

Derby-York
MAP: 134 miles/£5.99/NN6B

Public transport options
York: on the East Coast Line with services from London King's Cross and Edinburgh.

The Birmingham Canal Network offers numerous traffic-free routes for cyclists. The Main Line to Wolverhampton takes Route 5 north (West Midlands Route).

Nottingham: main line services from London. It is also possible to join the route from the following stations: **Doncaster**, **Sheffield**, **Rotherham** and **Worksop and Hucknall**.

THE WHITE ROSE CYCLE ROUTE (HULL -MIDDLESBROUGH)

Moderate: 123 miles (+ 99 miles of link routes)

Enjoy the splendours of Yorkshire between the bustling cities of Hull and Middlesbrough. You have a choice of two routes on leaving Hull: one runs west, parallel with the Humber, the other heads north across rolling wold country. They link in beautiful, historic York, one of Britain's most cycle-friendly cities. At Coxwold the route divides again: the easier western route runs through Sutton-under-Whitestonecliffe before crossing the North York Moors. The other option involves several challenging climbs through the spectacular heatherclad moorland.

Hull-Middlesbrough
MAP: 123 miles/£5.99/NN65

Public transport options
Kingston upon Hull: main line services via York, Leeds and Doncaster.
Middlesbrough: main line services from York, Darlington and Newcastle.

It is also possible to join the route from the following stations:
York, **Thirsk** and **Northallerton** are on the East Coast Line with main line services from London King's Cross and Edinburgh.

Local services operate between **Selby** and **Kingston upon Hull** and intermediate stations.

The Naburn Swing Bridge took the East Coast Main Line railway from King's Cross to Edinburgh over the Ouse south of York. Now it is a key link in the Network.

C2C (SEA TO SEA) CYCLE ROUTE

Cyclists enjoying a rest on the C2C.

(WHITEHAVEN/WORKINGTON-SUNDERLAND/NEWCASTLE)

Challenging: 140 miles (+ 73 miles of link routes)

Sustrans' most popular long distance route crosses northern England from coast to coast. Enjoy the (relatively!) gentle ride through the Lake District before the challenging crossing of the Pennines. Your efforts are rewarded with a long downhill stretch to the coast at Newcastle or Sunderland, passing many magnificent sculptures along the way. For those seeking even more adventurous options there are some parallel off-road alternatives. For a return route from Newcastle back to Whitehaven why not try the Reivers Cycle Route?

C2C Whitehaven/Workington-Newcastle/Sunderland

MAP: 140 miles/£5.99/NN7AA

The 1999 C2C and Reivers Routes Cycling Guide £5.99 RG08

Updated for 1999, this pocket-size 148-page book is packed with information about the accommodation along the course of the C2C and Reivers Cycle Route and has gradient profiles, and details of places of interest, refreshment stops, cycle shops and Tourist Information Centres.

Public transport options

It is best to buy a return ticket to Carlisle then catch a local train to get to the start and a local train back from the finish to Carlisle. This is a much cheaper option than buying two one-way tickets (one to the start and one back from the finish).

Carlisle: West Coast main line services from all parts of Britain.

Workington & Whitehaven: local train services from Carlisle.

Tynemouth: East Coast main line services to Newcastle from all parts of Britain. You will have to cycle back from Tynemouth to Newcastle via Route 72 along the north bank of the river as bikes are not allowed on the Metro (local train service).

Roker: Cycle from Roker to Sunderland then local trains to Newcastle (served by East Coast main line).

It is also possible to join the route from **Penrith.**

7 THE SCOTTISH NATIONAL CYCLE ROUTE
Moderate: 407 miles

Ride south from Inverness, 'capital' of the Scottish Highlands, through spectacular mountain scenery to the bonnie banks of Loch Lomond. Riverside paths, dismantled railways and canal towpaths take you through Glasgow and southwest to the Ayrshire Coast with dramatic views across to the Isle of Arran. Pedal through the forested heart of Dumfries and Galloway to the Solway Firth coastline, across the border into England and journey's end at Carlisle.

Inverness-Glasgow
MAP: 214 miles/£5.99/NN7C

Glasgow-Carlisle
MAP: 193 miles/£5.99/NN7B

Public transport options
Inverness: main line services from all parts of Britain via Glasgow Queen Street or Edinburgh Waverley.
Glasgow: main line services from all parts of Britain, services from south of Glasgow arrive at Glasgow Central and services north of Glasgow arrive at Glasgow Queen Street.
Carlisle: West Coast main line services from all parts of Britain

It is also possible to join the route from the following stations: **Dumbarton** from **Glasgow**, **Pitlochry**, **Blair Atholl**, **Dalwhinnie**, **Kingussie** and **Aviemore** are on the line to Inverness; **Paisley**, **Johnstone**, **Lochwinnoch**, **Kilwinning**, **Irvine** and stations to **Ayr** as well as **Dumfries** are all on the route.

71 CLYDE-FORTH CYCLE ROUTE (GLASGOW-EDINBURGH)

Easy: 86 miles (+ 85 miles of link routes)
Cycle across Scotland from Gourock on the Firth of Clyde to the spectacular city of Edinburgh on the Firth of Forth. Savour the panoramic views across the Clyde to the hills behind Helensburgh before turning inland. Pass through the heart of Glasgow and on to the Airdrie-Bathgate railway path before linking with the Union Canal into the centre of Edinburgh. The map also covers several

Glen Oglehead viaduct on the spectacular railway path section avoiding the A82 (Scottish National Route).

link routes: Glasgow-Loch Lomond, Glasgow-Kilmarnock (and Ardrossan), Edinburgh-Forth Road Bridge and Edinburgh-Musselburgh.

Glasgow-Edinburgh
MAP: 86 miles/£5.99/NN75

Public transport options
Numerous local stations on route are served from **Glasgow Central** or from **Queen Street.** From the latter you can catch the local train to **Drumgelloch** if you want to start at the end of the long railway path to **Bathgate.**
Edinburgh Waverley: main line services from all parts of Britain, and local trains to **Bathgate** and **Livingstone**.

It is also possible to join the route from many intermediate stations: there is an excellent network of railways around Glasgow operated by Strathclyde Passenger Transport – bikes are carried free of charge on all services.

LÔN LAS CYMRU – THE WELSH NATIONAL CYCLE ROUTE

Very challenging: 252 miles (+59 miles of link routes)
This spectacular route is the toughest in the National Cycle Network. It runs from the Bristol Channel to the island of Anglesey and frequently divides to offer challenging off-road options. Starting in either Cardiff or Chepstow, the route crosses several ranges of hills and mountains on its way through Wales, with east and west options linking at Builth Wells, Machynlleth, Dolgellau and near Porthmadog. North from here, the two routes become one, the gradients ease and railway paths whisk you north through Caernarfon and Bangor onto the gentle lanes of Anglesey.

Lôn Las Cymru South: Chepstow/Cardiff-Builth Wells
MAP: 136 miles/£5.99/NN8A

Poured Metal by Jeremy Cunningham can be found on the Airdrie and Bathgate section of the Clyde to Forth route. Watch out for other sculptures along this route.

Lôn Las Cymru North: Builth Wells-Holyhead
MAP: 175 miles/£5.99/NN8B

Cycling Wales FG08
56-page full colour booklet with details of
cycling opportunities in Wales. The publication
divides Wales into four regions and offers
information for all categories of rider from
families with young children to hard-core
mountain bikers.

Public transport options
Cardiff: main line services from all parts of
Britain.
Chepstow: on the Cardiff to Gloucester line.
Builth Wells: on the Swansea to Shrewsbury line.
Get off at Builth Road then cycle to Builth Wells
(1½ miles).

*One of the high points on Lôn Las Cymru, the Welsh
National Route crosses the Gospel Pass, on the way to
Abergavenny.*

Llanwrtyd Wells: on the Swansea to Shrewsbury
line.
Holyhead: on the Chester to Holyhead line.

It is also possible to join the route from the
following stations:
Abergavenny, **Merthyr Tydfil** (from Cardiff),
Machynlleth, **Barmouth**, **Porthmadog** and
Bangor.

*Stunning views can be seen from this route across
Talybont Reservoir (Lôn Las Cymru North).*

BELFAST-BALLYSHANNON CYCLE ROUTE
MAP: 233 miles/£5.99/NN9B

BALLYSHANNON-BALLYCASTLE CYCLE ROUTE
MAP: 244 miles/£5.99/NN9C

These two maps give coast to coast routes across Ireland from Ballyshannon, in Donegal, to Belfast, and to Ballycastle in the north east for the ferry to Campbeltown, around the corner from the Mull of Kintyre visible across the Irish Sea. Both of these routes make good use of the delightful network of quiet rural roads. At the same time new works take you to the centre of Omagh, to Derry, and a new bridge to Coleraine, with new roadside cycle routes to Portstewart. The Belfast option follows the Sperrins to Cookstown, Dungannon and Armagh, before picking up the cycling network through Craigavon to reach Oxford Island on the southern shores of Lough Neagh. From here the route mostly follows the canal towpath to Belfast with its magnificent new riverside promenades built by the Lagganside

Right: A wonderful new cycle route has been built around the head of Belfast Lough to link Whiteabbey with the City Centre (Belfast-Ballyshannon Route).

Development Corporation. The best is saved for the end where you cycle around the tidewater at the head of Belfast Lough on a new causeway set at the waters edge itself.

KINGFISHER TRAIL, NORTHERN IRELAND

Moderate: 230 miles
Follow minor country roads for 230 miles through the lovely green rolling countryside of Fermanagh, Leitrim and Cavan passing the beautiful Lough Erne, Lough Allen and a whole host of smaller loughs set amongst the Lackagh Hills. Discover the charms of villages with names like Swanlinbar, Ballinamallard, Drumshanbo and Killycluggin. Enjoy the warmth and friendliness of the locals and get a taste for Guinness in its home country.

Kingfisher Trail
MAP: 230 miles/£5.99/NN9A

The Cott Ferry to Crom Estate crosses Upper Lough Erne on the delightful Kingfisher Trail.

Details from two mileposts. Above: Andrew Rowe's design is nautical whilst right: The Fossil Tree (by Jon Mills) shows the eventual demise of the motor car, fossilised as surely as the Carboniferous plants which grew long ago to fuel it!

Stilwell's Britain Cycleway Companion
(Where to stop and stay along 20 long distance cycleways) £9.95/RG31
220-page guide packed with accommodation details for 20 of Britain's best known long distance cycle routes including the C2C, Lôn Las Cymru, the West Country Way, Hull to Harwich and the Scottish National Route. Additional background information about the places through which the routes pass.

Sustrans Stamping Scheme Information Sheet
Free/FF20
First introduced on the C2C, Sustrans' unique stamping scheme has proved so popular that it has been extended to all our mapped routes. If you are pedalling the Network, you can collect stamps as you cycle and qualify for the exclusive, commemorative T-shirt. Full details, with a list of stamping points are included (the Sustrans Information Service address, phone and website details are at the start of the chapter).

Millennium Log Book
£9.99/RG01
Keep a personal record of your journeys on the National Cycle Network in this beautifully designed log book. Each book is supplied with a full set of stamping cards.

Millennium Mileposts
Information sheet/Free/FF18
Standing just over two metres tall and made of cast iron, 1,000 Millennium Mileposts sponsored by the The Royal Bank of Scotland will be found all over the National Cycle Network. With four individual designs to choose from, you too can own one of these unique sculptures. Prices from £200 to £400. Please send for details and an order form (the Sustrans Information Service address, phone and website details are at the start of the chapter).

North Sea Cycle Route
Opened in its preliminary form for the Millennium, this 5500 km (3400 mile) route is a continuous, signed route encircling the North Sea passing through seven countries: Scotland, England, Holland, Germany, Denmark, Sweden and Norway. With many international ferry links along the way it can easily be divided into shorter sections. A high profile opening ride around the entire route will be arranged in 2001. The North Sea Cycle Route will become one of twelve long-distance routes in the EuroVelo network, a project initiated by the European Cyclists Federation.

THE TIME TRAIL

Sponsored by The Royal Bank of Scotland, the Time Trail is a voyage of discovery which we hope will add another dimension to your journeys along the National Cycle Network. It has been devised by artist Charlie Harrow.

Along most routes you will find tall cast iron Millennium Mileposts similar to the one pictured. They mark the opening of each new section of the 10,000 mile National Cycle Network, with almost 1,000 in place on Midsummer's Day 2000. On each you will find an embossed metal disc or Time Trail symbol similar to the one shown here (not to scale).

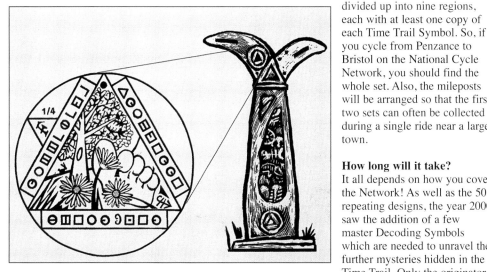

What are the Time Trail symbols about?
They are metal discs with pictures relating to the theme of Time and which show letters of a secret Code. If you collect copies of the discs (by placing a sheet of writing paper over the disc and rubbing all over with a pencil or wax crayon) as a record of your journey, you can start to piece together your own sculptures. You can purchase Time Treasures with more details, drawings and poetry from the Sustrans Information Service. If you are really dedicated, you can go further and try to solve the secrets of the Time Trail Code!

How many Time Trail symbols will there be?
There will be over 50 different designs, divided into five sets. Each set relates to a Time Treasure.

Where will the Millennium Mileposts be?
You will find them on National Cycle Network routes covered by our published maps, wherever you see a Millennium Milepost. As the maps are updated so the milepost locations will be added.

See the order form on page 253 for details of how to order maps covering these routes – or phone our information line (0117 929 0888) to request your free copy of our magazine.

How far will I have to travel?
You won't have to cycle around the whole National Cycle Network! The UK has been divided up into nine regions, each with at least one copy of each Time Trail Symbol. So, if you cycle from Penzance to Bristol on the National Cycle Network, you should find the whole set. Also, the mileposts will be arranged so that the first two sets can often be collected during a single ride near a large town.

How long will it take?
It all depends on how you cover the Network! As well as the 50 repeating designs, the year 2000 saw the addition of a few master Decoding Symbols which are needed to unravel the further mysteries hidden in the Time Trail. Only the originator of the Millennium Time Trail – Charlie Harrow knows what these are – so please don't ask anyone at Sustrans because they don't know!

For further information about the Time Trail
Contact Sustrans Information Service, PO Box 21, Bristol BS99 2HA.

Telephone:	0117 929 0888
Fax:	0117 915 0124
website:	www. sustrans.org.uk
e-mail:	info@sustrans.org.uk

The opening times of the office are 8.30am-5.30pm weekdays all year and 9am-1pm Saturdays from April to October.

Around the kingdom and across the seas
Stand mileposts of iron with symbols to tease.
It's no race against time our TIME TRAIL quest,
With Treasures for all who succeed in the test.
Made neither from silver, diamonds nor gold,
But elements, common and ancient and old.

Either by foot or your bike wheels spinning,
Finding time to find Time is just the beginning.
Brass rub the designs of triangles and squares,
And pentagons too, with a few other spares.
Claim treasures to solidify time well spent,
Discovering, perhaps, what Time actually meant.

Four dimensional jigsaws found in groups of
* fives,*
A sixth from them all makes it the Time of Our
* Lives.*
Layers upon layers, a rainbow coded rhyme,
In a universe of stars we join up space and time.
The Millennium Time Trail works out for all to
* see*
That Time in itself is still Time's mystery.

On the site of Consett's once renowned steelworks,
Tony Cragg's "Terris Novalis" pays homage to the
surveyors' instruments which set out the railways and
the landscape of the industrial age (C2C Route).

sustrans

GOOD CYCLING CODE

KEEP SAFE, BE COURTEOUS AND ENJOY CYCLING ON THE NATIONAL CYCLE NETWORK

The National Cycle Network will be 10,000 miles of cycle routes, running right through urban centres and reaching all parts of the UK. It is designed to encourage people to start cycling again and to be a safe and attractive resource for families, novices and experienced cyclists. One-third of the National Cycle Network is on traffic-free paths providing a major new amenity for walkers and people with disabilities.

On all routes..

Please be courteous. Always cycle with respect for others, whether other cyclists, pedestrians, people in wheelchairs, horse riders or drivers, and acknowledge those who give way to you.

On shared use paths...

One-third of the National Cycle Network is on traffic-free paths, such as disused railway routes. These are designed for shared use by cyclists and walkers. They are often suitable for wheelchairs and sometimes for horse riders.

Experience in the UK and abroad shows that such paths can benefit everyone and that they can be comfortably and safely shared if we show respect for others.

When cycling on shared use paths please:

- give way to pedestrians, leaving them plenty of room
- keep to your side of any dividing line
- be prepared to slow down or stop if necessary
- don't expect to cycle at high speeds
- be careful at junctions, bends and entrances
- **REMEMBER THAT MANY PEOPLE ARE HARD OF HEARING OR VISUALLY IMPAIRED – DON'T ASSUME THEY CAN SEE OR HEAR YOU**
- **CARRY A BELL AND USE IT – DON'T SURPRISE PEOPLE**
- give way where there are wheelchair users and horse riders.

On roads...

Much of the National Cycle Network is on traffic-calmed or minor roads through towns and the countryside.

When cycling on roads:

- always follow the Highway Code
- be seen – most accidents to cyclists happen at junctions
- fit lights and use them in poor visibility
- consider wearing a helmet and conspicuous clothing
- keep your bike roadworthy
- don't cycle on pavements except where designated – pavements are for pedestrians
- use your bell – not all pedestrians can see you.

And in the countryside...

- follow the Country Code
- respect other land management activities such as farming or forestry and take litter home
- keep erosion to a minimum if offroad
- be self-sufficient – in remote areas carry food, repair kit, map and waterproofs
- try to cycle or use public transport to travel to and from the start and finish of your ride
- cycle within your capabilities
- match your speed to the surface and your skills.

Thank you for cycling!

The bicycle does not cause pollution or contribute to climate change.

Thank you for choosing this environmentally-friendly form of transport.

PRACTICAL ADVICE FOR CYCLISTS

'Oh no, not another section of patronising tips from some know-it-all. Why do they bother with them?' Well, may we apologise now to anyone who is quite competent at mending a puncture, planning a route and knowing what to take with them on a bike ride. We suggest you skip this chapter and get on with the rides!

For those of you who are a little less certain or a bit rusty after a few years' absence from your bike, the good news is that almost everything related to cycling is simple, straightforward and rooted firmly in common sense.

The bike
Don't be put off by all the hype about bikes with thirty gears, full suspension and frames made of exotic metals. A Tour de France winner on an old butcher's bike would probably be faster than most of us on a bike costing £2,000! Enjoying cycling is in the mind, not in the equipment. If you want to enhance your enjoyment of cycling then try to get out more regularly and get used to spending a couple of hours on a bike saddle. Try out other people's bikes and see if you prefer the saddle/riding position/feel of the bike.

The Network consists of a mixture of minor roads, railway paths, forestry tracks, canal towpaths, sections on roads through towns and specially-built cycle tracks. The surfaces are not all sealed and may vary in quality so, for the unsurfaced sections, it is wise to use a bike with strong wheels (ie not a lightweight racing bike!).

Thames Cycle Route – be prepared to give way to other users of the riverside path.

Children's bikes tend to be robust enough anyway, but adults should opt for a strong touring bike, a hybrid bike or a mountain bike fitted with smooth tyres.

What to wear

You don't need lots of expensive, specialist gear: several thin layers of ordinary clothing will normally do. However, if you do want to invest, the most important items are padded cycling shorts and padded gloves. Leggings or tracksters on top of cycling shorts are best for the legs. T-shirts, thermal vests, shirts or fleeces should be long enough to cover the back even when you are stretched forward. The ideal top layer is a windproof/showerproof top with zips to help adjust for changes in temperature. Your extremities are much more susceptible to cold on a bike than when you are out walking: take gloves and a hat. Tight, non-stretch jeans are about the worst thing to wear.

Helmets

See the 'Helmets' section in 'Cycling with children' on page 247.

Punctures

They do not happen that often (unless the hedgerows have recently been cut) but they are the most common form of breakdown and they can ruin a day out if you are not prepared. A pump, spare tube and puncture repair kit are the only indispensable accessories you should carry with you at all times. If you don't know how to mend a puncture, it is worth learning – punctures can happen anywhere, anytime, to anyone, however experienced you are and whatever sort of bike you are riding. There are lots of maintenance books but better still is to get an experienced cyclist to show you what to do.

What else to take?

Besides pump and puncture repair kit, consider the following: money, map/guidebook, energy snacks and water, spare clothes (especially hat and gloves), waterproofs and a lock. If there is any chance of still being out at dusk, take front and rear lights (check they work before you set off). A reflective belt takes up little space and is useful for being seen in murky conditions. On those rare days when the sun is hot and bright take suntan cream and sunglasses. Drink much more water on hot days – you dehydrate far more quickly and are often not aware of it because your sweat evaporates in the breeze you create as you ride along.

Carrying equipment

What is the best way to carry equipment? For absolute minimalists, a water bottle and pump will fit on the frame, tools, keys and money will fit into a small bumbag. A larger bumbag will also carry a thin waterproof. More than this and it is best to carry food, spare clothing, waterproofs and lock in rear panniers rather than in a rucksack. Make sure the panniers are evenly loaded. If there is a chance of rain, put the contents of the panniers inside plastic bags. Handlebar bags are useful for easy access but they are not designed to carry heavy weights.

Cycling in a group

If you are cycling in a group of mixed ability and varying levels of fitness it is worth arranging regular rendezvous points for coffee/lunch/tea so that the slower people can catch up with the faster ones or so that the fitter people can do a longer route to get to the meeting point. The thought of getting to a good cafe, teashop or pub can do wonders in terms of encouraging people up hills! (It is worth checking the opening times of the refreshment stops to avoid disappointment.)

More experienced cyclists can do their bit for the group by checking the bikes of the novices, helping mend punctures or making adjustments to the position of the saddle or handlebars and generally giving encouragement or advice at difficult junctions. A more experienced cyclist should always bring up the rear to prevent a novice from being stranded at the back with a problem beyond his/her ability to fix. In strong headwinds it is possible to help a weaker cyclist by getting them to follow closely behind you in your slipstream. (Don't try this on unsurfaced sections – you need to keep an eye out for any rough patches!)

Hownsgill Viaduct. A well earned rest on the C2C high above Consett.

CYCLING WITH CHILDREN

A successful family cycle ride can satisfy so many different needs and provide such rich and long-lasting memories that it is worth knowing in advance the ingredients that make up a good, safe ride that will encourage children to get hooked on cycling from an early age.

Children and Bikes

Children can be carried in a child seat on an adult bike, pulled along in a trailer behind the bike, ride a bike that attaches to the adult bike or ride their own bikes. Looking at the options from birth onwards:

0 - 9 months: until babies can hold their heads up by themselves they should not be carried on bikes. This may happen between six months and a year. It is a good idea to get the baby used to the bike seat as early as possible so that they are quite happy in this environment. The adult will also get used to carrying the increasing weight and learn how this affects the handling of the bike.

9 months - 4 years: the child can be carried in a specially designed seat fitted to the back or the middle of a bike. There are many different bike seats and means of attachment. Look out for reviews in cycling magazines and ask friends and cycle shops for advice about which seat they recommend.

18 months +: a toddler graduates happily from a push-along tractor / car without pedals to a tricycle or a bike with stabilizers and eventually to a bike without stabilizers. A child interested in cycling will probably be cycling without stabilizers by the age of 4-6.

The child seat

The two most important factors for parents' peace of mind and the child's enjoyment are safety and comfort. Can the seat be adapted for different sized toddlers and children? Is there adequate padding? Is the child firmly held in place by straps and safety bars in case they fall asleep and nod forward or in case you have to brake suddenly? There are some seats which recline which allow the child to sleep comfortably and help to stop the child's head lolling forwards. Other things to consider are how easily or frequently you may wish to remove the seat entirely: having a seat that can easily be switched between the parents' bikes means that carrying the child can be shared during the course of a ride. Can the seat be used in conjunction with panniers?

There are some saddles which can be fitted to the crossbar. These give the child a much better view and allow conversation to take place, but obviously offer much less protection both from a safety aspect and from the wind and cold.

Trailers and trailer bikes

Trailers are a wonderful way to carry babies and children who are still too small to contribute pedal power. Babies as young as four months can be carried safely in a cycle trailer by fastening them in a small baby's car seat and then strapping that into the trailer. They can sleep when they wish and take a toy or a book with them. Trailers usually have accessible side pockets - children will enjoy disorganising their bits and pieces into them. The adult will find that towing a trailer affects bike handling far less than a child seat. Because of this, and despite the greater weight, cycling with a trailer can be less tiring than with a child seat.

Advantages to the whole family unit include the fact that a young child will be happier about longer excursions by bike (though it is still important to stop frequently to allow for play and leg-stretching). Another plus is that trailers are extremely conspicuous on the road and motorists tend to be overwhelmingly considerate. Also from the safety point of view trailers are designed so as to be very difficult to tip over – you can drop the bike horizontally without the trailer moving at all.

Having said that, drawbacks to trailer use are that they cannot be recommended in built-up areas. The extra length is obviously not helpful at busy junctions, and if you stop, and take the whole thing off the road, you block the pavement! However, on country lanes trailers are fine, though most weary parents will feel like avoiding very hilly areas. For peace of mind, it is worth avoiding the kind of countryside with twisting little lanes through dark woodland where drivers' vision is inevitably going to be restricted. Bought new, trailers are not cheap, but there is good availability of second-hand ones (try bike hire outlets selling stock at the end of summer).

Many railway paths are particularly suitable for wheelchairs and children.

Trailer bikes

Trailer bikes are the natural next step. By five years old, your child is going to be very burdensome either on a seat or in a trailer – yet is likely to have abundant energy! A trailer bike allows the child to contribute some pedal power without the responsibility for steering or braking. In effect the back half of a child's bike is attached to the adult's machine. There are various means of achieving this: the best are purpose-built trailer bikes which attach to a special frame you bolt to your own bike. This type works very well and adjusts with the growth of your child so that a single trailer bike will last them from around five years old to around nine. The worst are systems which encourage you to remove the front wheel from your child's bike and then clamp around its headset to attach it to your bike. These can wobble alarmingly – definitely try before you buy. As with trailers you get what you pay for. However, you are more likely to use a quality piece of equipment – and there is an avid second-hand market for purpose-built trailer bikes.

Helmets

Whatever your own views about wearing helmets, children should be encouraged to wear helmets for several reasons: until adolescence they are less able than adults to judge traffic speeds and

distances and are thus more likely to be at risk when they are on their bikes in the presence of traffic (even if this is on quiet back streets or quiet lanes); they are more likely to try out stunts and tricks which may end in a fall; in the event of an accident when children are being carried on the back of a bike, they will not be able to prepare themselves for a fall in the same way as the adult.

One of the easiest ways to put a child off wearing a helmet is accidentally to pinch the sensitive skin under its chin while securing the clips on the helmet straps. Take great care to avoid doing this. Insert your forefinger between the clip and the chin so that your finger may be pinched, but not the child's skin. Encourage children to put on the helmet themselves – they should be able to do this from about the age of three. A helmet which is not done up is no use whatsoever: it will be thrown off in the event of a fall, exposing the head to injury.

It is important that the helmet is the right size, neither too big nor too small. Good cycle shops should help you select the right size. As with bikes, children are likely to grow out of several helmets between birth and adolescence. If a helmet has been involved in a serious accident or fall then **replace** it.

Children's bikes

It is better to buy the right size than buy a bike

which is too large which the child can 'grow into'. Riding a bike which is too big is not only dangerous but is likely to put the child off cycling. Similarly once they have grown too big for a bike, think of passing it down or selling it secondhand. A child's first bike is better if it has no crossbar: this way the child falls through the bike and not off it. From the age a child can cycle, they should use and outgrow three bikes until they are old enough to ride an adult frame.

Hire bikes

At many of the more popular trails you can hire adult and children's bikes, kid seats, trailers and helmets. Look in the Yellow Pages or call the nearest Tourist Information Centre for details of hire centres. Ring in advance to book equipment, particularly on fine summer weekends. The hire centre staff are often the best people to ask about safe routes in the area.

Planning a ride: checking the bikes, what to take (food, drink, clothes)

Don't leave everything until the last moment: the evening before the ride check for punctures, check the brakes work properly, lubricate the chain and ensure that all the nuts on the rack and child carrier are tightly done up. Pack some food and drink (water or well-diluted squash is best). Oat bars, chocolate brownies and dried fruit travel well and give lots of energy, boiled sweets take up no room and are always good at stops. On cold days take something warm to drink (stainless steel thermos flasks are robust enough for the road). With regard to food and drink, little and often is better than one big midday meal.
You don't need a pannier full of tools but you should have the equipment to mend a puncture (tyre levers, spare inner tube, puncture repair kit, pump). Other tools worth taking are a small adjustable spanner, a reversible screwdriver and Allen keys. It is worth carrying sticking plasters and a clean handkerchief in case there is a fall.

British weather is notoriously fickle and a child on the back of a bike generates no heat thus is much more likely to get cold quickly; even if it is a fine day take extra clothes (hat, gloves and socks) and something waterproof. There are waterproof covers available for children's seats which will keep the child dry. Don't forget nappies and a plastic bag to carry any used nappies (and other litter) back home.

Trailer bikers enable all the family to enjoy the route.

Planning a ride: when to go, where to go

The best time to go is when it is warm and dry with no wind blowing. If cycling through urban areas, Sundays are the days when there is least traffic. Country lanes can often be quieter during the week than at the weekend.

The options for where to go are much greater if the child is being carried in a bike seat (ie you are in complete control of their safety and the limits are when you get tired and/or the child gets bored). If the child is cycling rather than being carried, cycle paths on dismantled railways are ideal places for children to learn to ride and to gain confidence and stamina – the routes tend to be broad, flat, with a good quality surface and, most important, they are traffic-free.

Forestry Commission tracks are traffic-free but may be steeper and slightly rougher than railway paths. Certain Forestry Commission holdings have waymarked trails, some of which are promoted as suitable for families. Only a small percentage of canal towpaths are appropriate for family cycling. Some reservoirs have a cyclepath around their edge.

How far to go?

When deciding how far to go the best advice is: don't be too ambitious! It is better that everyone has a good time and wants to go out cycling again rather than coming back home exhausted and tearful and permanently put off cycling! If the children are on their own bikes, the ride should be designed around them and not the adults. They are likely to be bored by a long, non-stop ride. If there are things to look forward to such as a picnic, a playground, a castle, a sculpture, a stream or river, or a field full of animals then the children will be happier.

On a still day, on good, flat surfaces, 3-4 miles on a bike is equivalent to one mile walking so a 12-mile bike ride on a dismantled railway line is the same as a 3-4 mile walk. Hills, rough surfaces, wind and heavy loads all make cycling considerably slower and harder. 5-10 miles is about the right length trip for young children on their own bikes. 10-30 miles makes for a good day out for older children or for adults carrying children.

Getting to the start of the ride

The best rides are often those that start from home: children will recognise familiar places and there is far less hassle about getting everything organised. Catching a train with bikes and children is also possible, and children certainly like travelling on trains, but you will need to do some research to find out which trains carry bikes and perhaps make a booking in advance. Some trains only take one or two bikes, making a family trip with adults and children impossible. The National Rail Enquiry Sevice (tel: 0345 484950) should be able to help with information about which trains are happy to carry bikes.

Cycling on roads with young children

Children must learn about the dangers of traffic and the need for safety whilst gaining confidence and stamina as they go out on longer rides. On the first few trips on quiet lanes it is worth teaching children to stop and pull into the side whenever a vehicle is heard. The best configuration is with adults ahead and behind. If there is only one adult, it is best to stay at the back to keep an eye on the children ahead. Always keep them in sight.

The most dangerous manoeuvre is a right turn from a main road on to a side road. Look behind you, wait for a gap in the traffic, indicate then turn. If there is a lot of traffic, pull in to the left and wait for a break in both flows of traffic. Teaching a child how to look behind them without wobbling and veering into the middle of the road is one of the most important skills of cycling confidently.

If you are carrying the child on the back of your bike it is well worth pushing the bike up a steep hill that you might have tried to cycle up if you were on your own: it can be very difficult to dismount on a steep hill with the weight of a child on the back.

Teaching a child how to cycle

The proverb 'pride comes before a fall' could have been written specifically about learning to cycle. Just when children have proudly mastered one skill they will take a tumble and feel disheartened. Praise any progress and don't push the child too far or too fast. Cycling should be associated with fun, not just a task to learn. Confidence will be gained and lost a hundred times during the course of learning to balance on two wheels.

Most aspects of learning to cycle are common sense: children have to progress from a tricycle or a bike with stabilizers to balancing on two wheels; they have to learn how to stop by using their brakes, not their feet; they should learn to anticipate when to put their feet on the ground just before stopping; and they need to understand that they must keep their eyes on what lies ahead. All this can only be done after many sessions of trial and error with frequent falls and tumbles. It is vital that you choose somewhere safe, free from traffic with a good surface and if possible a very gentle downhill (it is easier to learn to balance freewheeling down a gentle slope). The child's hands, elbows and knees should be covered as there are likely to be a few scrapes and bumps. Children must be made aware of the dangers of traffic so they do not practice their newly-found skills in areas where they may unexpectedly come across traffic.

If a bike has stabilizers then gradually raise them off the ground so that the child begins to spend more time with the bike on the main wheels than on the small stabilizer wheels. An open frame enables the child to fall 'through' the bike rather than off it. Once the basics have been learnt, build up the child's confidence and stamina on traffic-free cyclepaths, before letting them loose on streets and roads.

Hampton Court Palace from the Thames Cycle Route.

HELPING CREATE THE NATIONAL CYCLE NETWORK

Help from volunteers at a local level is crucial to the development of the National Cycle Network. There are a variety of tasks which Sustrans needs help with – volunteering might only take a couple of hours a month or it might become one of your principal pastimes!

The Ranger Scheme was implemented in 1998, drawing upon people who are keen to look after sections of route or pieces of land near their home. The two types of Rangers are:
Route Rangers who look after route signing, Mileposts, Time Trail disks and sculptures, and perform some routine maintenance such as sweeping up glass and cutting back brambles.
Land Rangers keep an eye on parcels of land which we are assembling for future use, but which for the time being lie fallow.

Trailblazing Works
Each year Sustrans runs a series of Trailblazing Work Camps throughout the UK. Volunteers can come along for the day or for the full 2-3 weeks and help build a key section of the National Cycle Network.

Other ways to help
Traffic counts, photography, administrative assistance, distribution of supporter recruitment leaflets and other work all rely on volunteers and we would be grateful for your help. Write to the Volunteer Co-ordinator, Sustrans, 35 King Street, Bristol, BS1 4DZ to receive further information.

Right: Volunteers on the 1998 Trailblazing Summer workcamp gather under Meldon Viaduct, Okehampton.

The route along the south side Loch Venachar, near Callander, was constructed entirely by volunteers.

Join Sustrans

Sustrans (it stands for sustainable transport) is a practical charity, designing and building routes for cyclists and walkers. Our lead project, the National Cycle Network, is creating 10,000 miles of traffic-free and on-road routes across the UK. We also work to create Safe Routes to Schools.

By joining Sustrans, you will be demonstrating your commitment to transport policies - with better provision for cyclists and walkers. As a Supporter, you will receive a **FREE** pack with information about routes already open, plus regular newsletters and invitations to openings and events.

YES I'll join...

NAME

ADDRESS

POSTCODE   PHONE

Complete either A or B below

A. YES I'll join with a donation

£15   £25   £50   £100

£_____ other *(please tick) (£15 is the minimum rate)*

Please EITHER enclose a cheque/PO/CAF voucher payable to Sustrans OR complete your Visa/Mastercard/Switch/CAFCard/ number here and sign:

_____ / _____ / _____ / _____

SIGNATURE

CARD EXPIRY DATE

ISSUE No. SWITCH

DATE

B. YES I'll join with a monthly standing order

FREE wallchart of the National Cycle Network when you make out a standing order of £3 per month or more.

£3   £5   £10   £15   £25

£_____ other *(please tick)*

NAME OF MY BANK

ADDRESS OF MY BANK

ACCOUNT NO   _/_/_/_/_/_/_/_/_/_

BANK SORT CODE   _/_/-_/_/-_/_/

MY NAME

DATE

SIGNATURE

☐ Please send me a covenant form *(Please tick)*

REMEMBER: You can cancel this standing order at any time by informing your bank.

BANK INSTRUCTIONS: Please pay the above amount on the 15th next and **monthly** thereafter to SUSTRANS, Acc No 1400978, Lloyds Bank, 55 Corn St, Bristol, BS99 7LE Sort Code 30-00-01.

PLEASE QUOTE REF:

Please remove this coupon and send with your payment to: Sustrans, PO Box 21, Bristol BS99 2HA.

National Cycle Network Route Maps

The National Route Map range is expanding all the time. The award-winning maps give easy-to-read contours, route profiles, mileages and essential visitor information. Latest editions are on waterproof paper.

Scotland
NN7B	Scottish National Route: Glasgow - Carlisle	£5.99
NN7C	Scottish National Route: Inverness - Glasgow	£5.99
NN75	Clyde to Forth Cycle Route: Glasgow - Edinburgh	£5.99
NN1D	Edinburgh - Aberdeen	£5.99
NN1E	Aberdeen - John o' Groats	£5.99

North of England
NN69A	Derby - Kendal	£5.99
NN69B	Kendal - Durham - Carlisle	£5.99
NN69C	Carlisle - Morpeth - Berwick	£5.99
NN7AA	Sea to Sea (C2C) Cycle Route	£5.99
NN65	White Rose Cycle Route: Hull - Middlesbrough	£5.99
NN6B	Derby - York	£5.99
NN14	Three Rivers Route	£5.99
NN1C	Coasts and Castles Cycle Route: Newcastle to Edinburgh	£5.99

Midlands
NN6A	South Midlands Cycle Route: Oxford - Derby, via Leicester	£5.99
NN5B	West Midlands Cycle Route: Oxford - Derby via Birmingham	£5.99

Wales
NN8A	Lôn Las Cymru - Welsh National Route South: Cardiff & Chepstow - Builth Wells	£5.99
NN8B	Lôn Las Cymru - Welsh National Route North: Builth Wells - Holyhead	£5.99
NN4B	Celtic Trail East: Swansea - Severn Bridge	£5.99
NN4C	Celtic Trail West: Fishguard - Swansea	£5.99

London
LN001	The National Cycle Network in London	£4.99

East of England
NN1A	Hull - Harwich Cycle Route: Hull - Fakenham	£5.99
NN1B	Hull - Harwich Cycle Route: Fakenham - Harwich	£5.99

South East
NN2A	London - Eastbourne - Hastings	£5.99
NN1X	London - Dover - Hastings	£5.99
NN4A	Severn & Thames Cycle Route: Gloucester - Newbury	£5.99
NN5A	Thames Valley Cycle Route: London - Oxford	£5.99

South West
NN3A	West Country Way: Padstow - Bristol/Bath	£5.99
NN3B	Cornish Way: - Land's End - Bude	£5.99
NN27	Devon Coast to Coast: Plymouth - Ilfracombe	£5.99

Northern Ireland
NN9A	Kingfisher Trail: N & S Ireland	£5.99
NN9B	Belfast - Ballyshannon	£5.99
NN9C	Ballyshannon - Ballycastle	£5.99

Family Guide
RB01	Family Cycling Trailguide: Superb value publication with details of over 300 traffic-free trails throughout Britain	£4.95

Please send me details of other maps and guides available from Sustrans

NAME

ADDRESS

POSTCODE   PHONE

Phone
0117 929 0888
to place your telephone order

Code	Product Name	Price	Total

Order total _____

UK orders, add P&P 10% of total, minimum £2 _____

Non-UK order, add P&P 20%, minimum £3 _____

Total with P&P _____

Donation _____

GRAND TOTAL _____

Order online or find more info - visit our website at **www.sustrans.org.uk**

Mastercard ☐   VISA ☐   Delta/ Connect ☐

Switch - issue no/_____/

Please EITHER enclose a cheque payable to Sustrans OR complete your credit/debit card number here and sign:

_____/_____/_____/_____

CARD EXPIRY DATE

SIGNATURE

DATE

Please return this coupon with your payment to: Sustrans, PO Box 21, Bristol BS99 2HA. For UK orders, we aim to deliver within 10 days of receipt of order. Phone for express service.

All prices are correct at time of going to press (April 2000) but may be subject to change without prior notice. Supply of all items is subject to availability.

OTHER PROJECTS

Although Sustrans has put a great deal of energy into creating the National Cycle Network, it has been a partnership project in which much of the work has been done by others, particularly a huge number of dedicated local authority officers, without whom the Network would still lie in fragments.

Sustrans is also pursuing a number of other projects which may conveniently be mentioned here.

Guardianship of Disused Railways
Over 10,000 miles of railways were abandoned at the time of the Beeching cuts in 1966. Although much of great value has been lost, a combination of local authorities and Sustrans has kept over 1,500 miles in public use. Sustrans owns about a third of these which it maintains against future transport use, and in the meantime uses for valuable walking and cycling routes.

Sustrans maintains over 700 bridges including some 40 railway viaducts. One of the invaluable roles played by our volunteers is that of Bridge Ranger where a volunteer can keep an eye on local structures.

Safe Routes to Stations
Scarcely a station in the UK has a dedicated walking and cycling route to it. We are working with Railtrack and the Government to turn this around so that the station becomes a focus of high quality routes leading from the town centre, nearby residential areas, and large employers.

These routes will both make it clear that walking and cycling are the natural partners of public transport, and at the same time extend the influence of each station more widely. Perhaps we can look forward to remote "entrances" where tickets can be bought and train times indicated in the centre of towns.

Safe Routes to Schools
Britain's treatment of children's journeys has been a disgrace. For example the Danish Government has, by patient work and policy, achieved 60% of children cycling to school whilst in Britain it is less than 2%. Not only does this lessen the independence of children, reduce their fitness and cause considerable congestion, not to say the waste of their driving parents' time, but it means that the next generation are not getting into the habit of cycling. Without young people cycling there will be no adult cyclists in the future.

Sustrans' Safe Routes to Schools Project has set out to change this with a combination of work in schools, coursework, exchanges, cycle racks and safe routes. If you need more information contact Sustrans Information Service.

At Huntington School, York the pupils redesigned their bike shed as part of their Safe Routes to Schools programme.

ACKNOWLEDGEMENTS

The National Cycle Network has been made possible by a huge co-operative effort over a period of years by hundreds of organisations and thousands of individuals. It is impossible to list all of them here. Particular thanks are due to:

Nearly 500 local authorities who have developed local sections of route.

The Millennium Commission for its visionary lead grant of £43.5 million.

Government departments including the Department of Environment, Transport and the Regions; the Scottish Executive and Welsh Assembly; the Department of Regional Development (NI); and the Highways Agency.

Utility and statutory bodies including British Waterways; Forest Enterprise and Forest Service; English Regional Development Agencies (fomerly English Partnerships); the Environment Agency; Ordnance Survey and Ordnance Survey Northern Ireland.

Countryside and regeneration bodies including the National Trust; English Heritage; the Countryside Agency, Countryside Council for Wales; Scottish Natural Heritage; the Groundwork Trusts; and many national parks, countryside and heritage sites, tourism bodies and wildlife groups.

Railtrack; Rail Property; British Railways Board; and the Railway Heritage Trust.

Partner bodies representing cyclists; walkers; people with disabilities; horse-riders; anglers; and other users of the routes.

Charitable trusts and individuals, in particular the AIM Foundation; the Sainsbury Family Charitable Trusts; the Serve All Trust; the Freshfield Foundation; the Gannochy Trust; the Ruben and Elizabeth Rausing Trust; the Southern Trust; the Manifold Trust; and many others who have given grants over the period.

The cycle trade and industry, in particular the Bicycle Association and Association of Cycle Traders, and the contributors to the Cycle Levy Scheme: Brompton, Cycleurope, Dawes, Giant, H & J Supplies, Halfords, Madison, Moore Large, Professional, Raleigh, Saracen, SBC, Trek and Universal.

Many local CTC and cycle campaign groups; the London Cycling Campaign.

Sister Millennium projects that have created routes including the Trans Pennine Trail; the Kingdom of Fife Millennium Cycleways; Peterborough Green Wheel; the Millennium Coastal Park at Llannelli; the Earth Centre; Mile End Park; Changing Places; Turning the Tide; and others.

Partners in the Ride the Net public events: the British Medical Association; the Variety Club of Great Britain; the Women's Institutes; the National Association of Scouts; the Times; the CTC; and many smaller bodies.

For corporate sponsorship particular gratitude is due to The Royal Bank of Scotland as well as to: Boots; INS/Edex; Halfords; Madison; and Giant.

And Sustrans' 40,000 supporters, rangers, volunteers, trailblazers, route developers and letter-writers who have kept up the positive momentum throughout the period.

Sustrans would also like to extend thanks to all those who have generously contributed to the creation of the Network who we have not been able to list here.

MAPS

Maps based on Ordnance Survey Strategi and OSCAR digital data with permission of the Controller of Her Majesty's Stationery Office © Crown copyright. Licence number GD 03181G0001.

Maps on pages 210, 211, 214, 216 and 217 based upon the 1984 Ordnance Survey of Northern Ireland 1:50,000 map with the permission of the Controller of Her Majesty's Stationery Office © Crown Copyright. Permit No. 1493

A-Z maps used on pages 73-81:
Reproduced by permission of Geographers' A-Z Map Co Ltd Licence Number B0283. Map based on Ordnance Survey mapping with the permission of the Controller of Her Majesty's Stationery Office. © Crown copyright; Licence Number 43472U.

CREATIVE TEAM

Sustrans
Nigel Brigham
Katie Dickson
Bryn Dowson
Peter Foster
Carol Freeman
Tony Grant
David Gray
John Grimshaw
David Hall
Ben Hamilton-Baillie
Barney Hill
Jeremy Iles
Penny Langley
Graham Lennard
Jane Ogilvie

John Palmer
Steven Patterson
Chris Sherrington
Lindsey Smith
Mark Strong
Simon Talbot-Ponsonby
Alison Tracey
Andy Whitehead

Project co-ordinators/Editors
Julian Holland
Lucy Thorp

Text and research
Nick Cotton and John Grimshaw

Design
Julian Holland
Nigel White
Lisa Bridge
Paul Taylor (cover)

Cartography
Stirling Surveys
Cycle City Guides
Sustrans

Picture Research
Julia Bayne
Lucy Keeler

PHOTOGRAPH CREDITS

Front cover Sustrans/Sculpture by Dave Holladay
Spine Steve Morgan
Back cover Sustrans

Robert Ashby
Julia Bayne
Graham Bell
Bristol Tourism & Conference Bureau
Bristol Tourist Information and Marketing
    Centre
British Waterways
Cadw: Welsh Historic Monuments. Crown
    Copyright
Caledonian MacBrayne Ferries
Canterbury Council Tourism
Cardiff City Council
Nick Cotton
Michael Cutter
Edinburgh & Lothians Tourist Board
Edinburgh City Council
Gwynedd Council

Martin Harrow
Highlands of Scotland Tourist Board
Ironbridge Gorge Museum Trust
Kai
Keswick Tourism Association
Gareth Lovett Jones
NMR (Crown copyright)
New Millennium Experience Company
Northumbria Tourist Board
Alan Pentland
Richard Robinson
Roger Sinek
Toby Smedley
Ian Smith
Sandwell Metropolitan Borough Council
Suffolk County Council
Sunderland Association Football Club Ltd
Sustrans
Trans Pennine Trail
Andy Tryner
Guy Woodland